OXFORD STUDIES IN EARLY MODERN PHILOSOPHY

VOLUME I

EDITED BY

DANIEL GARBER
(Princeton University)

AND

STEVEN NADLER
(University of Wisconsin, Madison)

CLARENDON PRESS · OXFORD

OXFORD

UNIVERSITY PRESS

Great Clarendon Street, Oxford OX2 6DP

Oxford University Press is a department of the University of Oxford.
It furthers the University's objective of excellence in research, scholarship,
and education by publishing worldwide in

Oxford New York

Auckland Bangkok Buenos Aires Cape Town Chennai
Dar es Salaam Delhi Hong Kong Istanbul Karachi Kolkata
Kuala Lumpur Madrid Melbourne Mexico City Mumbai Nairobi
São Paulo Shanghai Taipei Tokyo Toronto

Oxford is a registered trade mark of Oxford University Press
in the UK and in certain other countries

Published in the United States
by Oxford University Press Inc., New York

British Library Cataloguing in Publication Data
Data available

Library of Congress Cataloging in Publication Data
Data available

ISBN 0–19–926790–1
ISBN 0–19–926791–x (pbk.)

1 3 5 7 9 10 8 6 4 2

Typeset by Newgen Imaging Systems (P) Ltd., Chennai, India
Printed in Great Britain
on acid-free paper by
T.J. International Ltd., Padstow, Cornwall

Contents

Note from the Editors

The editors and Oxford University Press are very pleased to present this first volume of *Oxford Studies in Early Modern Philosophy*.

Oxford Studies in Early Modern Philosophy will cover the period that begins, very roughly, with Descartes and his contemporaries and ends with Kant. It will also publish articles on thinkers or movements outside that framework (including Kant), as long as they are important for illuminating early modern thought. The core of the subject matter will, of course, be philosophy and its history. But the volume's essays will reflect the fact that philosophy in this period was much broader in its scope than it is now taken to be, and included a great deal of what currently belongs to the natural sciences. Furthermore, philosophy in the period was closely connected with other disciplines, such as theology, and with larger questions of social, political, and religious history. While maintaining a focus on philosophy, the volume will include articles that examine the larger intellectual, social, and political context of early modern philosophy. Although the articles in the volume will be of importance to specialists in the various subfields of the discipline, our aim is to publish essays that appeal not only to scholars of one particular figure or another, but to the larger audience of philosophers, intellectual historians, and others who are interested in the period.

Oxford Studies in Early Modern Philosophy will be a single annual volume available in both hardcover and paperback and containing roughly 250–350 pages. Articles may be submitted at any time. It is strongly preferred that they be submitted by email attachment in MS Word (PC or Macintosh) or RTF to one of the editors. While everything will be published in English, articles may also be submitted in French, German, or Italian.

The editors of *Oxford Studies in Early Modern Philosophy* are Daniel Garber (Princeton University) and Steven Nadler (University of Wisconsin, Madison). The members of the editorial board are:

Edwin Curley (University of Michigan, USA)
Knud Haakonssen (Boston University, USA)
Sarah Hutton (Middlesex University, UK)

Susan James (Birkbeck College, University of London, UK)
Jean-Luc Marion (Université de Paris IV (Sorbonne), France)
Emanuela Scribano (Università di Siena, Italy)
Robert Sleigh, Jr. (University of Massachusetts, Amherst, USA)
Theo Verbeek (Rijksuniversiteit te Utrecht, the Netherlands)
Catherine Wilson (University of British Columbia, Canada)

The editorial office is:

Oxford Studies in Early Modern Philosophy
Department of Philosophy
Princeton University
1879 Hall
Princeton, NJ 08544–1006
USA

Email: dgarber@princeton.edu; smnadler@wisc.edu

FAX: 609-258-1502

Abbreviations

DESCARTES

AT   Charles Adam and Paul Tannery (eds.), *Œuvres de Descartes*, 11 vols. (Paris: CNRS/Vrin, 1964–74)

CSM   John Cottingham, Robert Stoothoff, and Dugald Murdoch, *The Philosophical Writings of Descartes*, 2 vols. (Cambridge: Cambridge University Press, 1984)

CSMK   John Cottingham, Robert Stoothoff, Dugald Murdoch, and Anthony Kenny (eds.), *The Philosophical Writings of Descartes*, vol. 3: *The Correspondence* (Cambridge: Cambridge University Press, 1991)

HOBBES

EW   Sir William Molesworth (ed.), *The English Works of Thomas Hobbes of Malmesbury*, 11 vols. (London, 1839–45)

LW   Sir William Molesworth (ed.), *Opera philosophica quae Latine scripsit omnia*, 5 vols. (London, 1839–45)

LEIBNIZ

A   Deutsche Akademie der Wissenschaften (eds.), *Gottfried Wilhelm Leibniz: Sämtliche Schriften und Briefe* (Berlin: Akademie Verlag, 1923—)

DM   *Discours de métaphysique*

GM   C. I. Gerhardt (ed.), *Mathematische Schriften*, 7 vols. (Berlin and Halle: 1849–63)

GP   C. I. Gerhardt (ed.), *Die philosophischen Schriften*, 7 vols. (Berlin: 1875–90)

LOCKE

E   *An Essay concerning Human Understanding*

MALEBRANCHE

Recherche   *De la recherche de la vérité*

OC   André Robinet (ed.), *Œuvres complètes de Malebranche*, 20 vols. (Paris: Vrin, 1958–84)

SPINOZA

C   Edwin Curley (trans.), *The Collected Works of Spinoza*, vol. 1 (Princeton: Princeton University Press, 1984)

E   *Ethics*

G   Carl Gebhardt (ed.), *Spinoza Opera*, 5 vols. (Heidelberg: C. Winter, 1925, 1987)

KV   *Short Treatise on God, Man and His Well-Being* (*Korte Verhandeling*)

TIE   *Treatise on the Emendation of the Intellect*

I

Conflicting Causalities:
The Jesuits, their Opponents, and Descartes
on the Causality of the Efficient Cause

HELEN HATTAB

What is causality? This was a stock question for Scholastic Aristotelians of the late sixteenth and early seventeenth centuries, as it is posed, again and again, in well-known commentaries on Aristotle's *Physics*, and in commonly used textbooks of Scholastic philosophy. It forms part of a standard set of questions philosophers at the time raised with respect to Aristotle's discussion of the efficient cause. To be precise, the question concerns the exact nature of the causality of the efficient cause and usually appears right after treatments of Aristotle's definition of the efficient cause, and the various kinds of efficient causes.

Early modern philosophers, having rejected Aristotelian natural philosophy and, along with it, the commentary form, no longer explicitly address this question. In fact, the whole transition from Aristotelianism to mechanism is often seen as involving a fundamental change in the conception of causation such that certain questions about causation simply become irrelevant. Having said that, the efficient cause is supposed to be the one cause that survived. One of the central tenets of mechanism is said to be the rejection of formal and final causation in favor of efficient causation, where efficient causation is understood by the mechanists in terms of impact. But this oversimplifies matters, for there are philosophers whom we would group with the so-called mechanical philosophers who do not reject final causes, such as Pierre Gassendi and G. W. F. Leibniz, as well as Scholastic Aristotelians who regard the efficient cause as primary in explanations of natural phenomena, such as Francisco Suárez and Antonio Rubio. Nor do the lines of demarcation become clearer if we say that mechanists redefine efficient causation and cast it solely in terms of impact, for one already finds this conception of physical causation in Sebastian Basso, who is not a mechanist in any straightforward sense.[1]

Perhaps all this means is that the terms 'Aristotelian' and 'mechanist' do not admit of straightforward definitions and that there may turn out to be as many mechanisms as there are Aristotelianisms. I am not concerned in this article to try and make these classifications. My goal is much more limited. I would like to take one instance of what many regard as a prime example of a mechanical philosophy, namely, that of René Descartes, and contrast the conception of efficient causation on which it is based to that of Descartes's immediate Scholastic Aristotelian predecessors. Despite a shared emphasis on efficient causation to explain natural phenomena, I will argue that there is a very fundamental difference between the two. The disagreement lies not so much in their conceptions of the status of the efficient cause in the domain of natural philosophy, but in its metaphysical grounding—i.e. the difference lies in the way in which the causality of the efficient cause is conceived.

There are two competing Scholastic Aristotelian accounts of the causality of the efficient cause that form part of Descartes's immediate context. The first is found in the commentaries of Jesuit philosophers that Descartes remembers from his school days at La Flèche, notably those by Francisco Toledo, Antonio Rubio, and the Coimbran commentators.[2] The same basic account is elaborated by Francisco Suárez in the *Metaphysical Disputations*.[3] The second account is found in the textbook of a Paris *doctor* by the name of Charles François d'Abra de Raconis. His *Tertia Pars Philosophiae* (the one on physics) was

---

[1] I argue for this in ch. 4 of 'The Origins of a Modern View of Causation: Descartes and his Predecessors on Efficient Causes (Ph.D. Diss., University of Pennsylvania, 1998), 171–227. This point is also made by Tullio Gregory in 'Sébastien Basson', in Marilène Raiola (trans.), *Genèse de la Raison Classique de Charron à Descartes* (Paris: Presses Universitaires de Paris, 2001) and by Christoph Lüthy in 'Thoughts and Circumstances of Sébastien Basson. Analysis, Micro-History, Questions', *Early Science and Medicine* 2/1 (1997), 1–73.

[2] All references will be to the following commentaries: [Manuel de Gois], *Commentarii Collegii Conimbricensis Societatis Iesu in Octo Libros Physicorum Aristotelis Stagiritae* [Coimbrans] (1593; repr. Hildesheim: Georg Olms Verlag, 1984); Antonio Rubio, *Commentarii in octo libros Aristotelis de Physico auditu unà cum dubiis & quaestionibus hac tempestate agitari solitis* [Rubio] (Lyons: Johannes Pillehotte, 1611); Francisco Toledo, *Commentaria una cum quaestionibus, in octo libros Aristotelis de Physica Auscultatione* [Toledo] (Cologne: In Officina Birckmannica Sumptibus, 1585).

[3] Alfred Freddoso (trans.), *On Efficient Causality Metaphysical Disputations 17, 18, and 19* [*MD*], (New Haven: Yale University Press, 1994). Unless otherwise indicated, all references are to this translation.

recommended to Descartes by Marin Mersenne at the time Descartes was preparing himself for objections to the *Meditations* from the Jesuits.[4] Descartes later indicated to Mersenne that he had de Raconis's text in his possession.[5] I will briefly outline both these accounts and then argue that Descartes appears to be relying on a conception of efficient causality that differs from both of these Aristotelian views.

For the Jesuits, causality is that which makes a thing be a cause in act, and lets us call it a cause in act. According to Rubio, this means that causality cannot possibly be the entity or its essence, nor its potential or power to produce an effect, for these are present whether the cause is in act or not.[6] Both Suárez and Rubio rule out that causality could be the actual relation between cause and effect, because that relation is the result of the causality. In other words, the relation between cause and effect presupposes a cause in act, and thus presupposes the causality that makes it a cause in act.[7] So the causality of an efficient cause must be whatever grounds the relation between cause and effect.[8] Following the logic of relations that prevailed at this time, whatever grounds a relation must inhere in at least one of the two relata.[9] In this case, the two relata

---

[4] AT iii, 234. All references to de Raconis's work will be to the following edition: Charles François d'Abra de Raconis, *Tertia Pars Philosophiae seu Physica* [de Raconis] (Lyons: Irenaei Barlet, 1651). [5] To Mersenne, 3 Dec. 1640, AT iii, 251.

[6] Rubio, bk. II, tract. 4, q. 1, 256.

[7] 'What is being discussed is not the relation *cause of* which is said to result once the effect has already been produced. For it is obvious that this relation is not the causality, since it instead presupposes the causality as the notion upon which it is founded' (Suárez, *MD*, 249; Rubio, 256).

[8] 'Therefore, the discussion is about causality, according as it means, in our way of understanding, that it [causality] is the proximate ground (*ratio*) of founding the relation; that indeed that ground (*ratio*) is what constitutes and denominates it as acting cause insofar as it is said to be prior in nature to the effect' (Suárez, *Disputaciones Metafísicas* Disp. XVI–XXIII [*DM*] (Madrid: Bibliotheca Hispanica de Filosofía, 1961), iii. 291).

[9] See Dennis Des Chene, *Physiologia: Natural Philosophy in Late Aristotelian and Cartesian Thought* [*Physiologia*] (Ithaca: Cornell University Press, 1996), 43, esp. n. 54: 'Every relation between two things must rest on non-relational accidents of those things, which are called the *fundamenta* of the relation. My being taller than Tom Thumb rests on my being such and such a height and Tom's being such and such a height. See, for example, Coimbra *In Log.* 1:465.' As Suárez points out, a relation is based on a real form and is not by nature distinct from that form: 'It must be clear that a relation expresses certainly a real form and that it denominates its own relative [term], which it constitutes. It is not, however, a reality or mode distinct *ex natura rei* from all absolute forms, but it is in reality an absolute form, although not taken absolutely, but rather as referring to another, which it includes or connotes with a relative denomination. In this way similarity, for example, is a real form existing in the thing called similar; but it is not distinct from whiteness in the thing, with respect to what it puts in the

are the agent and the patient. Our authors presuppose that the causality of the efficient cause must either be a mode intrinsic to the agent, or a mode extrinsic to it, and thus intrinsic to the patient.[10]

The Jesuits argue against the view that causality is a mode intrinsic to the agent such as a power or influx.[11] On their view, the action is what denominates the agent as actually acting and therefore action is the causality of the efficient cause. Suárez and Rubio both make it clear that action is an extrinsic rather than intrinsic denomination of the cause.[12] John P. Doyle has summarized Suárez's understanding of extrinsic denomination as 'a designation of something, not from anything inherent in itself, but from some other disposition, coordination, or relationship which it has toward something else'.[13] Common examples of extrinsic denominations are designating something as 'right' or 'left' in

---

thing which is said similar, but only with respect to the term it connotes. And so, in reality similarity is not other than the very white relating to another whiteness of the same or a similar nature *(rationis)*' (Francisco Suárez, *Metaphysical Disputation V: Individual Unity and its Principle* [*Individual Unity*], trans. Jorge J. E. Gracia (Milwaukee, Wis.: Marquette University Press, 1982), 257–8).

[10] According to St Thomas Aquinas a relation is a regard or orientation of its subject to something else. Each relation is made up of three elements: the subject, the term, and the foundation. The foundation is the reason why the subject is related to the term and it must exist and inhere in the subject. So the foundation of a relation must always be an accident. All foundations can be reduced to two basic categories: quantity or action (and passion). There is a fundamental difference between these two foundations. Relations rooted in quantity are reciprocal, e.g. A is unequal to B, and B is unequal to A. By contrast, the fire heats the pot, but the pot does not heat the fire. Hence relations grounded in the foundation of action are not reciprocal. Furthermore, for a relation to come into being there must be some change. In the case of relations based on quantity there can be a real change in both relata when the relation changes, e.g. if A and B become equal, this could be due to a change in both their quantitative measurements. But this is not the case in relations based on action and passion. In that case, the patient undergoes a change (e.g. the pot becomes hot) but the agent does not (the fire remains hot throughout). Cause and effect relations are thus non-reciprocal relations where only one of the two relata changes. See Robert W. Schmidt, S.J., *The Domain of Logic According to St Thomas Aquinas* [*Domain of Logic*] (The Hague: Martinus Nijhoff, 1966), 140–60.

[11] The Coimbrans attribute this view to Hervaeus, Soncinnas, and Javellus. Suárez argues against this view on the basis that what constitutes a cause as actually acting is thought of as immediately added to the power to act. In other words, the power alone is not enough to constitute a cause in act, and that is after all what causality does. Instead, the causality of the efficient cause is action, for that is what must be added to the power for there to be a cause in act. In fact, if the action is removed, the power cannot be thought of as acting, but once it is posited, the power is actually acting. See Suárez, *MD*, 252.

[12] Suárez, *MD*, 255; Rubio, 259.

[13] John P. Doyle, 'Prolegomena to a Study of Extrinsic Denomination in the Work of Francis Suárez, S.J.' [Prolegomena], *Vivarium* 22/2 (1984), 122–3.

relation to other things, or designating things as 'visible' or 'heard' or 'knowable' in relation to a knower.[14] Since these relations are rooted in real properties, Suárez locates extrinsic denomination under *ens realis*, not *ens rationis*.[15] In all cases the denomination is based on real features of things, namely, how they relate to other things, but the denomination in no way changes the thing that is denominated.[16] In other words, the thing in question remains the same, but its relation or disposition towards another thing changes. An intrinsic denomination, by contrast, does change the thing in question. For example, designating a thing as 'white' is an intrinsic denomination since whiteness is an intrinsic attribute that the thing has acquired. Since action is an extrinsic denomination, an action constitutes or denominates an agent as a cause in act, but extrinsically, that is, without conferring on it a new intrinsic property. The cause changes from potency to act only in regard to its relation to the effect.

This makes perfect sense on an Aristotelian metaphysics, for a substance, by its very nature, possesses the powers to produce certain effects and so its intrinsic properties do not change when it actually produces them. To produce the effect, it suffices for the substance to come into contact with something that has the appropriate passive powers. As soon as that happens, all change that occurs is within the affected substance, namely, the patient.[17] To take an example, fire by its very nature has the power to burn and is always ready to burn flammable substances, and so it possesses the same intrinsic properties whether it actually burns something or not. The moment it comes into contact with dry wood,

---

[14] Ibid. 123–4.   [15] Ibid. 133.   [16] Ibid. 129.

[17] Alfred Freddoso explains this point as follows: 'Suppose that all the prerequisites for an agent's acting are satisfied in a given case. These include the agent's having a sufficient power to produce a given effect in a properly disposed patient, the agent's being appropriately situated with respect to the patient, the patient's being properly disposed to receive the formal determination that the agent is ready to communicate, the absence of impediments, etc. Then what is the difference between the agent's acting in such a case and its not acting? The common scholastic adage is that the difference is just the coming to be of the relevant effect in the patient insofar as that effect is dependent on the agent. So no new entity need be added to the agent; instead the action consists in something being added to the patient.' Alfred Freddoso, 'God's General Concurrence with Secondary Causes: Pitfalls and Prospects,' *American Catholic Philosophical Quarterly* 68/2 (1994), 131–56. As Thomas Prendergast has pointed out, while Descartes rejects the Aristotelian metaphysics of potency and act, he seems to adopt this way of thinking when he states that motion is always in the mobile thing, not in that which moves it (Thomas Prendergast, 'Motion, Action and Tendency in Descartes's Physics', *Journal of the History of Philosophy* 13 (1975), 453–62).

the effect of burning is produced and thus one can conclude that the effect was produced, not by any change in the fire, but by the presence of the wood. It is the wood, as the patient, that then undergoes change and turns into ash. The fire as the agent remains unchanged. On this analysis, one can say that the action by which the agent, in this case the fire, produced the effect is an extrinsic denomination for the fire is designated as acting not due to any intrinsic change, but due to its relation to the patient, in this case the wood.

To sum up, the Jesuit position is that causality is whatever constitutes a cause in act. Action is what constitutes a cause in act and so action is the causality of the efficient cause. Furthermore, action is an extrinsic denomination and so it inheres as a mode in the patient, not the agent.

De Raconis argues directly against this account of causality, singling out Suárez and the Coimbrans by name. Whereas he agrees with them that action is an extrinsic denomination, inhering as a mode in the patient, he disagrees with them that action constitutes causality. Rather for de Raconis, the causality of the efficient cause cannot consist in something without which the cause is still formally a cause. Since the efficient cause is still formally a cause, even when it is not acting, on this criterion, the causality of the efficient cause does not consist in action.[18] Therefore, action cannot constitute the causality of the efficient cause.[19]

De Raconis claims that once you rule out that action constitutes causality, only the influx or power remains as something by which the efficient cause can be said to produce its act. In fact, it is by mediation of this influx that 'the cause itself bursts forth in act' and produces the action and the terminus.[20] This influx resides in the cause, and is thus an intrinsic mode of the agent not the patient. Having said that, de Raconis is rather fuzzy about what this influx is supposed to be.[21] He does distinguish between two senses of 'influx': influx in the first act which is 'the power of the same cause through which it concurs efficiently

---

[18] De Raconis, 125.   [19] Ibid. 125–6.   [20] Ibid. 126.

[21] In his 'Disputation about the heavens and the spheres' found in the *Tertia Pars Philosophiae* he argues that the heavenly bodies cannot influence lower bodies by motion and light alone, for some earthly effects cannot be explained in terms of just motion and light. He therefore posits a heavenly power or influx, but again does not explain exactly what it is. He is, however, very clear that these influxes do not determine earthly events with necessity. De Raconis also refers to the first cause and secondary causes as having diverse influxes, but denies that God's concurrence consists in a physical premotion since that would destroy free will. Therefore, it does not seem that an influx could consist in something physical that gets impressed on a cause before it acts, since that would seem to make the cause act by necessity.

towards the production of the effect', and influx in the second act which he describes as 'a certain mode or actual application of the efficient cause towards the work and action to be exerted'.[22]

To sum up, for de Raconis, causality cannot consist in action because a cause is still form-ally a cause without action. The only remaining option is that causality consists in an influx or power inhering as a mode in the agent. This influx can be either a power or an actual application of the cause to the effect but de Raconis does not say anything more explicit about its nature. In fact, he concludes by admitting that both the view that causality consists in action, and the view that it consists in an influx are problematic. Whereas the former is opposed by the strongest arguments, the latter is problematic because it is difficult to explain what an influx is. De Raconis explains that he nevertheless prefers the influx view because it is better to uphold a view that is difficult to explain than a false one that is easy to explain.[23]

Despite the opposition between the Jesuits and de Raconis with respect to the nature of causality, both base their analysis of causality on a shared Aristotelian metaphysics. Whether one identifies efficient causality as the action or power of a substance, both accounts presuppose that relations, such as the cause–effect relation, are dependent on substances. Furthermore, both theories presuppose that the relation must be grounded in some real feature of one of the two substances which constitute the relata. Whether that real feature is a mode intrinsic to the agent, or the patient, is a matter for debate, but that it has to be a mode

[22] De Raconis, 126. The distinction between first and second act was commonly used by Scholastics to distinguish the perfections or powers of an agent from the exercise of those perfections or powers. For example, St Thomas Aquinas distinguishes between the first act as the form and integrity of the thing and the second act as its operation; see Gracia, *Individual Unity*, 179–180 (cited in n. 9). This is based on the distinction Aristotle makes in *De Anima* II, ch. 1, 412ᵃ9–10, where he distinguishes between two senses in which form is actuality: one in the sense that knowledge is actuality, and the other in the sense that contemplation is. In other words, one can possess a form in the sense that one can possess knowledge, say of grammar, without exercising that knowledge at the time. This is an actuality in the sense that one possesses the knowledge, and thus one has realized one's potential to acquire knowledge of grammar. But one can also distinguish between the mere possession of the knowledge and the exercise of it at a certain time, which is a further level of actualization. At this level of actualization the person not only possesses knowledge but is engaged in the activity of contemplating or exercising that knowledge. Aristotle goes on to identify the soul as an actuality in the sense that knowledge is, and implies a distinction between a first actuality and a second actuality by defining the soul as 'the first actuality of a natural body which has life potentially' (412ᵃ27). See D. W. Hamlyn (trans.), *Aristotle's De Anima Books II, III* (Oxford: Clarendon Press, 1968), 8–9. [23] De Raconis, 127.

inhering in one or the other is not. Thus, on a more fundamental level, one could say that both the Scholastic accounts of efficient causality that Descartes was exposed to, agree with respect to basic metaphysical categories. When it comes to the grounding of efficient causation, it is clear that these competing Aristotelian camps both agree that relations are dependent on modes that in turn inhere in a substance. The disagreement is not about the order of dependence, but about which of the two substances causality inheres in.

Interestingly, these broadly speaking Aristotelian metaphysical categories, and the order of dependence that they imply, seem to be presupposed in the two most common current interpretations of Descartes's account of causation. In other words, interpreters seem to assume that despite Descartes's overt rejection of Aristotelianism, he still holds to a basically Aristotelian ontology in which attributes and modes inhering in substance ground the relations between substances. The problem is that this Aristotelian ontology does not gel with Descartes's mechanistic conception of matter. Although they are not Scholastic modes, matter as *res extensa* certainly has attributes and modes, namely, geometrical properties.[24] But there is nothing inhering in matter that could provide the grounding for real causal relations as matter possesses no intrinsic powers or actions. Following the assumption that causal relations must be grounded in a substance capable of generating actions by its own causal powers, interpreters have found two solutions.

The first way out, which was already taken by seventeenth-century Cartesians, is to claim that, in Descartes's physical world, causal relations are not grounded in the intrinsic powers of material substance, for it has none, but in the power of the divine substance. More recently this interpretation of Descartes as an occasionalist with respect to body–body causation has been defended by Gary Hatfield and Dan Garber. It is admittedly an appealing solution as it allows one to preserve the onto-logical order of dependence, namely, that relations are dependent on

---

[24] Suárez says of modes:'I assume that in created things, besides their entities which are, as it were, substantial and (if I may use the term) radical, there are apprehended certain real modes that are something positive and of themselves modify the very entities by conferring on them something that is over and above the complete essence as individual and as existing in nature' (Cyril Vollert S.J. (trans.) *On the Various Kinds of Distinctions: Metaphysical Disputation 7* (Milwaukee, Wis.: Marquette University Press, 1947), 28). For Descartes there can be no modes over and above a thing's essence, e.g. the modes of matter are merely ways of being extended, extension being the essence of matter.

powers which inhere in substance, while at the same time recognizing that Descartes's conception of material substance rules out that it could be what grounds causal relations.

The alternative solution is to try and find a way in which powers and forces can be said to inhere in bodies without violating the geometrical conception of matter. On this interpretation, causal relations are grounded in real features of material substance. The appealing thing about this interpretation is that it preserves real natural causation. This is more consistent with Descartes's texts for he explicitly distinguishes secondary natural causes from the first divine cause, and frequently refers to created things as causing, acting, and possessing forces when giving physical explanations. However, finding ways in which Descartes could consistently attribute intrinsic forces to matter turns out to be very challenging indeed. Martial Gueroult argued that while force cannot be a mode of extension, it is a different kind of mode, not derivable from the essence of matter but from its existence and duration. In other words, force is simply another aspect of existence and duration that a body receives from God's creative act.[25] But as Garber has correctly noted, equating force with existence and duration fails to account for the variability of forces, for duration and existence do not vary, whereas forces do.[26] At most Gueroult's solution can account for the force of rest.

More recently, Desmond Clarke has also argued that bodies have modes other than the modes of extension, and that Cartesian forces are to be understood as a special kind of mode bodies receive from God. Clarke thus agrees that bodies on their own are inert, inactive, and incapable of moving themselves. However, God injects a quantity of force into the material world that gets distributed among bodies. Once bodies receive these forces they are endowed with active powers by which they produce motions.[27] While this interpretation accounts for the variability of forces, there is no evidence that Descartes's metaphysics allows for this special kind of mode. In fact, by its very nature

---

[25] Martial Gueroult, 'The Metaphysics and Physics of Force in Descartes', in Stephen Gaukroger (ed.), *Descartes: Philosophy, Mathematics and Physics* (Totowa, NJ: Barnes and Noble, 1980), 197.

[26] Daniel Garber, *Descartes' Metaphysical Physics* (Chicago: University of Chicago Press, 1992), 296–7.

[27] Desmond M. Clarke, 'The Concept of *Vis* in Part II of the Principia', in Jean-Robert Armogathe and Giulia Belgioioso (eds.), *Descartes: Principia Philosophiae (1644–1994)* (Naples: Vivarium, 1996), 331–9.

a mode is only understood through the concept of the thing in which it inheres, and it can only change when there is a change in that in which or through which it exists.[28] The idea that bodies could have forces that are not conceived through extension, nor changed as a result of changes in extension, violates the very definition of what it is to be a mode.[29]

In short, there are two ways of reading Descartes's views on body–body causation if we presuppose that he shares with his Scholastic Aristotelian predecessors some basic assumptions about metaphysical categories and their grounding. Assuming that Descartes shares the view that causality must be grounded in actions or powers that inhere in substance, then he must either be an occasionalist about body–body causation or committed to forces that inhere as modes in matter. The problem is that the occasionalist reading is inconsistent with Descartes's claims about causes, and the forces reading is inconsistent with his claims about modes. I argue that Descartes does not unequivocally support either account of causality we find in the Aristotelian texts he read. In fact, there are passages where he seems to reject them entirely and instead seems to be relying on a very different conception of what grounds the relation between cause and effect. I am going to go so far as to suggest that the conception of causality Descartes implicitly adheres to changes the entire order of dependence on which the Aristotelian accounts of causality rely. Since Descartes makes no explicit claims about the nature of causality and the grounding of causal relations, I make no claim that Descartes was conscious of introducing these changes. I will merely try to show that Descartes's references to secondary causes, forces, and actions can be made consistent with his metaphysics if we read him as,

---

[28] Whenever Descartes speaks of modes, he stresses that they are dependent on the substance in which they inhere, and he characterizes them as modifications of substance, or ways in which the substance is affected. Unlike a substance, modes cannot exist without the thing on which they depend. As a result, modes are not changed or destroyed by God without a corresponding change in the substance that they modify. Descartes illustrates this to Mesland in his letter of 9 Feb. 1645: 'By "surface" I do not mean any substance or real nature which could be destroyed by the omnipotence of God, but only a mode or a manner of being, which cannot be changed without a change in that in which or through which it exists; just as it involves a contradiction for the square shape of the wax to be taken away from it without any of the parts of the wax changing their place' (CSMK 241). In his *Comments on a Certain Broadsheet* Descartes writes: 'the nature of a mode is such that it cannot be understood at all unless the concept of the thing of which it is a mode is implied in its own concept' (CSM i, 301).

[29] I make this argument in more detail in 'The Problem of Secondary Causation in Descartes: A Response to Des Chene', *Perspectives on Science* 8/2 (2000), 100–1.

at least in part, rejecting the Aristotelian view of the ontological grounding of causal relations.

References to causes, forces, tendencies, and inclinations abound in Descartes's physics. I will show that one need not dismiss them as metaphorical ways of speaking of God's causality, nor posit irreducible powers in matter to explain them. These powers are reducible for Descartes but they are not directly reducible to the actions of the divine substance, rather they have a real grounding in the natural world. However, the way in which these powers are dependent on more fundamental categories goes against the Aristotelian order of dependence. Implicitly, Descartes's account of the causes of natural phenomena relies on a new account of causality. Descartes's physics, I will show, hints at a radically different ontological grounding of causation, one that he did not realize to its full extent.

To make my case I will examine three basic types of forces or tendencies Descartes relies on in his physics. I will be primarily concerned with the forces involved in the three laws of nature, namely, the force of a body to persist in its states, to resist the motion of another body, and the centrifugal force that results when the second law of motion is applied to motion in a vortex. I will then indicate how my account of these forces can be extended to more particular forces, specifically, the agitation force Descartes attributes to the sun, planets, and stars and the action or tendency to move, which defines light. In short, I will give a unified explanation of these different forces and argue that the common basis for all these forces points to a new understanding of causality.

The first law of nature is that 'each thing, in so far as it is simple and undivided, always remains, in so far as it is in itself (*quantum in se est*), in the same state and is never changed, except by external causes.'[30] According to the second law of nature, 'each part of matter, regarded separately, never tends to continue to be moved according to oblique lines, but only according to straight lines; although many are often forced to turn aside on account of the encounter of others.'[31] Finally, on the third law of nature,

when a body which is moved meets another, if it has less force to continue according to a straight line than the other has to resist it, then it is turned aside in another direction, retaining its motion and losing only the determination of

---

[30] AT viii, 62.   [31] AT viii, 63.

motion. If, however, it has greater force then it moves the other body with it, and gives it as much of its motion as it loses.[32]

Taken on their own, these three laws may convey the impression that individual particles of matter possess intrinsic powers to persist in their states, tend towards rectilinear motion, and resist the actions of bodies with which they collide. But in the *Principles of Philosophy* II, article 43, Descartes explains what the force to persist or resist consists in: 'namely, in this one fact, that each thing strives, in so far as it is in itself (*quantum in se est*), to remain in the same state in which it is, according to the first law posited in the previous place'.[33] Thus it would appear that for Descartes, the forces referred to in the laws of nature are not reducible to more basic powers, but that the powers themselves are explainable in terms of the first law. For Descartes, the notion of a power is a derivative one, dependent on the content of the laws of nature. That this dependence is an ontological one is indicated by the elaboration that follows. Descartes explains that from the first law of nature it follows that a body which is joined to another has some force or power to resist being separated from it, while a body that is separate has some power to remain separate. Later on Descartes explains that what joins bodies together is their relative rest to one another.[34] So the force to resist separation amounts to the power to remain in the same state of rest, which is fully explained by the first law of nature. Similarly bodies in motion with respect to each other are separate, and the power to remain separate turns out to be nothing but the power a moving body has to continue to move at the same speed and in the same direction. Thus there is nothing mysterious about these powers to persist and resist on Descartes's account. The powers are direct results of the fact that bodies remain in the same state they are in, as far as they can, and so a body already in motion will continue to move and thus appear to resist being stopped and joined to other bodies, whereas a body at rest will appear to resist being put in motion and thus being separated from bodies.

One might still think that the continued state of motion or rest, which is supposed to explain the resulting powers, must itself be explained in terms of an inherent tendency the body has to continue in its state of motion or rest. But Descartes makes it very clear that the initial states of motion and rest and their continuation are due to the action

---

[32] AT viii, 64.   [33] AT viii, 66.   [34] AT viii, 66–7.

of the divine first cause 'who in the beginning created matter, at the same time as motion and rest; and now, through his ordinary concourse alone, conserves as much motion and rest in the whole as he then placed in it.'[35] Furthermore, God always acts in the same way: 'For we understand that perfection is in God, not only because he is immutable in himself, but also because he operates in a manner that is most constant and immutable.'[36] Descartes claims that it is, 'most suitable to reason to conclude from this alone that, since God moved the parts of matter in diverse ways, when he first created them, and now certainly conserves that matter in the same way and by the same reason by which he previously created it, he also always conserves just as much motion in it.'[37]

Rather than attributing forces to bodies which then generate motions, God directly causes the states of body and preserves them in the same way in accordance with the immutability and simplicity of his action. The first and second laws of nature specify what results when God, by his immutable and simple operation, acts on the existing matter. But since the world is a plenum, bodies being moved rectilinearly or being maintained in a state of rest will encounter one another, and so Descartes claims that God's preservation of the total quantity of motion dictates that motion will have to be transferred or be altered in its direction when bodies come into contact. How exactly God distributes the different motions among bodies is determined by the third law of nature and the rules of collision.

So far, it looks as though this reading of the laws of nature makes forces completely reducible to God's action thus committing Descartes to occasionalism. But this would leave out an important aspect of Descartes's account which becomes especially salient with respect to the third law of nature. The fact is that the laws of nature, and resultant powers to persist and resist, do not follow straightforwardly from God's immutable action. Rather we must presuppose that particles of matter and their states have some basic features which determine how God is to transfer or alter motions in the case of collisions. The most fundamental feature is the opposition between motion and rest. That the state of motion in one body should oppose the state of rest in another is in no way dictated by the immutability of God's action, but it just seems to be inherent to these states that they are incompatible. This basic principle forms the basis of the third law of nature such that whenever bodies with these

---

[35] AT viii, 61.   [36] AT viii, 61.   [37] AT viii, 61–2.

opposing states come into contact, the opposition must be resolved. When there is an opposition between motion and rest, or even between a rapid movement and a slow one (for Descartes claims that slow motions partake of the nature of rest), then motion must either be transferred from one to another or the direction of motion must be altered depending on the size and speed of the bodies. Given bodies of equal size, the more extreme the difference in their speeds, the greater the opposition that must be overcome. Motion is itself not opposed to another motion of equal speed, and so when two bodies of equal size and speed collide, they lose none of their speed, but only the direction of the motion is altered.

One might conclude from this that there must be some irreducible forces in matter after all, namely, the ones that produce this basic opposition between motion and rest, and between different directional determinations of motion. But there is no indication that Descartes thinks there are. Rather motion and rest are simply states of matter given to particles of matter by God. Their opposition is not explained by any mediating forces, nor is it derivable from God's immutable action. It just seems to be a basic principle of the material world, once created and preserved by God, that states of motion and rest, and motions in opposing directions, are incompatible with one another.

This is not the only instance when Descartes relies on a fundamental principle that is not reducible to the nature of God's action in formulating his laws of nature. The second law of nature is said to result from 'the immutability and simplicity of the operation by which God conserves motion in matter'.[38] In *Le Monde* Descartes had already articulated this rule and justified it on the basis that, 'of all the motions, only the rectilinear one is entirely simple and has a nature which may be comprehended in an instant'.[39] There is one obvious sense in which one could say that motion in a straight line is simple whereas circular motion along a curved line requires at least two instants or parts and the relation between them. If one tries to trace a straight line (leaving aside the particular direction), one can do this through any one point. If one further assumes, as Descartes does, that motion in an instant has a direction, then a body in motion will follow a straight line in the same direction when God preserves it in the same state in the next instant. By contrast, to trace a curved path, one must have at least two points and so

---

[38] AT viii, 63.   [39] AT xi, 45.

God would have to consider at least two instants to preserve a body in motion along a curved line. According to Descartes, this would violate the simplicity and immutability of God's action.

God appears as the divine geometer limited to whatever is in front of him at every moment. Descartes specifies: 'I am not saying that rectilinear motion can take place in an instant, but only that everything required to produce it is found in bodies at each instant which could be determined while they are moving, but not everything which is required to produce circular motion.'[40] It is not entirely clear why it should be simpler for an omnipotent, omniscient being to consider one instant instead of two or more, nor is God's immutability violated unless we accept Descartes's assumption that motion along a curved path involves a change in the state of motion whereas motion along a rectilinear path does not.[41] If one regarded circular motion as natural to bodies, then God, by acting always in the same way, could produce motions along curved lines. This highlights the fact that Descartes is not so much concerned with what follows from God's nature, but with what is compatible with a geometrical conception of matter and its states. Just as there is a basic opposition between the states of motion and rest, it is basic to the geometer's conception of local motion that only motion in a straight line is simple because everything required to produce it is contained in bodies in each instant.

These two basic principles, which arise not from the nature of God, but seem to be fundamental features of extended matter and its states, are arguably the most fruitful in Descartes's physics. The fundamental opposition between motion and rest, which forms the basis for the third law of nature, also allows Descartes to distinguish between two different kinds of bodies: solid bodies and fluid bodies. Rest becomes the principle whereby Descartes explains what causes the parts of a body to cohere.[42] Bodies with parts that are at relative rest with respect to one another oppose motion and so they can only be driven out of their places with difficulty. Thus all we mean when we say that a body is solid is that it appears to resist being divided because its parts are at rest

---

[40] *Le Monde*, ch. 7; AT xi, 45.

[41] But as Gregory Brown has pointed out to me, the assumption that God produces what amounts to the simplest mathematical solution is shared by other seventeenth-century philosophers, most notably Leibniz. Similar assumptions are also apparent in the works of earlier figures such as Nicholas Copernicus and Johannes Kepler.

[42] *Principles of Philosophy* II. 55; AT viii, 71.

and oppose motion. By contrast, bodies whose parts are in motion do not oppose motion and so are easily moved out of their places. So all we mean by fluid bodies, according to Descartes, are bodies that do not resist motion because they 'are divided into many small parts agitated by motions reciprocally diverse from one another'.[43] In other words, there is nothing over and above the extended parts of bodies and their states of motion and rest that accounts for their solidity and fluidity. The power to resist that solid bodies display is solely due to the opposition between the rest of their parts, and the motion of our hands, whereas the force our hands seem to possess to modify fluid bodies is simply due to the fact that the motions of the parts of fluid bodies do not oppose the motion of our hands. We can see that the basic principle that motion and rest oppose one another becomes explanatory even of the different kinds of matter in the universe.

Once the distinction between solid and fluid matter is made on the basis of this principle, Descartes can proceed to articulate how bodies will move in the fluid matter of the heavens and attribute forces to them on the basis of their relative solidity. What Descartes calls the 'agitation force' of various celestial bodies turns out to be a function of solidity, which is a result of the motions of their parts in relation to their volume and surface area. In *Principles of Philosophy* III, article 121 Descartes explains that the solidity of a star consists in the third element matter[44] which makes up the spots surrounding it, in proportion to its volume and surface. Third element particles are larger and more angular and thus they cohere more easily with each other and acquire a greater force to resist motion as a result. This force, which Descartes calls 'agitation force', allows the star to maintain its movement and not succumb completely to the motions of the more volatile, and hence less solid and less resistant, globules of the second element matter surrounding it.[45]

The principle that only rectilinear motion is simple, which forms the basis for the second law of nature, similarly provides the backbone for

---

[43] *Principles of Philosophy* II. 54; AT viii, 71.

[44] In *Le Monde* and the *Principles of Philosophy* Descartes makes it clear that the various motions God attributes to the divided matter will lead to the formation of three elements of matter. First element matter consists in the small pointed edges that break off the larger pieces as a result of the motions of surrounding material particles. Owing to this continual wearing down, these larger pieces become smaller and rounded thus forming the second element of matter. Third element matter consists of large, jagged particles that have not been completely worn down. [45] AT viii, 170–2.

many of Descartes's explanations of specific natural phenomena. In the context of illustrating the second law of nature Descartes uses the example of a stone being rotated in a sling. Even though the stone will move along a circular path while in the sling, it is inclined to move in a straight line along a tangent to the circle, in accordance with the second law. This is confirmed by the fact that if the stone leaves the sling, it will not continue in its circular motion, but will move along a straight line. Descartes concludes from this that 'any body which is moved circularly constantly tends to recede from the center of the circle which it describes'.[46]

Descartes returns to the analogy of the stone in the sling in Part III of the *Principles of Philosophy*, article 57. He now identifies different strivings or tendencies to motion in relation to the different causes of the motion of the stone. He claims that if all the causes are taken together, i.e. the force of the stone's movement as well as the impeding motion of the sling, then the stone tends towards a circular motion. But if we consider only the force of motion of the stone in accordance with the second law of motion, then it tends to move in a straight line at a tangent to the circle. Lastly, if we only consider the part of the stone's force of motion that is hindered by the sling, then the stone tends to recede from the center of the circle along a straight line.[47]

Note that the tendencies described here are not separate powers inherent to the stone. That would imply that the stone possessed conflicting powers pulling it in one direction and another. Rather the different tendencies are a product of opposing states of motion and are understood in terms of counterfactuals, e.g. this is the way the stone would move absent the opposing motion of the sling.[48] The important point is that a tendency is always understood in terms of an impeding cause. In other words, all tendencies arise from an analysis of the motion dictated by the laws of nature, in relation to opposing motions.

---

[46] *Principles of Philosophy* II. 39; AT viii, 64.   [47] AT viii, 108–9.

[48] The stone's motion taken on its own is rectilinear, at a tangent to the circle. But this motion is opposed, and thus altered directionally, by the motion of the sling. Descartes then further divides the tendency of the stone to move at a tangent to the circle into a tendency to revolve around a fixed point and a tendency to move in a straight line along a rotating radius of a circle. Only the latter motion is opposed by the sling, which allows Descartes to identify it as the part of the stone's tendency to motion that is hindered by the sling. He then generalizes and claims that this tendency to recede from the center is a tendency of all bodies being carried along in a circular motion.

Tendencies designate the motions that would occur absent the opposing motions that are always present in a plenum.[49]

This tendency of bodies to recede from the center of a circle also plays
a central role in Descartes's explanations of celestial phenomena. The globules of the second element matter strive to recede from the center of the
vortex in which they rotate and are restrained by the globules beyond them
as the stone was by the sling.[50] Light itself is defined by Descartes as this
tendency of globules to recede from the center of the vortex. Descartes also
refers to this tendency, which constitutes light, as the 'first preparation to
motion'.[51] This tendency to motion is transmitted instantaneously along
an infinite number of straight lines through the medium to our eyes.

It is clear that one can account for the forces and tendencies Descartes
refers to by reducing them to more basic principles. Agitation force, and
forces to resist motion in general, derive from a body's solidity, which in
turn is reducible to the relative rest of its parts in relation to its surface
area. The various tendencies to move, such as the tendency to recede
from the center in a straight line which constitutes light, are fully
explained in terms of the motions that would occur absent opposing
motions. Ultimately, the forces to persist in a state and resist opposing
motions are reducible to the three laws of nature. These in turn reflect
God's immutable and simple action. However, as we saw, the laws also
presuppose some basic principles inherent to the nature of matter and
its states, namely: (1) the states of motion and rest oppose one another,
(2) different directions of motion oppose one another, (3) only rectilinear motion is simple and can be grasped in an instant.

What are the implications of this analysis for Descartes's conception
of the causality of the efficient cause? With respect to physical phenomena, Descartes identifies God as the universal and primary cause of all
the motions in the world and the laws of nature as the secondary and

---

[49] Descartes makes this clear in *Le Monde* when he writes: 'To this end, it should be noted
that when I say that a body tends in some direction, I do not thereby want anyone to imagine
that there is a thought or will in the body that bears it there, but that it is disposed to move
there, whether it actually moves or whether some other body prevents it from doing so. And
it is principally in this last sense that I use the word "tend", because it seems to signify some
exertion and because every exertion presupposes some resistance. Now in so far as there are
often a number of different causes which, acting together on the same body, impede one
another's effect, one can, depending on the various considerations, say that the same body
tends in different directions at the same time' (AT xi. 84; translation by H.H.).

[50] *Principles of Philosophy* III. 60; AT viii, 112.

[51] *Principles of Philosophy* III. 63; AT viii, 115.

particular causes of particular motions and their variations.[52] The division between a first, universal cause and second, particular causes was a standard distinction made by Scholastic Aristotelians with respect to efficient causes.[53] Descartes is making an analogous division among his efficient causes of motion.[54]

Problems arise when trying to determine in what sense one could attribute causality to the laws of nature in so far as they are the secondary and particular efficient causes of motion. If we take the Jesuit criterion and claim that action is what constitutes the causality of the efficient cause, then the laws of nature do not appear to be genuine efficient causes since laws are not sources of action. Thus it has been common to regard the laws as expressions of, or reasons for, God's action. In other words, their causality is identical to God's causality and thus the primary universal cause is the only true efficient cause of all motions. But this is inconsistent with Descartes's claim that particular causes, not God, account for particular and changing motions, for God's action does not change.[55] De Raconis's account, which identifies the causality of the efficient cause with an influx or power the cause acquires, is equally problematic for Descartes. In what sense can an influx or power inhere in a law as a mode? Modes inhere in substances and since the laws of nature are not substances, it seems that they could only be said to be causes in the loose sense that they describe the powers inhering in material substances. The causality of the secondary and particular causes would thus have to consist in powers intrinsic to bodies, but as we already saw, this is inconsistent with Descartes's conception of matter and its modes.

---

[52] *Principles of Philosophy* II, a. 36–7; AT viiia, 61–2.

[53] See for example Toledo: 'the universal cause is that which produces many effects of different species, like the sun, the heavens, the celestial movers and glorious God. . . . The particular cause is that which produces one principal effect of one species, for example fire produces fire, man produces man' (Bk. II, ch. 3, q. 7, 60).

[54] See my essay on 'One Cause or Many? Jesuit Influences on Descartes' Division of Causes', in Stephen Brown (ed.), *Meeting of the Minds* (Turn out (Belgium): Brepols, 1998), 105–120.

[55] Descartes writes in *Le Monde*: 'According to this rule, then, [the third rule that the parts of a moving body individually always tend to continue moving along a straight line] it must be said that God alone is the author of all the motions in the world in so far as they exist and in so far as they are rectilinear; but it is the various dispositions of matter which render them irregular and curved. Likewise, the theologians teach us that God is also the author of all our actions, in so far as they exist and in so far as they have some goodness, but it is the various dispositions of our wills that can render them evil' (CSM i, 97; AT xi, 46–7).

At this point one might be tempted to throw one's hands up in the air and claim that Descartes is confused about the metaphysics of causal relations, or that he simply had no interest in providing a consistent account of the causality of the particular causes of motion. On my view, whether he realized it or not, Descartes actually has the resources to give such an account, but it requires a rethinking of the metaphysical categories and the order of dependence presupposed by Aristotelian accounts.

As mentioned earlier, on an Aristotelian metaphysics, relations are dependent on individual substances, and whatever grounds the relation between them. For the Scholastics a relation, such as the one between cause and effect, has to be grounded in a real accident of at least one of the two relata. In other words, there has to be a mode, inhering in at least one of the two related substances, that forms the basis for that relationship. Thus relations are dependent on modes to exist, and modes are dependent on substances to exist. As modes, actions and powers are ontologically and explanatorily more basic than relations, and substances in turn precede modes by nature.

What we find, by contrast, in Descartes's physics is that substances, as we know them, such as solid and fluid bodies, are results of the forces of matter either to act on other bodies and resist their actions, or be acted on. But these apparent powers and actions turn out not to be irreducible modes inhering in these substances. Rather they turn out to be a result of the states of motion or rest of the microscopic parts of bodies, and the opposition between these states. The causal relations we observe are thus not the results of actions or powers inhering in one of the related individual bodies, but the result of a complex set of relations at the microscopic level. Nor can one say that the relations among the microscopic parts of bodies are explained by powers or actions inherent to the related particles, for God preserves these particles and their current states at every instant thus giving them the actions and powers they appear to exert. One might think that God's immutable action alone grounds the relations between these particles, but this too is incorrect since particles will cohere, or seem to resist each other, and tend away from each other as a result of the compatibility of similar states and the incompatibility of differing states. The oppositions between certain states are not explainable in terms of God's simple and immutable action, but seem to be inherent in matter once it is preserved in a certain state. The relationship of God's immutable action to these inherent principles of matter forms the basis for the three laws of nature. These laws, as they apply to particular contexts, account for particular motions and changes in motion.

The causality of the laws of nature consists not in any intrinsic powers or actions inhering in them as modes. Rather what forms the basis of the laws of nature is another set of relations, the most obvious one being the relation between God's immutable action and the states of matter. But as we have seen, the states of matter are not fully determined by the simplicity and immutability of God's action, rather, God's action has to be accommodated to certain principles basic to the nature of matter. These principles themselves express certain relations between the states of matter, such as the relation between the state of matter at one instant and the next, and the opposition between states of motion and rest, and different directions of motion. As we saw, these principles are not further reducible to intrinsic powers in matter. In terms of finding a grounding for the laws of nature in material substance, this is as far as we are going to get. Thus the causal relationship between laws of nature and the particular motions that follow from them is dependent on a further set of relations which determine why the laws of nature have the character that they do, and produce the kinds of motions they do in specific contexts.

The causality of the laws of nature then consists partly in God's immutable action, which provides the power by which the states of matter are preserved. But it also consists in the fundamental features of the states of matter and their relations. It is in this sense that Descartes reverses the ontological order of dependence found in the Aristotelian accounts of what grounds causal relations. The causal relations between individual bodies are for Descartes not dependent on powers intrinsic to those bodies. Instead, at the most basic level one has a set of relations between the states of material particles. This set of relations produces powers to resist division and displacement, or tendencies to be divided and displaced, depending on whether the particles are in a state of rest or in motion with respect to one another. These powers and tendencies in turn determine whether particles will cohere to form one individual body or be divided.

The Aristotelian conception of the order of ontological dependencies is from individual substances, as the most basic reality, to the powers and other modes which inhere in them, to the relations which derive from these modes. By contrast, Descartes's physical explanations indicate that for him certain relations between states of motion and rest are prior by nature to the powers of matter to resist and persist. These powers, which are reducible to the laws of nature, in turn, determine what kinds of individual substances are formed. The ontological order implied by Descartes's physics, is from relations between states of matter as governed by the laws of nature, to the powers that derive from them, to individual substances as we know them. If we hold to the common view at the time that the causality of the efficient cause is that which grounds the relation between cause and effect, then Descartes's laws of nature can be said to have a causality that consists in a set of fundamental relations among states of matter, and their relation to God's immutable action.[56]

Whether or not we want to accept this as a legitimate conception of causality, the ontological reversal at its base, which is implied by Descartes's physics, makes his view of efficient causation fundamentally different from the accounts of both his Aristotelian and non-Aristotelian predecessors. But neither Descartes nor his successors were ready to embrace it, hence the attempts by both Cartesians and their critics, such as Leibniz, to reinstate an Aristotelian conception of onto-logical dependencies, and adapt it to the new physics. In this process, real causal relations grounded in features inherent to the natural world gave way to occasionalism and pre-established harmony.

University of Houston

---

[56] St Thomas Aquinas denied that a real relation could hold between two relata, one of which was itself a real relation. Even when the more fundamental relation making up one of the two relata is real, the second-order relation is merely a relation of reason. One of the reasons for rejecting the idea that real relations could themselves be grounded in relations is that this would lead to an infinite regress. Schmidt, *Domain of Logic*, 165. However, Suárez seems to allow for the possibility that relations could themselves give rise to further real relations: 'Thus in the present context, just as we said above that an accident can result from a substance, so too from any accident there can result another accident that is either really or at least modally distinct from it, as long as the former has the capacity for such a property. For it is in this way that a shape or a relation of equality (if the latter is a distinct mode) results from a quantity; and it is in this way that, according to many authors, one relation can result from another—for example, a similarity from a paternity and so forth' (Suárez, *MD*, 111–12). However, Suárez's discussion of fate indicates that ultimately such relations must be grounded in substances and their accidents. He states that fate is not just the relations but an arrangement of causes which 'bespeaks, within each and every cause, the application that is appropriate in order for a given effect to be able to follow' (ibid. 396–7).

2

The Cartesian God and the Eternal Truths

GREGORY WALSKI

Throughout his works, from his letters to Mersenne as early as 1630 to a letter to More dated 5 February 1649 (just months before his death), Descartes advances his doctrine of the creation of the eternal truths, according to which the laws and truths of mathematics, logic, and metaphysics—what we call 'necessary' truths—were determined by God's free will. In his letter to Mersenne of 27 May 1630, he writes that God 'was free to make it not true that all the radii of the circle are equal—just as he was free not to create the world' (AT i. 152; CSMK 25).[1] In the *Sixth Replies*, he claims that God's will is responsible for 'all order, every law, and every reason for anything's being true or good' (AT vii. 435; CSM ii. 293–4). And in his letter to Arnauld of 19 July 1648, he asserts that 'every basis of truth and goodness depends on [God's] omnipotence', and so that he 'would not dare say that God cannot make a mountain without a valley, or bring it about that 1 and 2 are not 3' (AT v. 223–4; CSMK 358–9).

In her celebrated *L'Œuvre de Descartes*, Geneviève Rodis-Lewis has claimed that 'in proposing this thesis . . . Descartes broke not only with his Augustinian version of Platonism and with Neo-Platonist emanationism, but also with the Scholastic accounts of what makes an object possible'.[2] This is certainly true, but at the same time it is an understatement: by advancing his eternal truths doctrine, Descartes largely broke *with the traditional conception of God*. We do not simply find in his works the traditional God along with a superadded doctrine about his power over the eternal truths. Instead, we find a God who, while he has the traditional divine attributes, has them in a way conceived so uniquely that from them it follows that he created the eternal truths.

---

[1] In some places I make changes to the CSM(K) translations, citing the original language in the text or in the notes where the changes are substantive.

[2] Geneviève Rodis-Lewis, *L'Œuvre de Descartes* (Paris: J. Vrin, 1971), 128.

Descartes's doctrine of the creation of the eternal truths strikes most philosophers as patently false, if not absurd. As a result, a growing number of his commentators have asked why Descartes thought that the doctrine was true. The common view is that Descartes thought that it was necessary in order to maintain God's omnipotence. In his influential study of the doctrine, Edwin Curley asks, 'Why did Descartes hold this doctrine?' He answers that 'Clearly he thought that God's omnipotence required it', yet admits that 'this simple, obvious answer does not take us very far'.[3] This answer does not take us very far for two reasons. First, it does not explain *why* Descartes should think that God's omnipotence requires that God created the eternal truths. Second, it does not account for the fact that Descartes also appeals to the indifference of God's will and God's simplicity in support of his eternal truths doctrine, and that he thinks that it is *primarily God's simplicity* that requires that God created the eternal truths. So the question becomes this: Why did Descartes hold that God's omnipotence, the indifference of his will, and primarily his simplicity, require that he created the eternal truths?

I

The traditional conception of God's causal relation to the eternal truths is bound up with what I shall call the 'theory of divine ideas', according to which God knows the natures of all possible things by understanding how potential objects of his creation can share or 'participate' in his essence. By performing a reflexive act on his own essence, as it were, he knows the natures of humans, horses, and even things such as stones. So for instance, by understanding how something can share in his knowledge, will, power, etc., he understands the nature of a human being. The nature of every possible thing is contained in God's intellect prior to his act of creation, and each nature is comprehended by a 'divine idea'.

---

[3] Edwin Curley, 'Descartes on the Creation of the Eternal Truths', *Philosophical Review*, 93 (1984), 569–97, at 583. Similarly, Peter Geach claims that 'Descartes' motive for believing in absolute omnipotence was not contemptible: it seemed to him that otherwise God would be *subject* to the inexorable laws of logic as Jove was to the decrees of the Fates' ('Omnipotence', *Philosophy* 48 (1973), 7–20, at 10–1). In all fairness, the way in which Descartes states his doctrine in his letter to Mersenne of 15 Apr. 1630 invites Curley's and Geach's reading: 'It is indeed to speak of God as if he were Jupiter or Saturn and subject to the Styx and the Fates to say that these truths are independent of him' (AT i. 145; CSMK 23). Nevertheless, there is no implication here that Descartes regards his view of God's relation to the eternal truths and the view that they are independent of God as the only two possible positions.

As Aquinas writes in the *Summa Theologica* (*ST*):

> Inasmuch as God knows His essence perfectly, He knows it according to every mode in which it can be known. Now it can be known not only as it is in itself, but as it can be participated in by creatures according to some kind of likeness. But every creature has its own proper species, according to which it participates in some way in the likeness of the divine essence. Therefore, as God knows His essence as so imitable by such a creature, He knows it as the particular model and idea of that creature: and in like manner as regards other creatures. So it is clear that God understands many models proper to many things; and these are many ideas.   (*ST* I, 15, 2)[4]

Upon understanding the proper natures of all possible things, God chooses to create some of them (e.g., humans), but refrains from creating others (e.g., unicorns). And with understanding of all possible natures comes knowledge of the essential truths about them: 'God knows not only that things are in Him, but, by the mere fact that they are in Him, He knows them in their own nature' (*ST* I, 14, 6). So if we were to suppose along with Aristotle that the nature of a human being is 'rational animal', then by understanding his own essence, and hence understanding the nature of a human being, God knows the eternal truths 'All humans are rational', 'All humans are animals', and so on.

On this theory, God is not the efficient cause of essences and eternal truths, as he is of the world and everything that occupies it; instead, he is their *exemplary* cause. And since God necessarily understands himself and because his nature could not have been otherwise, it follows that he necessarily understands himself in the way that he does. In turn, it follows that the essences of things and eternal truths are what they are necessarily. So for example, 'human being' is necessarily an essence, the essence of humanity is necessarily what it is, and all truths about the essence of humanity are necessary. One of the important consequences of the theory of divine ideas is that the modal properties of things are determined entirely by God's understanding of his own nature and in no way by his will. God does not *will* or *decide* that things should have the modal properties they do; instead, the modal properties of things are determined by how God understands them. If God understands that a property is essential to x, then x necessarily has that property; if a

---

[4] Citations from Aquinas's *Summa Theologica* are from Anton C. Pegis (ed. and trans.), *Basic Writings of Saint Thomas Aquinas*, i (New York: Random House, 1945), and cited by '*ST*' followed by book, question, and article numbers.

property is incompatible with y, then it is impossible that y should have that property; and if a property is neither essential nor incompatible with z, then whether or not z has that property is contingent.

Another important consequence of the theory of divine ideas is that it makes the natures of things and eternal truths identical to God. Since they arise from God's understanding of his own nature, they exist 'in' the divine intellect. In the divine intellect, however, there are no real distinctions (*ST* I, 15, 2), and the divine intellect is identical to the divine essence (*ST* I, 14, 4). To quote from Aquinas, 'an idea in God is nothing other than his essence' (*ST* I, 15, 2), and 'the truth of the divine intellect is God himself' (*ST* I, 16, 7). These natures and ideas are not limited to natures of substances and the eternal truths about them, but also include mathematical natures and truths: 'The nature of a circle, and the fact that two and three make five, have eternity in the mind of God' (ibid.). And since God is identical to the eternal truths, the contrary of an eternal truth is, in effect, a negation of the divine nature itself. When we say that it belongs to the nature of a human to be an animal, we are expressing one of the requirements of the *being* of a human. As Aquinas writes in the *Summa contra Gentiles* (*SCG*), 'To take away an essential principle of any thing is to take away the thing itself' (*SCG* II, 25, 13).[5] Hence, a man could not be an inanimate thing because inanimateness is contrary to humanity. Were a human not an animal, it would not be a human, but a *chimera*, i.e. a *non-being*. And since the nature of a human being arises from God's nature, which could not have been otherwise, it follows that if it were not an eternal truth that all humans are animals, the Being of *God himself* would be negated.

II

Descartes rejects the theory of divine ideas based on the indifference of the divine will. In his letter to Mesland of 9 February 1645, he explains that by 'indifference' he means 'that state of the will when it is not impelled one way rather than another by *any* perception of truth or goodness' (AT iv. 173; CSMK 244–5; emphasis added). I emphasize 'any' here because not even ideas in God's intellect can influence his will. Descartes makes this clear in the *Sixth Replies*. In reply to the objection

---

[5] Citations from Aquinas's *Summa contra Gentiles* are from James F. Anderson (ed. and trans.), *On the Truth of the Catholic Faith: Summa contra Gentiles, Book Two: Creation* (Garden City, NY: Hanover House, 1955), and cited by '*SCG*' followed by book, question, and article numbers.

that 'if indifference cannot be a proper part of human freedom, neither will it find a place in divine freedom' (AT vii. 417; CSM ii. 281), Descartes first claims that freedom of the will exists in humans in a different way from the way in which it exists in God. While he doesn't explain just what the difference consists in, *Meditations* IV makes it clear that what he means is that while indifference of the will is a perfection in God, it is an imperfection in human beings.[6] Descartes goes on to write that 'it is self-contradictory to suppose that the will of God was not indifferent from eternity with respect to everything which has happened or ever will happen', and then claims that 'it cannot be imagined that an idea might have existed in the divine intellect of any good, truth, belief, or object of God's creation or omission from his creation, prior to the determination of his will to make it so' (AT vii. 431–2; CSM ii. 291).[7] In other words, the exercise of God's will does not in any sense presuppose ideas in his intellect. This is the case for *at least* the reason that, if there were such ideas, 'God would not have been completely indifferent with respect to the creation of what he did in fact create' (AT vii. 435; CSM ii. 294). If we were to suppose that God had an indefinite number of ideas in his intellect prior to his creation, each comprehending the nature of something, and also suppose that he 'then' chose to create some of them, leaving others uncreated, we would be left with the question, 'Why did God choose to create the things he did?' Any answer to this question would imply that there was something about the particular natures he chose to actualize that influenced his will to create them. This consequence also extends itself to truths. For instance, if there were an idea of the essence of a triangle in God's intellect prior to his creation, he would have been impelled to make the Pythagorean theorem true. But if God were impelled to make it true, he would not have indifferently made it true. If he is to be truly indifferent, then *not even his own nature* can determine or influence his will. It cannot be the case, as

---

[6] 'But the indifference I feel when there is no reason pushing me in one direction rather than another is the lowest grade of freedom; it is evidence not of any perfection of freedom, but rather a defect in knowledge or a kind of negation' (AT vii. 58; CSM ii. 40).

[7] The CSM II translation omits Descartes's reference to divine ideas. Here is the Latin: 'nullum bonum, vel verum, nullumve credendum, vel faciendum, vel omittendum, fingi potest, cujus idea in intellectu divino prius fuerit, quam ejus voluntas se determinarit ad efficiendum ut id tale esset.' For a translation of this passage similar to my own, see Roger Ariew (ed. and trans.), *Philosophical Essays and Correspondence* (Indianapolis: Hackett Publishing Co., 2000), 199.

Descartes explains, that God willed 'that the three angles of a triangle should be equal to two right angles because he recognized that it could not be otherwise'. Instead, it must be the other way around: 'it is because he willed that the three angles of a triangle should necessarily equal to two right angles that this is true and cannot be otherwise' (AT vii. 432; CSM ii. 291).

Also in the *Sixth Replies*, Descartes writes that if it were not the case that God's will is responsible for 'all order, every law, and every reason for anything's being true or good', then

God would not have been completely indifferent with respect to what he did in fact create. If some reason for something's being good has existed prior to his preordination, this would have determined God to prefer those things which it was best to do. But on the contrary, just because he resolved to prefer those things which are now to be done, for this very reason, in the words of Genesis, 'they are very good'; in other words, the reason for their goodness depends on the fact that he exercised his will to make them so.   (AT vii. 435–6; CSM ii. 294)

Simply put, God's indifference *requires* that he created the eternal truths. For if God's will cannot be impelled by anything, then he cannot have had ideas of natures or eternal truths in his intellect prior to his creation. But we know that things do have natures and that there are eternal truths, and that everything depends on God. Since these natures and eternal truths are not products of God's exemplary causality, they must be products of his efficient causality, 'in the sense that a king may be called the efficient cause of a law' (AT vii. 436; CSM ii. 294). This is precisely what Descartes had told Mersenne back in his letters of 1630. In the letter of 15 April, he had claimed that God has established the eternal truths 'just as a king lays down laws in his kingdom' (AT i. 145; CSMK 23); and in the letter of 27 May 1630, he had claimed that God established the eternal truths 'by the same kind of causality as he created all things, that is to say, as their efficient and total cause' (AT i. 152; CSMK 25).

It is worth pausing for a moment here to point out that, unlike the traditional conception of the eternal truths, which are products of God's exemplary causality and so are identical to God, Descartes's eternal truths are products of God's efficient causality, and so distinct from God—just as the laws legislated by a king are distinct from the king. This is precisely the sense of Descartes's claim, in his letter to Mersenne of 27 May 1630, that 'it is certain that these truths are no more necessarily conjoined to [God's] essence than are other created things' (AT i. 152; CSMK 25).This explains why Descartes can hold—and *does* hold—that God was free to will them otherwise: willing them otherwise would be in no way willing against his own nature.[8] Hence, in the *Sixth Replies*, soon after claiming that God's indifference requires that he is the efficient cause of 'other truths, both mathematical and metaphysical' in addition to truths about goodness, Descartes proclaims that 'God could have brought it about from eternity that it was not true that twice four makes eight' (AT vii. 436; CSM ii. 294). So against the authors of the Sixth Set of Objections, God's power over the eternal truths is not only consistent with God's indifference, but *required* by God's indifference.

It certainly comes as no surprise that Descartes also thinks that God's omnipotence requires that he created the eternal truths.While advancing his doctrine of the creation to the eternal truths in his letter to Mersenne of 15 April 1630, he appeals to the 'incomprehensible' power of God (AT i. 146; CSMK 23); in the same context, he writes in his letter to Mersenne of 6 May 1630 that God is being 'who is infinite and incomprehensible, the sole author on whom all things depend' (AT i. 150; CSMK 24–5); in his letter to Mersenne of 27 May 1630, he claims that he knows that his eternal truths doctrine is true because he knows that God is 'infinite and all-powerful' (AT i. 152; CSMK 25); in his letter to Mesland of 2 May 1644, he claims that the difficulty of conceiving how his eternal truths doctrine is consistent with God's freedom and indifference can be easily dispelled by considering that 'the power of God cannot have any limits' (AT vi. 118; CSMK 235); in his letter to Arnauld of 29 July 1648, he claims that 'every basis of truth and goodness depends on [God's] omnipotence' (AT v. 224; CSMK 358–9); in his letter to More of 5 February 1649, he writes that since 'God's power is infinite', he will 'not be so bold to assert . . . that he cannot do what conflicts with [his] conceptions of things' (AT v. 272; CSMK 363); and in the *Sixth Replies*, he writes that 'anyone who attends to the immeasurable greatness of God will find it manifestly clear that there can be nothing whatsoever which does not depend on him' (AT vii. 435; CSM ii. 293).

---

[8] This is true even if one holds that God's ability to have willed the eternal truths 'otherwise' does not include the ability to have made contradictories true together. For the most compelling argument for this interpretation, see Jonathan Bennett, 'Descartes's Theory of Modality', ['Modality'], *The Philosophical Review* 103 (1994), 639–67.

Descartes doesn't think that God has power over the eternal truths
because he thinks naïvely that God is 'super-omnipotent', or simply
because he thinks that God is *more* powerful than his predecessors
thought. Rather, he comes to this judgment from his rejection of the
theory of divine ideas. According to the traditional conception of
omnipotence, as voiced by Aquinas, 'since power is relative to what is
possible, this phrase, *God can do all things*, is rightly understood to mean
that God can do all things that are possible; and for this reason he is said
to be omnipotent' (*ST* I, 25, 3). Here we must recall that 'what is possible' is determined by God's understanding of his own nature: this provides him with exemplary ideas of what is a possible object of creation
and what is not. Since Descartes rejects this theory, however, there are no
restrictions on what God can create, and so *anything*, whether or not its
description is logically coherent, is a possible object of creation for the
Cartesian God.[9] This explains why 'the supreme indifference to be found
in God is the supreme indication of his omnipotence' (AT vii. 432; CSM
ii. 292). God's indifference is 'supreme' because not even ideas of *possibilia* in his intellect can impel his will; and God's supreme indifference
supremely indicates his omnipotence because there are no divine ideas of
what God can and cannot create to place restrictions on his power.

III

Similarly, the Cartesian God has supreme simplicity, a nature *so* simple
that it requires that he created the eternal truths. The thesis of divine

---

[9] I am of the view that Descartes's God *could* have made contradictories true together.
Jonathan Bennett's argument against this interpretation rests primarily on attributing to
Descartes a position according to which 'not impossible' and 'possible' are not equivalent, and
pointing out that Descartes never offers an actual contradiction as an example of a statement
that God could have made true. Bennett holds that Descartes regards the proposition, 'it is
not the case that God absolutely could have made two plus two equal five' as 'not impossible',
but regards the proposition, 'God could have made two plus two equal five' as 'possible', and
claims that, for Descartes, the former does not entail the latter ('Modality', 653–4). On this
reading, it doesn't follow from Descartes's claims that God could have made actual eternal
truths not true that he could have made contradictory statements true. In my judgment,
however, the textual evidence for attributing this position to Descartes is grossly insufficient,
and Descartes's claim in his letter to Mesland of 2 May 1644, that 'God cannot have been
determined to make it true that contradictories cannot be true together, and . . . he could
have done the opposite' (AT iv. 118; CSMK 235), speaks directly against it. For other interpretations similar to Bennett's, see Hide Ishiguro, 'The Status of Necessity and Impossibility in
Descartes', in Amélie Rorty (ed.), *Essays on Descartes' Meditations* (Los Angeles and Berkeley:
University of California Press, 1986), 459–71, and Amos Funkenstein, *Theology and the Scientific*

simplicity states that there can be no metaphysical complexity whatsoever in God, and is generally acknowledged as consisting of at least three tenets. First, God cannot have any spatial or temporal parts. As such, he lacks physical extension; he is also timeless, and so has no duration or temporal extension. He also lacks temporal location, which is to say that no temporal predicates of any kind can be applied to him. Second, there cannot be any real distinctions between God's essential attributes, which is to deny that they can be distinguished from one another. We describe God's power, knowledge, will, etc., as though they are distinct attributes, but what we are in fact describing is a single reality, which, as it were, we view from different perspectives. God's knowledge is identical to his power, which is identical to his will, and so on. Moreover, the *acts* of the essential divine attributes are one and the same. According to Aquinas, 'the multifarious actions attributed to God, as understanding, willing, producing things, and the like are not diverse realities, since each of these actions in God is his very being, which is one and the same' (*SCG* II, 10, 2). Third, there cannot be a real distinction between God's essence and his existence. According to this tenet, we cannot distinguish God's existence from his essence: God does not simply exist; his essence is identical to his existence.[10]

The tenet of divine simplicity that Descartes employs to support his eternal truths doctrine is the identity of God's essential attributes, and more specifically the identity of the *acts* of the essential divine attributes. In his letter to Mersenne of 6 May 1630, he writes that the eternal truths

are true or possible only because God knows them as true or possible. They are not known as true by God in any way which would imply that they are true independently of him. If men really understood the sense of their words, they could not say without blasphemy that the truth of anything is prior to the knowledge which God has

---

Imagination from the Middle Ages to the Seventeenth Century (Princeton: Princeton University Press, 1986), 188–92.

[10] Eleonore Stump and Norman Kretzmann, 'Absolute Simplicity', *Faith and Philosophy* 2 (1985), 353–82, and Stump, 'Simplicity', in Philip Quinn and Charles Taliaferro (eds.), *A Companion to Philosophy of Religion* (Oxford: Blackwell Publishers, 1997), 250–6. Stump and Kretzmann add a fourth tenet to the doctrine of divine simplicity, that God cannot have any intrinsic accidental properties. Due to the apparent counterintuitive and necessitarian consequences of this thesis (which Stump and Kretzmann argue are *only* apparent), others shy away from it. See Brian Leftow, 'Is God an Abstract Object?', *Nous* 24 (1990), 581–98; William Vallicella, 'Divine Simplicity: A New Defense', *Faith and Philosophy* 9 (1992), 508–25; and Daniel Bennett, 'The Divine Simplicity', *The Journal of Philosophy* 66 (1969), 628–37. Below I shall discuss the connection between this fourth tenet and Descartes's thought.

of it. For in God willing and knowing are a single thing in such a way that by the very fact of willing something he knows it and it is only for this reason that such a thing is true. So we must not say that *if God did not exist nevertheless these truths would be true.* (AT i. 149; CSMK 24)

In this passage, Descartes is contrasting his conception of God's relation to the eternal truths with Suárez's position—the portions in this passage in italics are paraphrases from Suárez's *Disputationes metaphysicae.*[11] There is much debate about just what Suárez's position is on God's relation to the eternal truths, but that is not my concern here.[12] For my purposes, all that is important about Suárez's position is that Descartes *understands* it as asserting something that implies that the eternal truths are true independently of God. But Suárez, according to Descartes, doesn't quite understand the 'sense of [his] words'. More specifically, he doesn't understand *the identity of the divine attributes.*

Descartes's appeal to the identity of God's willing and knowing in this passage is intended to *explain* the dependence of the eternal truths on God's will. Since God is omniscient, he surely knows the eternal truths. If they were true independently of his will, however, there would be a divine act of knowing the eternal truths, but no identical act of willing them. Consequently, God's essential attributes of knowing and willing would not have identical properties—knowledge of the eternal truths could be predicated of his knowing but not of his willing—and his simplicity would be undermined. Yet, this argument is an *ad hominem* against Suárez, and more specifically against Descartes's *understanding* of Suárez's position. And this is an easy target: God's perfection cannot possibly be maintained if there exist eternal truths that do not depend on him.

---

[11] The first italicized portion of the passage reads as follows: 'sunt tantum verae aut possibiles, quia Deus illas veras aut possibiles cognoscit, non autem contra veras à Deo cognosci quasi independenter ab illo sint verae.' In his *Disputationes metaphysicae* [*Disputationes*] (Hildesheim: Georg Olms, 1965), Suárez wrote the following: 'Rursus neque illae enuntiationes sunt verae quia cognoscuntur a Deo, sed potius ideo cognoscuntur, quia verae sunt . . .' (Disp. 31, sect. 12, art. 40). The second italicized portions of the passage says that 'si Deus non esset, nihilominus istae veritates essent verae.' Also in his *Disputationes*, Suárez wrote of the proposition 'every animal is able to sense' that 'si per impossibile nulla esset talis causa [i.e. Deus], nihilominus illa enunciatio vera esset' (Disp. 31, sect. 12, art. 45).

[12] For differing interpretations on Suárez's position on the eternal truths, see esp. Amy D. Karofsky's 'Suárez' Doctrine of Eternal Truths', *Journal of the History of Philosophy* 39 (2001), 23–47; Norman J. Wells's 'Suárez on the Eternal Truths: Part I', *The Modern Schoolman* 58 (1981), 73–104 and his 'Suárez on the Eternal Truths: Part II', *The Modern Schoolman* 58 (1981), 159–74; and John P. Doyle's 'Suárez on the Reality of the Possibiles,' *The Modern Schoolman* 45 (1967), 29–48.

Yet, Descartes thinks that even Aquinas's traditional view, according to which the eternal truths are dependent on God but independent of God's will, violates the simplicity of the divine nature.

In his letter to Mersenne of 27 May 1630, Descartes again appeals to divine simplicity in support of his eternal truths doctrine. In response to Mersenne's question of 'what God did in order to produce [the mathematical truths]' he writes:

> From all eternity he willed and understood them to be, and by that very fact he created them. Or, if you reserve the word 'created' for the existence of things, then he established them and made them. For in God, willing, understanding and creating are all the same thing without one being prior to the other *even rationally (ne quidem ratione)*.   (AT i. 152–3; CSMK 25)

Here we have a much stronger and more sweeping claim about the identity of God's essential attributes. The *ne quidem ratione* indicates that there cannot be a relationship of *conceptual presupposition* between God's willing, understanding, and creating. Descartes makes this point again, both in the *Sixth Replies* and in his letter to Mesland of 2 May 1644. In the former, he writes that between God's intellect and will 'there is not even any priority of order, or nature, or of "reasoned reason" as they call it' (AT vii. 432; CSM ii. 291). And in the latter, he writes that we should not

> conceive any precedence or priority between his intellect and his will; for the idea which we have of God teaches us that there is in him only a single activity, entirely simple and entirely pure. This is well expressed by the words of St. Augustine: 'They are so because thou see'est them to be so'; because in God *seeing* and *willing* are one in the same.   (AT iv. 119; CSMK 235)[13]

This is a bold and, as far as I am aware, unprecedented requirement of a simple God. Why does Descartes insist on it?

---

[13] In *Descartes and Augustine* (Cambridge: Cambridge University Press, 1994), 340, Stephen Menn claims, partly on the basis of this passage, that 'Descartes attributes his doctrine of the creation of the eternal truths to Augustine.' This is clearly not the case: Descartes is simply citing Augustine as an authority on divine simplicity. Menn also apparently reads Descartes as having adopted the theory of divine ideas, as evidenced by his attribution to Descartes of a position according to which knowledge is mediated by divine ideas, whereby one can perform acts of 'contemplating incorporeal divine Ideas' (217) and 'looking at a divine archetype which eminently contains all the perfections of horseness' (277).

Henri Gouhier and Jean-Luc Marion have rightly looked back at Aquinas's account of divine simplicity to assist in answering this question, and both correctly point out that Aquinas's account of divine simplicity, which permits a rational distinction between the divine intellect and the divine will, gives the former priority over the latter.[14] However, neither author explains satisfactorily or in sufficient detail, at least in my judgment, just how Descartes's doctrine of the creation of the eternal truths follows from his insistence on the *ne quidem ratione*.

If acts of the divine will cannot presuppose acts of the divine intellect, then acts of the former can in no way depend on acts of the latter. However, Descartes sees most clearly that the acts of the will of Aquinas's God, with ideas in his intellect prior to his creation, depend on acts of his intellect, and this is why Descartes regards Aquinas's account of divine simplicity to be unacceptable. Moreover, it is precisely from denying that acts of God's will conceptually presuppose acts of God's intellect that Descartes's eternal truths doctrine follows. Those who subscribe to the theory of divine ideas must hold that acts of God's will presuppose acts of God's intellect in order to preserve God's freedom. For on the theory of divine ideas, God knows what he knows necessarily. So if it is to be the case that God does not will what he wills necessarily, they must hold that God's will is conceptually posterior to his intellect; this provides God with conceptual space, as it were, to choose what to create and what to refrain from creating. But the rational distinction which must be posited to provide this conceptual space, and which appears innocuous enough, ultimately collapses into a distinction in reality. For if two things are identical, it must be the case that whatever is true of one of them is also true of the other. Since the eternal truths depend on the intellect of a God with divine ideas but not on his will, however, it follows that they are not truly identical—which is a manifest violation of divine simplicity. By contrast, since Descartes rejects the theory of divine ideas, he isn't committed to the position that God necessarily knows what he knows—which enables him to affirm that God's intellect has no priority *whatsoever* over God's will, while at the same to preserve God's freedom. Moreover, once there is no relationship of presupposition between God's intellect and will, it follows

---

[14] Henri Gouhier, *La pensée métaphysique de Descartes* [*La pensée métaphysique*] (Paris: J. Vrin, 1962), 233–5; Jean-Luc Marion, *Sur la théologie blanche de Descartes: Analogie, creation des vérités éternelles et fondement* [*Sur la théologie blanche*] (Paris: Presses Universitaires de France, 1981), 283–4.

that he creates the eternal truths: his omniscience ensures that he understands the eternal truths, from which it follows, in conjunction with the identity of the essential divine attributes, that he also wills them. Descartes's God, then, neither knows what he knows necessarily, nor wills what he wills necessarily: he knows and wills what he does with complete freedom.

Rejecting the theory of divine ideas also enables Descartes to maintain *consistently* in *Principles* I. 23 that there is 'a single identical and perfectly simple act by means of which [God] simultaneously understands, wills, and accomplishes everything' (AT viiia. 14; CSM i. 201). If committed to the theory of divine ideas, one must hold that God accomplishes his creation by a first act which is conceptually presupposed by a second: the first whereby God understands himself and all possible objects of his creation, and the second whereby he exercises his will and creates the world and everything in it. But as we have seen, such a god is not truly simple. Nor is such a god truly indifferent or omnipotent: for if there exist ideas of *possibilia* in his intellect prior to the determination of his will, then these ideas impel his will, hence undermining his freedom, and dictate what he can and cannot create, hence undermining his power.

IV

Descartes's God, divested of the traditional divine ideas, is not the traditional God with added power over the eternal truths; instead, he is a radically different God—the *Cartesian* God. While this God is attractive in so far as his attributes of indifference, simplicity, and omnipotence are purged of the inconsistencies created by the theory of divine ideas, he certainly might be regarded as unattractive for a number of reasons. The basis for these reasons is well expressed by Richard La Croix:

On Descartes's view God did not bring about something by first consulting a list of alternative possibilities and then *choosing* one of these possibilities to actualize because, on Descartes's view, there are no possibilities or goods or truths prior to God's creative activity or from which he could choose.[15]

---

[15] 'Descartes on God's Ability to do the Logically Impossible', *Canadian Journal of Philosophy* 3 (1984), 455–75, at 461. Leibniz makes virtually the same point in his *Theodicy:* 'if the affirmations of necessary truths were the actions of the will of the most perfect mind, these actions would be anything but free, for there is nothing to choose' (GPVI, 228). Citation from E. M. Huggard (ed. and trans.), *Theodicy* (LaSalle: Open Court, 1985), 245.

This might appear unattractive because it implies that God does not deliberate, make choices, or think before he creates. This in turn implies that he is no artisan or designer, since he could not have had any purpose in mind when creating the world. Nor can he be regarded as having aimed at producing good in his creation. And finally, his creation of the world would have been completely random—more like the big bang than the effect of the will of a personal being.

For reasons such as these, Harry Frankfurt writes that 'if God is to be compared to a king who lays down laws for his kingdom, He might be compared to a king who is utterly capricious and quite mad'.[16] Marion draws similar conclusions about a God who creates the eternal truths:

First, God is incomprehensible because He acts before any rationality determines or delimits his actions; therefore from the point of view of our minds, finite and endowed with a limited rationality, the God who creates them remains inaccessible in a sense, even if He is known in another, weaker sense. And second, God is a power, because in the absence of any common rationality and of any analogy of being between the finite and the infinite, only a relation of power remains: even if the understanding does not comprehend it, we are acquainted with that power. In short, as 'an infinite and incomprehensible being', God is known only as 'a cause whose power surpasses the limits of human understanding'.[17]

---

[16] Harry Frankfurt, 'Descartes on the Creation of the Eternal Truths', ['Creation'], *The Philosophical Review* 86 (1977), 36–57, at 42. Frankfurt adds, however, that 'these characterizations are not *entirely* apt since they suggest an indifference to or a flouting of the canons of rationality, which cannot be ascribed to God's determination of those canons. In any event, on Descartes's account God has no reasons whatsoever for His decrees and His choices are in no way submissive to any moral or rational constraints at all' (ibid.).

[17] 'The Idea of God', in Daniel Garber and Michael Ayers (eds.), *The Cambridge History of Seventeenth-Century Philosophy* (Cambridge: Cambridge University Press, 1998), 65–304, at 274. In *Sur la théologie blanche*, Marion draws the same conclusion, characterizing Descartes's theology as 'blank' because it is 'anonymous and undetermined' (450). I do, however, have a fundamental disagreement with Marion about Descartes's reason for advancing his eternal truths doctrine. In *Sur la théologie blanche*, Marion argues that Descartes advanced his doctrine in response to Suárez's doctrine of univocity. Marion's argument is largely based on the fact that, in his 1630 eternal truths letters to Mersenne, Descartes advances his doctrine in close paraphrases from Suárez's *Disputationes*. I reject Marion's argument because I am of the view that there is little evidence to suggest that Descartes was familiar with Suárez's *Disputationes* in 1630. It is not listed in the 1586 version of the *Ratio studiorum* or in the definitive 1599 version. I judge it to be much more likely that Mersenne introduced the passages from the *Disputationes* in the lost half of his 1630 eternal truths correspondence with Descartes, and that Descartes referenced the *Disputationes* only because Mersenne did so first. For a full treatment of this topic, see my 'The Opponent and Motivation Behind Descartes's Eternal Truths Doctrine', in A. Del Prete (ed.), *Studi cartésiani II: Atti del seminario 'Descartes et ses adversaires,' Parigi 10–12 dicembre 2000* (Lecce: Centro Studi Cartésiani, 2003).

In virtue of the consequences of Descartes's incomprehensible God, whose acts are not determined or delineated by rationality, we find Leibniz, clearly alluding to Descartes, claim that those who say 'that things are good . . . solely by virtue of the will of God . . . destroy all of God's love and all his glory' (*DM* 2; GP iv. 428).[18] Descartes's God, Leibniz thinks, 'would be equally praiseworthy in doing the exact contrary'. There is no justice and wisdom in Descartes's God, according to Leibniz, but 'only a certain despotic power' (DM2; GP iv. 428).

On this basis, in a letter to Molanus *c*. 1679, Leibniz likens Descartes's God of 'despotic power' to the God of Spinoza:

Descartes's God, or perfect being, is not a God like the one we imagine or hope for, that is, a God just and wise, doing everything possible for the good of creatures. Rather, Descartes's God is something approaching the God of Spinoza . . . Descartes's God has neither *will* nor *understanding*, since according to Descartes he does not have the *good* as the object of his will, nor the *true* as the object of his understanding.   (GP iv. 299)[19]

Unlike Leibniz's God, Spinoza's God has no will or intellect. Spinoza claims that, *if* will and intellect are to be attributed to God,

we must of course understand by each of these attributes something different from what men commonly understand. For the intellect and will which would constitute God's essence would have to differ entirely from our intellect and will, and could not agree with them in anything except the name. They would not agree with one another any more than do the dog that is a heavenly constellation and the dog that is a barking animal.   (*E*IP17S2; G ii. 73)

It might at first seem that Leibniz is misguided in comparing Descartes's God, who has a will and an intellect, and who acts out of absolute freedom, to Spinoza's God, which has no will and no intellect, and which acts out of necessity.[20] Yet upon reflection, it is not too difficult to see why Leibniz should judge that Descartes's God, *in effect*, has no will

---

[18] Citation from Roger Ariew and Daniel Garber (eds. and trans.), *Philosophical Essays* (Indianapolis: Hackett Publishing Co., 1989), 36. Further citations from Ariew and Garber are cited by 'AG' followed by page numbers.   [19] AG 242.

[20] A remark by Spinoza in *E*IP33S2 is worth pointing out here. Clearly alluding to Descartes's view and to the view that Leibniz would endorse, respectively, Spinoza claims that the opinion that 'subjects all things to a certain indifferent will of God, and makes all things depend on his good pleasure, is nearer to the truth than that of those who maintain that God does all things for the sake of the good. For they seem to place something outside of God, which does not depend on God, to which God attends, as a model, in what he does, and at which he aims, as at a certain goal. This is simply to subject God to fate. Nothing more absurd

or intellect. If God does not have the good as the object of his will, or the true as the object of his understanding, then 'will' and 'intellect', when attributed to God, arguably lose their sense.

But it is Leibniz, like Aquinas, who violates the requirements of the identity of the divine will and intellect.[21] At *DM* 2, he also writes that

> it seems that all acts of will presuppose a reason for willing and that this reason is naturally prior to the act of will. That is why I also find completely strange the expression of some other philosophers who say that the eternal truths of metaphysics and geometry and consequently all the rules of goodness, justice, and perfection are merely the effects of the will of God; instead, it seems to me, they are only the consequences of the understanding, which, assuredly, does not depend on his will, any more than does his essence.   (GP iv. 428)[22]

If acts of divine will 'presuppose a reason for willing' and 'this reason is naturally prior to the act of will', then, like Aquinas, Leibniz is committed to a God whose creative act of will is conceptually presupposed by an act of his understanding—and hence to a God whose will and intellect are not truly identical, and so to a God who is not simple.

By insisting on the identity of the actions of the essential divine attributes, Descartes is not advancing a 'radical' conception of divine simplicity,[23] but instead a *consistent* one—one that embraces the logical consequences of the identity of the essential divine attributes and in fact *preserves* their identity. Many don't see it this way, however, charging Descartes with giving God's will priority over his intellect. Gouhier does not endorse this charge, but raises the issue as follows: 'While reading the passages on the creation of the eternal truths, one might ask if Descartes does not reestablish a certain distinction between God's intellect and will, in subordinating the former to the latter instead of subordinating the latter to the former.'[24] Some of the passages in which

---

can be maintained about God' (C 438–9; G ii. 76). As for Spinoza's remark about the position Leibniz would endorse, however, he is attacking a straw man: Leibniz would never claim that God attends to or aims at goals 'outside' of himself.

[21] Leibniz's commitment to divine simplicity can be seen in his correspondence with Arnauld. See H. Mason (ed. and trans.), *The Leibniz–Arnauld Correspondence* (Manchester: Manchester University Press, 1967), 48; GP ii. 44.

[22] AG 36. AG informs us that, where Leibniz writes 'some other philosophers', Descartes's name was mentioned in an earlier draft but subsequently deleted (n. 9).

[23] In *Descartes and Augustine*, 340–1, n. 3, Menn criticizes Gouhier and Marion for taking 'Descartes' doctrine of the creation of the eternal truths as . . . dictated by a new Cartesian insistence on God's radical simplicity'.   [24] Gouhier, *La Pensée métaphysique*, 235–6.

Descartes asserts his eternal truths doctrine make it appear that this is the case. For instance, he writes in his letter to Mersenne of 6 May 1630 that 'by the very fact of willing something [God] knows it and it is only for this reason that such a thing is true' (AT i. 149; CSMK 24). But this appearance is misleading. We can add to Gouhier's point by affirming with confidence that Descartes would not hesitate to assert the converse, namely, 'by the very fact of *knowing* something God *wills* it and it is only for this reason that such a thing is true'. If Descartes indeed subordinated God's intellect to God's will, then God's understanding of the eternal truths would presuppose his willing of them. But Descartes says nothing that suggests or implies this position. Moreover, it would be absurd, since it would require that God would have to 'look' outside himself at his creation in order to understand the objects of his creation. So far from giving precedence to God's will at the expense of God's intellect, the *ne quidem ratione*, as Gouhier explains, 'implies not a *change* of priority but the *refusal* of any priority' (emphases added).[25] It is precisely this refusal, this consistent application of the thesis of divine simplicity across the essential divine attributes, that provides Descartes with the ultimate justification for his eternal truths doctrine.

V

Most paradoxically, while divine simplicity seems to provide God with ultimate freedom, it also seems to strip it away. In the *Conversation with Burman*, in the context of querying Descartes on various passages from the *Meditations* and the *Principles*, Burman asks Descartes about the claim in *Principles* I. 23 that 'there is always a single identical and perfectly simple act by means of which [God] simultaneously understands, wills, and accomplishes everything' (AT viiia. 14; CSM i. 201). Burman objects to this position with the following:

> It seems that this cannot be, since there are some of God's decrees which we can conceive of as not having been enacted and as alterable. These decrees, then, do not come about by means of the single act which is identical with God, since they can be separated from him, or at least could have been. One example of this, among others, is the decree concerning the creation of the world, with respect to which God was quite indifferent.   (AT v, 165–6; CSMK 347)

---

[25] Ibid. 237.

In his reply, Descartes advances the following, most stunning remark:

> We should not make a separation here between the necessity and the indif-
> ference that apply to God's decrees; although his actions were completely
> indifferent, they were also completely necessary. In reality the decrees could not
> have been separated from God: he is not prior to them or distinct from them,
> nor could he have existed without them.   (AT v. 166; CSMK 348)

The claim that God could not have existed without his decrees is nothing short of necessitarianism. One of the things that God decreed was
that the world should exist. If God could not have existed without this
decree, then the existence of the world—along with every state of affairs
in it—would be just as necessary as God's existence, i.e. *absolutely, uncon-
ditionally necessary*. And not only does this necessitarian remark blatantly
contradict Descartes's eternal truths doctrine, it also flies directly in the
face of his comment to Mersenne, in his letter of 27 May 1630, that the
eternal truths are 'no more necessarily attached to [God's] essence than
are other created things' (AT i. 152; CSMK 25).

What are we to make of this remark? On the one hand, we can call
into question the reliability of the *Conversation*. After all, it is not a work
written by Descartes, but a record of a conversation between Descartes
and Burman, *written by Burman*. Even though their meeting was formal
and prearranged, and Burman prided himself on having obtained his
material 'straight from the horse's mouth',[26] we certainly cannot assume
that his notes of the conversation are reliable, let alone infallible. Hence,
the *Conversation* is by no means authoritative. On the other hand, we can
work under the assumption that Descartes indeed made this remark, and
see if we can make sense of it. Since I hold, as a principle of interpretation,
that we should not discard a text—or even a record of a conversation—
without strong evidence on the basis of which to do so, I shall opt for the
latter course of action.[27] In doing so, I hope to show that divine simplicity
creates a tension in Descartes's thought which he never worked through—
a tension which continues to plague philosophers of religion today.

---

[26] John Cottingham (ed. and trans.), *Descartes' Conversation with Burman* [*Conversation*]
(Oxford: Oxford University Press, 1976), p. xvi.

[27] One might naturally object to my application of my principle of interpretation in this
particular case on the grounds that the passage in question introduces a major inconsistency
into Descartes's thought—which is as good a reason as any for discarding the passage. While
I certainly agree that the passage introduces a major inconsistency into Descartes's thought,
I believe it is reasonable to think that Descartes said it. And I think that this is reasonable,

According to some philosophers of religion, one of the requirements of divine simplicity is that God cannot have any intrinsic accidental properties, i.e. that all of his intrinsic properties must be essential. Following Eleonore Stump and Norman Kretzmann, I shall say that 'a change in x's extrinsic properties can occur without a change in x, while a change in x's intrinsic properties is as such a change in x'.[28] For instance, my mentioning of Stump in this essay is one of her extrinsic accidental properties, while her belief that there is a simple God is one of her intrinsic accidental properties. On this account, if I did not mention her in this essay, no change in her would occur. But if she ceased to believe in the existence in a simple God, a change in her would occur. The thesis that God cannot have any intrinsic accidental properties is regarded by some philosophers as required of divine simplicity because nothing simple is supposed to be able to change; but since intrinsic accidental properties can change, if God had such properties, he too could change, and hence would not be simple.

But this requirement, as Stump and Kretzmann claim, seems to 'entail that God could not do anything other or otherwise than he actually does'.[29] They elaborate on this by saying that

it seems to follow, for instance, that God's knowledge is identical with God's power and also with anything that can be considered an intrinsic property of his, such as one of God's actions—his talking to Cain, for instance . . . If God's talking to Cain is essential to God, it is necessary and thus not something God could refrain from doing.[30]

In short, it would appear that a simple God must also be God who acts out of necessity.[31]

I do not at all mean to suggest that Descartes thought about the distinction between intrinsic and extrinsic properties in the way that

as I shall explain in detail below, because I believe it likely that Descartes came to see a problem about the coherence of divine simplicity, a problem that has received much attention among contemporary philosophers of religion. For a brief evaluation and argument in favor of the reliability of the *Conversation*, see Cottingham, *Conversation*, pp. xvi–xviii.

[28] Stump and Kretzmann, 'Absolute Simplicity', 354.

[29] Ibid. 355. Similarly, while speaking of the same tenet of divine simplicity (though expressed a bit differently), Daniel Bennett claims that 'this is Spinozism' ('The Divine Simplicity', 634).   [30] Stump and Kretzmann, 'Absolute Simplicity', 355.

[31] Stump and Kretzmann argue at length against this apparent consequence by rejecting the assumption that God's free will 'is essentially an independent, neutral capacity for choosing among alternatives' ('Absolute Simplicity', 359). They replace this assumption with

Stump and Kretzmann do, or in the way that other contemporary philosophers do. Nevertheless, I think that the passage under consideration from the *Conversation* gives us compelling reason to think that Descartes caught a glimpse of the (at least apparent) necessitarian consequences of the thesis that God cannot have intrinsic, accidental properties.[32] This would explain why he claims that God could not have existed without his decrees. For God's decrees are among his intrinsic properties. And if all of God's intrinsic properties are *essential*, i.e. if God could not have existed without them, then he is *necessitated* to decree what he does. In light of this, Leibniz's charge that Descartes's conception of God borders on the Spinozistic does not appear to be too far off the mark.

VI

But just as it would be inconsistent with God's simplicity for him to know the eternal truths but not to will them, it would be equally inconsistent with his simplicity for him to know allegedly *contingent* truths but not to will *them*. The most striking instances of allegedly contingent truths for which the will of Descartes's simple God must be regarded as responsible are those about the effects of our allegedly free wills. And most surprisingly, in his letter to Elizabeth of 3 November 1645, Descartes concedes that the effects of our wills in fact depend on God:

As for free will, I agree that if we think only of ourselves we cannot help regarding ourselves as independent; but when we think of the infinite power of God, we cannot help believing that all things depend on him, and hence that our free will is not exempt from this dependence. For it involves a contradiction to say that God has created human beings of such a nature that the actions of their will do not depend on his.   (AT iv. 332; CSMK 277)

Here we have Descartes saying that the actions of our wills depend on God's will in virtue of 'the infinite power of God', not in virtue of God's

---

Aquinas's account of the will 'as a natural inclination toward goodness associated with the agent's understanding of goodness' (ibid.). While God's will is naturally necessitated toward goodness, this 'natural necessity, far from threatening freedom', they claim, 'is a precondition of the will's making choices' (ibid. 361).

[32] That Descartes held that God cannot have intrinsic, accidental properties is also suggested by *Principles* I. 56, where he writes that 'we do not . . . say that there are modes or qualities in God' (AT viiia. 26)—modes which, in *Meditations III*, he identifies with accidents ('modos, sive accidentia'). (AT vii. 40; CSM ii. 28)

simplicity. Nevertheless, his conception of divine simplicity, as we have seen, commits him to the very same position. It would have been perfectly consistent with his conception of God had Descartes told Elizabeth that the actions of our wills depend on God's because of God's simplicity—and even because of the indifference of God's will, for that matter. Now, I certainly don't think that Descartes *wants* to be committed to the position that God is ultimately responsible for human actions. We all know that he insists on freedom of the human will in many places throughout his works, and we are all familiar with his treatment of what we might call the 'epistemological problem of evil' in *Meditations* IV. God is not the cause of our false beliefs: he has given us wills free of all defects, and we acquire false beliefs by extending our will beyond our understanding, that is, by assenting to what we do not clearly and distinctly perceive (AT vii. 58–9; CSM ii. 39–41). Nevertheless, the passages from the *Conversation with Burman*, in conjunction with the passage from the letter to Elizabeth, make it reasonably certain that Descartes ultimately realized that he is indeed committed to God being the author of the effects of our wills, and hence not only for our false beliefs but also for our immoral actions.

These considerations call to our attention just how problematic Descartes's eternal truths doctrine is, as well as how problematic divine simplicity is. Of course we have the traditional problems associated with divine simplicity, for instance, of how attributes such as omnipotence, omniscience, and omnibenevolence can be identical, and how these, along with God's existence and essence, can be identical to God himself. And if we follow Descartes in his consistent application of the thesis of divine simplicity across the essential divine attributes, we are pulled in opposite directions. While the Cartesian God must be regarded as absolutely free and unrestricted in his creation to the extent that he created the eternal truths, he must also be regarded as a God who could not have rendered human actions free—and perhaps even a God who acts completely out of necessity. These considerations, moreover, leave to one side the problem of whether or not Descartes's eternal truths doctrine is *itself* incoherent, as many commentators have charged. For instance, Frankfurt claims that the doctrine entails 'the possibility of what is logically impossible',[33] and James Van Cleve claims that

---

[33] 'Creation', 44.

Gregory Walski

'Descartes's total view is inconsistent: he holds that some facts about God are necessary, yet is forced . . . to maintain that *nothing* is necessary.'[34] If the doctrine is indeed incoherent, then Descartes's arguments from the divine nature to his doctrine of the creation of the eternal truths do not provide us with reason to believe that God created the eternal truths, but instead with a *reductio* of the Cartesian God.[35]

University of San Diego

[34] James Van Cleve, 'Descartes and the Destruction of the Eternal Truths', *Ratio* 7 (1994), 58–62, at 61.

[35] I would like to thank Edwin Curley, Daniel Garber, Louis Loeb, Alan Nelson, and an anonymous reader for their comments and suggestions on much of the content of this essay, along with the audience at the Fall 2001 Midwest Seminar in the History of Early Modern Philosophy at Miami University (Ohio) for their comments on an abbreviated version of it, especially Marleen Rozemond.

3

What Do the Expressions of the Passions Tell Us?

LISA SHAPIRO

I. INTRODUCTION

In this essay I examine Descartes's treatment of the expressions of the passions. Descartes takes our emotions to be made manifest by what he terms 'the external signs of the passions'—that is, 'the actions of the eyes and face, changes in color, trembling, languor, fainting, laughter, tears, groans and sighs' (*Passions* a.112; AT xi. 411). There is a puzzle in understanding just how these manifestations can be signs of the passions. While it seems clear that our expressions signify our passions in virtue of the body's relation to the soul—they are expressions of the passions *of the soul* after all—what is not clear is *how* our emotive expressions gain content. I aim to work through this puzzle here.

I begin by considering what might seem like the most obvious explanation: our expressions signify what they do because the soul causes them. While this account might seem plausible, I argue that this *causal account* fails to accord with Descartes's claims, in the *Passions of the Soul*, that our expressions are caused simply by the workings of our body. One way of addressing this failure is to explain the significance of our expressions by their sharing a physiological cause with the passions they represent. While this *common causal account* does accord with what Descartes claims about the causes of our expressions, it too fails, for it is not clear how to reconcile it with Descartes's account of the regulation of the passions. I go on to suggest a third possible explanation of

This essay grows out of a paper presented jointly with Annette Baier at the University of Toronto: 'Why do All the Passions of the Cartesian Soul get Expression in the Cartesian Body?' I thank Annette for the opportunity to think about the issue of the expressions. While this essay expands on the discussion we began in that paper, the errors in it are my own. An earlier version of this essay was presented at the Midwest Seminar in Early Modern Philosophy and at the University of New Mexico. It has benefited from the comments of those audiences, as well as those of the editors of this journal.

the significance of our expressions, one that attends to the reasons for the connections between physical and mental states. In so far as these reasons are tied to Descartes's account of human nature, this third explanation might be called a *human naturalist account*. While this account is in many ways more satisfying than the first two, I am not sure it succeeds in the end either. That Descartes may not have a coherent account of our expressions might well be a problem for him, but in this analysis of the possible accounts I hope to make some headway in articulating just where the problem lies, and so in clarifying some sources of tension within Descartes's account of a human being.

2. SOME PRELIMINARY REMARKS: GETTING CLEAR ON THE QUESTION

Before I begin trying to unravel Descartes's account of the expressions of the passions, let me situate my topic here with respect to two related issues. First, I am only concerned to understand what might be called the naive expressions of our passions. Certainly, it is an important part of our passionate lives that we can dissimulate what we feel. We can affect an air of coolness when we are in love or put on a cheerful grin when we are annoyed. And Descartes does recognize this,[1] but it is not his primary concern. I follow him here.

Second, it is perhaps remarkable that Descartes hardly considers how our emotive expressions gain currency as a language. This reticence might be due to his taking the expressions of the passions to be *natural* signs rather than conventional signs.[2] Words, on the one hand, are conventional signs and demand rules governing their usage so that we

---

[1] He writes: 'And in general all the actions of both the face and the eyes can be changed by the soul, when, willing to conceal its passion, it forcefully imagines one in opposition to it; thus one can use them to dissimulate one's passions as well as to manifest them' (*Passions* a. 113; AT xi. 412–13).

[2] It is hard to know how to cash out this distinction for Descartes. On the one hand we might turn to the Port Royal *Logic*. (Antoine Arnauld and Pierre Nicole, *Logic or the Art of Thinking*, trans. Jill Vance Buroker [*Logic*] (Cambridge, Cambridge University Press, 1996).) There, a natural sign is one which represents what it does independently of human fancy (*Logic*, 36–7); there is an 'obvious connection' between the sign and the object signified, and because of this there are no problems making claims involving them (ibid. 120). Our expressions do seem to be natural signs of our passions in this sense. Conventional signs, on the other hand, are instituted by human beings; they need bear no relation to what they represent, and

affirm only true propositions, whereas what expressions signify just seems obvious to us.[3] Yet still, it does seem, from the discussion in the *Passions of the Soul*, that the communicative aspect of our expressions is supposed to follow somehow from the way in which those physical movements express our thoughts. I do take it that any account of the expressiveness of our expressions in the second sense—how our thoughts are able to be signified externally through our body—should be able to support a reasonable account of how our expressions speak to other people, and I will touch on the connection between these two issues in my discussion.[4]

3. A FIRST ATTEMPT TO UNDERSTAND THE EXPRESSION OF THE PASSIONS

It is natural to start to make sense of Descartes's account of the expressions of our passions by looking at the titles of the relevant articles: 'How

so they demand rules for proper usage. However, if we probe further, things become more confused. An 'image that appears in a mirror is a natural sign of what it represents' (ibid. 37) and a painting of Caesar is a natural sign of Caesar, a map of Italy a natural sign of Italy (ibid. 120). In these cases, we can without issue identify the sign with its object, and we can do so just because the sign resembles what it refers to. Thus, there does seem to be something distinctive about a Cartesian natural sign: the emotive expressions do not resemble what they might be said to represent. A smile does not resemble the joy we feel, blushing does not resemble the feeling of embarrassment or shame. Though Descartes, in discussing how representation might be possible without resemblance, appeals to the words we use—that is, by the *Logic's* account, conventional rather than natural signs—it seems to me that here he can be read as pointing to a sort of natural sign which does not involve resemblance. I will not be able to explore this point further here.

[3] Descartes's claims that 'there is no passion which is not manifested by some particular action of the eyes' and that the meaning of these expressions is obvious even to the stupidest of servants (*Passions* a.113; AT xi, 412) would seem to imply that we naturally recognize the import of emotive expressions.

Moreover, Charles Le Brun, in his *Conférence sur l'Expression des Passions*—a work greatly influenced by, if not largely plagiarized from, Descartes's *Passions*—claims that emotional expressions are natural signs. (Charles LeBrun, *Conférence sur l'Expression des Passions*, trans. and ed. Jennifer Montagu [*Le Brun*] (New Haven: Yale University Press, 1994).) Just as expression in painting 'is a simple and natural image of the thing we wish to represent . . ., indicat[ing] the true character of each object', so too, Le Brun wants to demonstrate, is expression 'that which reflects the movements of the heart and which makes visible the effects of the passions' (*Le Brun*, 126). Montagu, in her outstanding edition of this work and its background and influence, details the precise instances of plagiarism on Le Brun's part.

[4] The significance of our emotive expressions gains prominence in eighteenth-century French thought, both in theories of language and in theories of human understanding which

joy makes one flush' (*Passions* a.115); 'How *sadness makes one* turn pale'
(*Passions* a.116); languor is '*caused by love* and by desire' (*Passions* a.120);
'How *one cries from sadness*' (*Passions* a.131) (emphasis added). They
suggest that the passions themselves, thoughts in the soul, cause their
particular expressions. And, since a causal account of reference is one
that, though flawed, is at least familiar and intelligible, we might well
think that, for Descartes, our expressions refer to our passions in virtue
of the causal relation between them.

The content of the explanations contained in these articles only
seems to confirm such a causal account. Take, for instance, the discussion
of the way joy makes us flush. Descartes writes:

Joy renders the color more vivid and rosy because in opening the heart's sluices,
it make blood flow more quickly into all the veins, and, as [the blood] becomes
warmer and finer, it gently swells all the parts of the face, rendering its demeanor
more smiling and cheerful.   (*Passions* a.115; AT xi. 413)

Here it seems that joy, the passion of the soul, causes the heart valves to
open, letting in more blood, which in turn leads to our appearing
flushed.[5] A similar sort of causal efficacy is lent the passions in the other
articles.[6] In all these cases, Descartes talks as if the passions themselves
effect the physiological state which leads to our expressions. And it

lend primacy to human discursive abilities. Both Condillac and Diderot, for instance, take
human understanding to be a discursive faculty, and they find the origin of our language in
our natural gestures or emotive expressions. See Etienne Bonnot de Condillac, *Essay on the
Origin of Human Knowledge*, trans. Hans Aarsleff (Cambridge: Cambridge University Press,
2001) and Denis Diderot, *Lettre sur les sourds et les muets*, 1751, ed. Marian Hobson and Simon
Harvey (Paris: Garnier Flammarion, 2000).

[5] Joy also has other effects. By opening the cavities of the heart too wide, it causes an excess
of blood to flow into it, thereby smothering the fire which is the principle of life and bringing on a fainting spell (*Passions* a.122; AT xi. 418); and laughter (when we are naturally indignant as opposed to feigning indignance) 'seems to spring from the joy one gets from seeing
that one cannot be injured by the evil one is indignant about, and along with this, from finding oneself surprised by the novelty of or the unexpected encounter with this evil—so that
joy, hatred, and wonder contribute to it' just because these passions send 'blood from
the spleen to the heart, where it is rarefied and driven on into the lungs'. This redirection of
the blood causes just the sort of physiological motions which lead to our emitting sounds
of laughter (*Passions* a.127; AT xi. 422).

[6] Sadness contracts the heart's orifices (*Passions* a.116; AT xi. 414); shame makes the blood
flow from internal organs to the heart and then to the face (*Passions* a.117; AT xi. 414–15); and
in the case of languor 'love so engrosses the soul with the consideration of the object loved
that [the soul] employs all the spirits in the brain to represent its image to it, and stops all the
movements of the gland not conducive to this effect' (*Passions* a.120; AT xi. 417); and so on.

seems that they do so just by causing the physiological changes that result in our expressions; we might reasonably presume that they do this by effecting the shift in the pineal gland which sets the appropriate physiological mechanism to work.

This account has a further advantage of seeming to mirror Descartes's account of how bodily states are significant to the mind. Some commentators have tried to explain just how, for Descartes, our sensations can refer to what they do by appealing to the causal interaction between the soul and the body. In doing so they draw on Descartes's explanation in *Meditations* VI of how we feel a pain in our foot. On this view, our sensations have the content they do in virtue of standing in the causal relations they do; Descartes claims that we feel a pain-in-our-foot just in virtue of the fact that a particular bodily state (a tilt of the pineal gland) causes that thought, and that bodily state stands in a causal relation to the object of our thought (the damage to our foot has caused the motion in the nerves that leads to the tilt of the gland which causes the thought).[7] So in general, on this view, our thoughts have the content they do just because of the causal relation in which they figure.[8] It would be a tidy package if we could also understand the expressiveness of emotive expressions to consist simply in the causal relation between soul and body. Just as thoughts have the content they do just because they stand in the causal relations they do, so too, one might think, the movements of our face and eyes, our laughter, have the content they do—signify the passions they do—just because *they* stand in the causal relations *they* do.

There are two serious problems with this account. First, there are the problems inherent in any causal account of how signs are invested with meaning. The standard problem with causal accounts of content concerns a sign's referring to the particular link in the causal chain it does. In the case of sensations, there is nothing in the causal story that

---

[7] This sort of interpretation starts from this passage: 'when the nerves of the foot are set in motion in a violent and unusual manner, this motion, by way of the spinal cord, reaches the inner parts of the brain, and there gives the mind its signal (*signum*) for having a certain sensation, namely the sensation of pain as occurring in the foot' (AT vii. 88; CSM ii. 60). Other passages support this reading. See for instance *Principles of Philosophy* IV. 189, 197, AT viii. 316, 320; CSM i. 280, 284; *Treatise of Man*, AT xi. 144–5. This account is not the only reading of this passage. Margaret Wilson, for one, wants to distinguish a causal account from a signification account of sensation. See Margaret Wilson, 'Descartes on the Origin of Sensation', in her *Ideas and Mechanism: Essays on Early Modern Philosophy* (Princeton: Princeton University Press, 1999), 41–68.

[8] There still remains the problem of understanding the metaphysics of body–mind interaction. I will not address this concern at all here.

mandates that our thought (a pain-in-our-foot) represent the pain in our foot—motions in the nerves of the foot—rather than the motions of the nerves more proximate to the pineal gland. In the case of the expressions, there seems to be no reason that our being flushed, say, should be expressive of our embarrassment rather than, say, some physiological state along the causal chain leading up to the expression.[9]

There is a second, more immediate, problem with the causal account: it ends up being inconsistent with a large part of the text. Despite Descartes's manner of talking about them, it does not seem that the soul itself causes the expressions of its passions. They are not, after all, voluntary actions. And moreover, Descartes implies that the expressions have a physiological cause. The initial physiological motions that first shift the position of the pineal gland, and thereby engender the passion in the soul, do not terminate at the gland. The gland's shifting orientation redirects the animal spirits in ways that can strengthen and sustain the passion (as the definition of the passions suggests), as well as dispose the body to action. So Descartes writes in a.38:

Just as the course these spirits take toward the nerves of the heart suffices to impart the movement to the gland by which fear is put in the soul, so too, simply in virtue of the fact that certain spirits proceed at the same time toward the nerves that move the legs to flee, they cause another movement in the same gland by means of which the soul feels and perceives this flight—*which can in this way be excited by the body merely by the disposition of the organs without the soul contributing to it.* (AT xi. 358; emphasis added)

And he continues in the next article, explaining that our responses to emotions differ just because 'all brains are not disposed in the same manner, and the same movement of the gland which in some excites

---

[9] One might see Descartes as attempting to solve this problem in the case of sensation by appealing to the preservation of the human being: a sensation of pain-in-our-foot signifies damage to the foot, rather than to say, the tilt of the pineal gland which is the proximate cause of that sensation, because its doing so is most conducive to the continued well-being of a healthy man. See AT vii. 87, CSM ii. 60. It is not clear that a similar story can be told about our expressions: Is it most conducive to the preservation of the human being that our blushing signifies shame? Tears, sadness?

Considerations of the place of well-being in this story has led some, for instance Alison Simmons, to take our sensations simply to represent the way things benefit or harm us. While Simmons does not deny the causal interaction of mind and body, she does not link this account of the content of sensation to this causal interaction. See Alison Simmons, 'Are Cartesian Sensations Representational?', ['Cartesian Sensations'] *Nous*, 33/3 (1999), 347–69. I will return to consider this passage from this point of view in Section 5.

[the move to flee], in others makes the spirits enter the brain's pores that guide part of them into the nerves that move the hands for self-defense'. (ibid.). It only makes sense that our expressions too would have a purely physiological cause, and so that what we take to be external displays of emotion are simply the result of the design of the human body-machine.[10] In so far as they occur independently of the soul, it is not clear what basis we have for claiming these bodily motions are signs of our mental states.

It is also worth pausing to consider what sort of accounts of how our expressions are meaningful to others are available on this line. There are three ways Descartes might go, and none seems particularly satisfactory. First, he might claim that others could understand what our expressions mean only by first understanding their causal history. That is, one would have to work through the *Passions of the Soul, comme physicien*, and then some. Elisabeth, in her letter of 25 April 1646, remarking on a draft of the *Passions*, seems to read Descartes to be suggesting as much. And she none too innocently raises a question of how such detailed knowledge not only of microphysiology but also of its correlation with the different passions is possible (AT iv. 404). Moreover, this demand certainly does not seem to accord with our experience: it just does not take that much to understand a smile or a scowl. And Descartes himself seems to recognize this—after all the stupidest servant would not be able to grasp all this. He might reply to this sort of objection by claiming rather that just as objects affect us in such a way that we naturally feel the passions we do on encountering them, so too do our expressions naturally signify the passions. Malebranche, in *The Search After Truth* seems to take this line. He writes:

I cannot overemphasize the fact that all the passions excited in us by the sight of some external object mechanically produce their particular facial expression in

---

[10] Indeed, it is because Descartes understands our expressions as simply the result of the mechanics of physiology in this way that he feels comfortable attributing passions and their expressions to animals (though animal expressions would undoubtedly depend on animal physiology). See Part V of the *Discourse*: 'and we should not confuse speech with the natural movements which express passions and which can be imitated by machines as well as animals' (AT vi. 58); as well the Letter to More, 5 Feb. 1649: 'I am not at all disturbed by the astuteness and cunning of dogs and foxes, or by all the things which animals do for the sake of food, sex, and fear; I claim that I can easily explain all of them as originating from the structure of their bodily parts' (AT v. 276; CSMK 365); and the remarks about the training of animals in the Letter to the Marquess of Newcastle, 23 Nov. 1646: 'If you teach a magpie to say good-day to its mistress when it sees her approach, this can only be by making the utterance of this word the expression of its passions. . . . Similarly all the things which dogs, horses, and monkeys are taught to perform are only expressions of their fear, their hope, or their joy; and consequently can be performed without any thought' (AT iv. 574, CSMK 303).

those struck by them, i.e. an appearance that by its impression mechanically disposes everyone seeing it to those passions and actions useful to the good of society. (*Recherche*, v. 7)[11]

This certainly makes more sense, and indeed seems continuous with many contemporary accounts of how we understand expressions. More, however, needs to be said about the nature of this mechanism. For it is not clear how a mechanism can explain the way in which these expressions engage our moral sensibilities. After all, why should seeing another's tears, say, excite in us compassion rather than simply the belief that the person's eyes are watery. If Descartes wanted to avoid this problem he could, of course, take a behaviorist line and simply explain our facility at understanding others' expressions by our establishing correlations between outward physical appearances and passions. This would certainly explain the facility with which the servant reads his master's face; the servant may be stupid, but he learns quickly how to survive in a household with a demanding master. Although this account would be the more plausible one, there is little evidence that Descartes takes it up. So it is at least unclear on the causal account how Descartes would go on to explain how others are able to understand our expressions.

There are thus at least two core problems with the causal account of the significance of our passionate expressions. The first is endemic to causal accounts of reference: we need a way of picking out the referent from the many elements in the causal chain. The second is one of textual inadequacy. And hovering in the background is a concern about how a causal account of our expressions can be consistent with the way we actually read off those expressions. I want now to consider the second core problem, for one might hope that in getting Descartes right we can avoid the other problems.

4. ADJUSTING THE CAUSAL ACCOUNT:
A COMMON CAUSAL ACCOUNT

We might try to resolve the textual problems of the causal account by adjusting the picture a bit. While it may well be the case that the

---

[11] See also *Recherche*, II. 1. 4, v. 3, as well as other passages in v. 7. Notice, however, that Malebranche here does not suggest that the soul's thoughts cause our passionate expressions: they are produced mechanically by the external object.

physiological motions which constitute our expressions are not *caused* by the soul on Descartes's account, it does seem that these physiological states are still correlated with mental states: in particular, we might think, they share a common cause. The physiological state resulting from our interaction with the world seems to have two parallel effects: a physiological reaction and a mental state. Our outwardly directed bodily states can be understood to be expressive of our passions just because both are caused by a particular way in which the world impacts on us. This too is an intelligible model of reference, for this is sometimes the way a set of symptoms are taken to be signs of a disease.[12]

   This account does require that we reread Descartes's discussion of the expressions, but this seems straightforward enough. For one, in saying that joy or sadness or shame or love causes certain physiological changes, Descartes might simply be invoking the thought to refer metonymically to the physiology. Or, perhaps more likely, he might be adopting the way people speak colloquially about the passions and their effects. We just say things like 'I blushed because I was embarrassed' even though we think that our blushing has a physiological aetiology.

   And if we go this way, it seems that at least part of the problem with the causal account can be resolved. For on this common causal account, the significance of an expression is not explained through its direct causal relation to the referent. Rather, the common causal account depends simply on the two sets of determinate connections working in concert with one another.[13] That is, the common causal account invokes two things: (1) the causal connection between physiological states; and (2) the causal connection between bodily states and mental states. Our expressions are causally connected to the physiological states that precede them, and one of those states, a tilt of the pineal gland, is directly causally connected to a mental state, a passion. Through that pivotal physiological state, our passions are linked to our expressions, and

---

[12] The symptoms of muscular sclerosis, for instance, are taken to be signs of the disease, though, on one theory of MS, both the symptoms and the disease are thought to be caused by an as yet unidentified virus.

[13] I am using the word 'determinate' here to avoid the confusions of 'necessary'. While the causal connections between bodies may well be necessary, Descartes is clear that, in the case of body–mind connections, God could have made things otherwise. In this sense body–mind connections are not necessary. On the face of it, however, it does seem that once God institutes body–mind associations the way they are, a bodily state determines a thought in the mind, and vice versa. I will presently call this assumption into question, however.

through this linkage our expressions can be said to signify the passions they do.[14]

But why are we able to turn on that pivotal state? Why are we able to claim that our expressions signify our passions? We are able to do so just because we take the connections both between physiological states and between physiological and mental states to be determinate connections.

It must be the case that our being in a certain physiological state *always* leads (1) to the movements constituting our expressions *and* (2) to our having a certain thought, a passion. We can elide the move through their common cause and go directly to the passion just because of these determinate connections.[15]

Both of these assumptions seem to be entirely uncontroversial. Certainly, in so far as Descartes understands the body to function as a machine, he takes the workings of the body to consist in a chain of physiological causes, one state determinately leading to another. Equally, the assumption that the connections between particular physiological states and thoughts are determinate seems unproblematic. Descartes does claim that certain thoughts are joined to certain bodily states by a natural institution,[16] and this natural institution seems to consist in nothing but the establishment of determinate associations between bodily states and mental states.[17]

However, there is a problem. It seems that this account as it stands cannot accommodate a basic feature of our passionate lives, a feature Descartes recognizes: our capacity for emotional development, for changing how we feel about things. In the *Passions of the Soul*, it becomes clear that Descartes

---

[14] On this view, we might well say that any physiological state on the causal pathway leading up to (or indeed following from) the expression could signify the passion. I don't think this is a problem; there can be multiple signs of the same thing, after all. This is not to say that there aren't other problems with this account. I turn to one of them presently.

[15] In cases of dissimulation, of course, the expression only seems to be a sign of our passion: the physiology thus exists without the passion in the soul. But dissimulation is an intentional act of a sort, and one that depends on there being a connection between the physiology of the expression and the passion in the soul. We willfully direct our body to assume a particular expression so that it seems that we feel a certain way.

[16] With regard to the passions see *Passions* a.36, AT xi. 357, *Passions* a.89, AT xi. 394, *Passions* a.90, AT xi. 395, and *Passions* a.94, AT xi. 399 f.

[17] Most commentators subscribe to the position that body–mind associations are fixed in this way at least tacitly. See for example, Alison Laywine, 'Malebranche, Jansenism and the Sixth Meditation', *Archiv für Geschichte der Philosophie*, 81 (1999), 148–73, at 150, and Margaret Wilson, *Descartes* (New York: Routledge and Kegan Paul, 1978), 217. The textual basis for it comes in *Meditation* VI. See AT vii. 88–9, CSM ii. 61.

does not think that the association between a given physiological state and a thought (or at least a passion) is fixed; that is, Descartes does not think that mind–body associations are determinate in the sense in play here. So the account of the *Passions* challenges the second of the two assumptions of the common causal account, and without that assumption the common causal account of our passionate expressions is inadequate.

This idea that the associations between bodily and mental states are not fixed comes out in Descartes's remarks about the regulation of the passions. First remark that at the end of the *Passions*, Descartes details this remedy for the misuses and excesses of our passions:

> I have included among those remedies the forethought and diligence through which we can correct our natural faults by striving to separate within ourselves the movements of the blood and spirits from the thoughts to which they are usually joined.   (*Passions* a.211, AT xi.486.)

In order to feel the passions we should feel to the degree we should feel them, we are supposed to separate in ourselves the connection between the physiological state and the thought, and then we are, presumably, to institute a new connection—one which conforms to our 'firm and determinate judgements bearing on the knowledge of good and evil' (*Passions* a.48; AT xi.367). Thus, Descartes here avers that we have a capacity for changing our feelings about things by reforming the natural associations between mental and physical states.

What does Descartes mean in proposing this remedy? Consider first *Passions* a.44, an article with the title 'That each volition is naturally joined to some movement of the gland but that *by artifice or habituation one can join it to others*' (AT xi.361; emphasis added). While the title here is certainly suggestive of the remedy he will prescribe later, in the text of the article he does not yet go that far. Rather his focus is on the way we act on our passions, and he rightly notes that we can train ourselves to respond to our occurrent thoughts in new ways.[18] So, for example, although our natural fear of dogs might incline us to run away, we can, through judging that we are in fact in no danger from dogs, make ourselves stay. Indeed, we can train ourselves to react this way reflexively. Nothing in this suggested way of controlling our passions indicates that

---

[18] It is here where Descartes treats of language learning, whereby we come to associate certain movements of the mouth with meanings of words rather than with the desire to make those movements.

the natural institution between physical and mental states themselves is not fixed. I still feel the fear I am naturally disposed to in the face of dogs. I just no longer react to it in the same way.

However, in a.50 the promise of the title of a.44 is realized. In this article Descartes extends his discussion and suggests that we can change the way we are given to feel in certain situations: he asserts that 'although nature seems to have joined every movement of the gland to certain of our thoughts from the beginning of our life, yet we may join them to others through habit' (AT xi. 368). Thus, Descartes implies that we can change our feelings about things at the most basic level; we can, through a process of rejoining physical and mental states, change the way in which the world affects us so that we have the thoughts we do. To continue with the dog example: we not only can overcome our fear of dogs by controlling our reaction to them, but also we can come to be simply not afraid of dogs any longer.[19] According to the former course of regulating the passions, I will still feel fear upon seeing a dog; my fear will be under control. However, on the latter course of regulating the passions, I will reach a point where I just do not fear dogs; my fear has been overcome not because I am able to control it but because I no longer feel it at all.

That we can reform ourselves in this second way, according to Descartes, poses a problem for the common causal account of our expressions. For on that account our expressions signify our passions just because they share a common cause, a physiological state. But given our capacity to reform ourselves, a physiological state that once led us to feel fear, and also led to an expression of fear, might come to lead us to feel another passion through our efforts to regulate our passions. There is nothing in the common causal account as it stands, however, to lead us to think that anything at all has changed physiologically. We are given no reason to think that those efforts at regulation that involve a reinstitution of mind–body associations should have any effects on the causal mechanisms through which other bodies affect our body and which

---

[19] I offer a more detailed account of this capacity to reform ourselves in my 'Descartes's *Passions of the Soul* and the Union of Mind and Body' ['Passions and Union'], *Archiv für Geschichte der Philosophie* (forthcoming 2003). That Descartes holds this view might require that we rethink our understanding of what it is for the connections between bodily states and mental states to be instituted by nature. I cannot undertake this here, but I offer a suggestion of how such a story might go in 'The Structure of the *Passions of the Soul*', in *Passion and Virtue in Descartes*, ed. Byron Williston and André Gombay (Buffalo: Prometheus Books, 2003). I intend to develop this suggestion further in future work.

govern the operations of our own body. And with our physiology a constant, our expressions should also remain the same. Our bodies would, on this account, still be affected in the same way by dogs, say, and we would present the same expression when confronted with a dog. But through our efforts to regulate our passions that same physiology would lead to a different thought; we might feel affection rather than fear when faced with a dog. If we are to say that our expressions are expressive of our passions just because they share a physiological cause with them, then it seems we are committed to claiming that our expressions change significance with our efforts at controlling our passions.

Thus, Descartes's account of the regulation of the passions effectively undermines the second of the assumptions of the common causal account, and without that assumption it is unclear just what the basis is for any claim that our expressions signify our passions. Indeed, it is not clear which passion a given expression signifies.

In this way, the common causal account as it stands does not seem to accord with our experience. While changing how we feel about things is not commonplace—we are set in our ways about many things—it is not extraordinary either. We often overcome our fears, likes, and dislikes to such an extent that we can hardly imagine ourselves as we once were. If, with these changes of feeling, our various facial expressions remain constant, we would be effectively inscrutable, or at least very difficult to negotiate. And moreover, it does seem that our expressions *do* change with our feelings. So, now that I am over my fear of dogs, when I see a dog, I will not wear the same expression I did before, when I was afraid of them. Our expressions are consistent in signifying what they do, and the common causal account as it stands would suggest that they are not.[20]

One possible resolution of this problem is to claim that in some cases the significance of our passionate expressions can be explained through the common causal account, while in other cases, that significance is to be explained through the causal involvement of the soul. In particular, we might think that while the common causal account is an adequate explanation of the passions we feel pre-reflectively, the soul is to figure in explaining our expressions when we find our feelings change. The

---

[20] It is also worth noting that nothing in this common causal account as it stands would seem to resolve the problems surrounding the communication of our passions through our expressions that surfaced with the causal account. Thus it is still less than clear how we are able to read off the expressions of others.

text of the *Passions* might well be consistent with such a reading, though it does not support it directly. However, in order for this sort of resolution to afford a philosophically viable position, more would need to be said about how the soul effects changes of expression with its changes of feeling. For it is not the case, even with these changes of feeling, that our emotive expressions are voluntary actions. In the case of voluntary action, the thought itself is associated with a motion of the pineal gland, and that motion of the gland in turn moves the animal spirits in such a way as to effect the action at issue. In the case of changes of feeling the motion of gland remains constant—what changes is the association between that motion and a thought—but somehow the physiological effects of that motion are different, so that we wear a different expression. If the soul had the power to effect *that* change, it would seem it would challenge Descartes's physics. Descartes, however, does admit that animals can be trained, and indeed retrained. Presumably, this training would involve simply a configuration of bodily dispositions (a tweaking of the body-machine, as it were), and he could appeal to this sort of bodily training to account for how our expressions come to match our change of feeling. This, however, seems to me overly theatrical. For it is not as if we come to inhabit the mask proper to the portrayal of our new feelings. Rather, it seems that our change of feeling and change of expression come together.

We are thus left asking: can any more be said about how the soul might effect a change of expression coordinate with its change of feeling? Is there any other way Descartes can be left making some sense about our emotive expressions?[21]

5. A THIRD ALTERNATIVE: AN APPEAL TO HUMAN NATURE

One thing to note is that both the causal and the common causal account presuppose a thin notion of efficient causation, that is, one in which no further explanation of that efficient causal relation is offered or required.

[21] Spinoza doesn't seem to think so. In *EIIIP59S* he denies that there are any expressions of the passions, properly speaking: 'As for the external affections of the body, which are observed in the affects —such as trembling, paleness, sobbing, laughter, and the like —I have neglected them because they are related to the body only without any relation to the mind'. One can read this as an acknowledgment that there is no good way of account for the expressiveness of bodily states (after all, for Spinoza, modes of body do not represent).

There is good reason for this: Descartes's rejection of final causes in physics and his rejection of substantial forms would seem to leave him with just that to account for causal relations. Moreover a notion of efficient causation seems just that simple:[22] one thing is the efficient cause of the other if it has the power, or the efficacy, to move the other in some way, and without a notion of formal or final causation to appeal to, it seems there is nothing more to say in this regard. However, in the case of the human being, Descartes does appeal to a thicker notion of efficient causation: that is, he aims to offer an explanation for why bodily states bring about the mental states they do.[23]

What can explain the associations between thoughts and physical states? In *Meditations* VI, Descartes invokes the institution of nature to explain why it is we feel a pain in our foot when our foot is injured. We feel the pain we do, he says, just because 'nature has laid it down that this motion [of the pineal gland] should produce in the mind a sensation of pain, as occurring in the foot' (AT vii. 87; CSM ii. 60). Descartes's explanation, however, does not stop there. Particular mental–physical associations are instituted by nature to be the way they are because:

the best system that could be devised is that it [the gland] should produce the one sensation which, of all possible sensations, is most especially and most frequently conducive to the preservation of the healthy man. And experience shows that the sensations which nature has given us are all of this kind.   (ibid.)

---

[22] There are, of course, many problems in understanding the details of Descartes's account of causation, and a vast literature that aims to flesh out these details. See for instance Daniel Garber, 'Descartes and Occasionalism', in Steven Nadler (ed.), *Causation in Early Modern Philosophy* (University Park, PA: Penn State University Press, 1993), 9–26; Gary Hatfield, 'Force (God) in Descartes' Philosophy', *Studies in Philosophy of Science*, 10 (1979): 113–40; and Janet Broughton, 'Adequate Causes and Natural Change in Descartes's Philosophy', in Alan Donagan, Anthony Provich, Jr., and Michael Wedin (eds.), *Human Nature and Natural Knowledge* (Dordrecht: D. Reidel, 1986), 107–27. Kenneth Clatterbaugh, *The Causation Debate in Modern Philosophy 1637–1739* (New York: Routledge, 1999) provides a nice overview of the seventeenth-century debates. My claim here is simply that often the notion of efficient causation under discussion is one that comprises only the ability of one thing to effect another, and not any further explanation of that ability.

[23] In n. 9 above, I suggested that in the passage I will consider presently, Descartes attempts to resolve problems with a causal account of the reference of our sensations. Reading the passage in that way does not require taking Descartes to be explaining the causal relation between bodily states and mental states. The discussion that follows takes Descartes to be explaining not only the reference of our body-caused thoughts but also the causal relations themselves. That is, I take the natural institution to be a causal relation and not simply a referential relation. Simmons, 'Cartesian Sensations', has the most detailed discussion of this passage. I cannot here settle the question of which interpretation is preferable.

States of the pineal gland are instituted so as to produce certain thoughts *for our own good*, so that we might better preserve ourselves as human beings. Thus, our good as human beings is meant to explain the natural causal associations between bodily and mental states.

A similar sort of explanation figures in a curious way in the *Passions of the Soul*, aa.107–11. There Descartes provides a natural history of the primitive passions; he tells a story about the origins of our passions. In the immediately preceding articles (aa.97–106) Descartes has set out the physical symptoms of each passion, and then considered the physiological causes of these symptoms. It is clear from the order of presentation that the natural history is meant to explain just why that physiology is associated with the particular passion it is. And interestingly, the articles on the expressions of the passions follow immediately from this natural history. It thus seems that the explanation Descartes offers of these associations is meant to contribute to an explanation of how our expressions can signify what they do. Since any further account of our expressions we might arrive at here will emerge out of an understanding of this natural history of the mind–body union, that is, of human beings, I will call this account the *human naturalist account*. Let us look at this natural history further.[24]

According to this natural history, Descartes claims that when our soul 'began to be joined with our body' the heart contained a nutriment particularly well-suited to maintaining the life of the body. The soul then loved these juices in the heart:

> For it seems to me that the first passions that our soul had, when it began to be joined to our body, had to have been at a time when the blood or other juice which entered in the heart, was an aliment more suitable than the usual for maintaining the heat which is the principle of life; this was cause for the soul to join itself willingly with this aliment, that is, to love it. (*Passions* a.107; AT xi. 407)

Descartes continues, explaining our first feelings of hate, joy, sadness, and desire in a similar way.[25] While the story is a strange one, and not in the

---

[24] There is much to be said about these very peculiar articles, but here I will only present the general shape of the picture, and draw out some select points. See my 'Passions and Union' for a more thorough discussion.

[25] We first felt hate when there was some bad blood, insufficient for maintaining life, circulating in the body, first felt joy when our blood was so well-nourished that our body had no need to replenish itself, first felt sadness when our body lacked sustenance, and first felt desire to receive things suitable to the body. See *Passions* aa. 108–11; AT xi. 408–11.

least because of its appeal to our feelings towards our blood,[26] the *Passions* is not the only place he tells it. In the letter to Chanut of 1 February 1647, Descartes also tries to explain why we feel the primitive passions when we do, also by appealing to an original moment of the soul's union with the body (AT iv. 604 ff.; CSMK, 307 ff.). In so far as Descartes does seem to be insistent about offering this sort of explanation of primordial associations between mental and physical states, it seems we can take this set of articles in the *Passions* seriously.

According to Descartes's natural history, our passions come to be associated with their proper physiology in so far as that physiological state indicates our state of physical well-being. We feel love when the body is functioning particularly well, sadness when it is functioning poorly, and so on. In feeling the passions it does, the soul has some sort of access to the state of the body, but this access alone is insufficient to explain its passions. That it feels what it does on the occasion it does is also due to the soul's relating itself to its body, to its taking up a certain sort of attitude towards that state. In the case of love, the soul not only is aware that the body is functioning well, it is also pleased at that well-functioning. The soul in a way takes what is good for the body as its own good. This aspect of the soul's first experience of love establishes the association which will guide future feelings of love. It explains the causal efficacy of that bodily state in bringing about a passion.[27]

So this account suggests that there is a thick, rather than a thin, notion of efficient causation in play, at least in the case of body–mind interaction. That is, Descartes thinks there is an explanation of the efficient causal relations between mind and body. Moreover, just as it does in *Meditations* VI, the explanation appeals to our good.

---

[26] It is also strange in virtue of the fact that he is trying to account for the beginnings of a soul–body union he elsewhere attributes to God.

[27] The questions coming out of this story are many: what is the difference between the soul's having access to a bodily state and its assuming an attitude towards it? How does this attitude serve to establish a body–mind association? How is that association related to the causal interaction between body and mind? In addition, there is an important difference between this account and that of the *Meditations*. In the latter, Descartes does not seem to assign the soul any agency in effecting the natural institution between mind and body. In the *Passions* the soul does seem to play an active role. It is an interesting question whether we can read the account of passions back into the *Meditations* VI account. It can certainly seem as if the natural history we are given in the *Passions* constitutes a development in Descartes's view, and if it does we need to ask what prompts him to make this change. I cannot begin to address these questions here.

I want also to note two other elements of this natural history. First, a certain physiological state still causes a thought, but the way in which it does affords the possibility of reforming mind–body associations. The causal efficacy of a bodily state with respect to a thought is due to associations between physiological states and passions. These associations in turn are due to the soul's concern for the body, for through this concern an association is forged between them. We might think that these associations can change in accordance with the changes in the soul's concern for the body. It can thus potentially avoid the problem of the common causal account.

The second point concerns the conception of our physiology. By all accounts our physiology is described mechanistically. However, what Descartes's natural history of the passions makes clear is that what physiological state we are in is not, as is commonly thought, divested of value. It is important on the view I am suggesting here that a physiological state can be either better or worse for the functioning of the machine of the human body. That is to say, it is clear here that Descartes sees the body as having its own good—just its functioning well or preserving the heat that is the principle of life.[28]

We are now in a position to return to the question of Descartes's account of the significance of our emotive expressions. How does an explanation of the associations between bodily states and passions in terms of the human good help us to understand our expressions as signifying our passions? That is, what is the human naturalist account of our emotive expressions?

---

[28] Standard views of Cartesian efficient causation would have us break down the physiology of the body into discrete causal events linked together in a chain. There is no place for any purpose or end built into these mechanical workings and in light of which we could say that one bodily state is better or worse than another. The standard interpretation does have its justification: for Descartes disavows repeatedly the appropriateness of final causes, and hence of final causal explanations, in physics. Thus, there is a real question as to whether this notion of the 'body's good' is consistent with Descartes's disavowal of teleological explanations in physics. Denis Des Chene, *Spirits and Clocks: Machine and Organism in Descartes* (Ithaca: Cornell University Press, 2001), offers a very clear statement of this concern, and even argues against the suggestion I am advancing here. (See pp. 116–52 in particular.) I do think, however, that there is no inconsistency here. That the body has a good is not what explains the body's physiology—the motions of the body are governed by the laws of motion, just as much as those of any other matter—and so it does not provide us with a final cause in this sense. Rather, the body's good can be explained in terms of the mechanics of the body: it is simply the continued functioning of the body-machine, which is something determined entirely by the interrelation of the body's parts. The body simply strives to maintain its mechanical integrity, an integrity defined internally to the body itself. See my 'The Health of the Body-Machine? Or 17th Century Mechanism and the Concept of Health' (MS) for a further defense of this suggestion.

On this account our expressions are the result of the physiology of our body. Our expressions are just the manifestations on the surface of our body of a particular physiological state. And equally, on this account, our feelings of the passions are caused by the physiological state we are in, in virtue of the established associations between body and mind. But we also have an explanation of these causal associations: they serve the good of a human being.

Through this explanation we can understand our expressions to signify our passions because they both reflect the same thing: our well-being, or the way in which things harm or benefit us. To see this, recall first that our expressions are integrated into the causal nexus constituting our body. And as we have seen, the body on its own functions either well or poorly, depending on how well the machine of our body is maintaining itself. Thus, our expressions can be understood as manifestations of the workings of the body as whole, and as such they present whether the body is functioning well or poorly.[29] And our passions represent how things are affecting our well-being. Indeed, that is just what the passions are. As Descartes indicates in a.52, our passions represent the way that things 'can harm or profit us or, generally, be important to us' (AT xi. 372). Both our physiology and our thoughts thus reflect the same thing: the effect of things on our well-being.[30]

I have already suggested that this account can accommodate Descartes's account of the regulation of the passions and so avoid the central problem that faced the common causal account. I now want to consider this in more detail. First, on the human naturalist account, the associations

[29] In this regard, I draw attention again to what Descartes includes among our expressions. He is not primarily interested in smiles or frowns, though he does include movements of the eyes and face as expressions; rather his focus is on our coloring, languor, laughter, and tears. And we do associate these expressions with our states of bodily well-being. Thanks to Amy Schmitter for drawing my attention to this point.

[30] On the surface, this human naturalist account of the expressions of our passions has a similar structure to the common causal account. Our expressions signify the passions they do in virtue of their shared aetiology. But what is significant in this aetiology is no longer a discrete element of this physiological state. We have our expressions in virtue of the physiological state the body is in, and as such they might certainly be said to be caused by a preceding event in the causal chain of events leading up to them. But they are *expressions* in virtue of the physiological state of the body as a whole. They figure in a body which is functioning well or poorly. And a particular element (the state of the gland) of this physiological state as a whole gives rise to the passions. The passions and their expressions do have a common cause, but what is salient here is not so much the efficient causal history as the way that causal history pertains to our bodily well-being.

between mental and physical states are explained by the soul's conception of our well-being. As we develop our understanding of our well-being, it makes sense that we would then reinstitute mind–body associations. Can this consistency with Descartes's account of the regulation of the passions resolve the problem the common causal account faced, that of understanding how our expressions might change with our change of feelings?

There are two ways Descartes might go here. First, on this model the body is conceived as a whole which functions better or worse, and our expressions reflect that functioning. One might think that Descartes could claim that mind and body are intertwined with one another such that as the mind gets better understanding of our good, the body adjusts its functioning to conform to that understanding—akin to a symbiotic relationship. He seems to suggest something similar to this in his correspondence with Elisabeth, where his investigation of the passions and their regulation begins in the summer of 1645.[31] And more, it seems that our feeling generosity, that passion which makes us master of our passions and is key to all the virtues, has a real physiological effect, keeping us calm both physically and mentally. So long as our changing the way we are given to feel about things does have this real physiological effect, our expressions should change along with our feelings. But to make good on this promise, more needs to be said about how such a responsiveness might be consistent with the causal interaction of mind and body. Descartes is here not envisioning intentional voluntary action on the part of the soul. And it is not clear that the natural institution model of causal interaction can handle the complexity of our reconception of the good. That model seems tailored to explaining the associations between particular ideas and bodily states rather than that between our overall way of approaching the world and our overall bodily condition.

---

[31] There Descartes aims to cure Elisabeth's physical troubles by helping her through a difficult period emotionally; in Elisabeth's terms, he aims to cure her body by curing her soul. See the Letter from Elisabeth to Descartes, 24 May 1645, AT iv. 208. Indeed, in this correspondence Descartes suggests that his own efforts in feeling things properly helped him to overcome his own chronic illness in adolescence. See the Letter to Elisabeth, May or June 1645, AT iv. 218 ff.; CSMK 249 ff. These letters are consistent with the line Descartes takes in an earlier one, from 8 July 1644, in which he writes: 'the construction of our body is such that certain movements follow in it naturally from certain thoughts, as one sees that redness of the face follows from shame, tears from compassion, and laughter from joy. And I know of no other thought more proper to the conservation of health than that which consists in a strong persuasion and firm belief that the architecture of our body is so good that, once one is healthy once, one cannot easily fall ill' (AT v. 65: CSMK 237).

The responsiveness of mind and body to one another seems more in keeping with an Aristotelian model of their union, one rooted in formal causation. If Descartes were to appeal to this here, in the case of the human being, he would compromise his more general rejection of formal causation.

There is, however, another way Descartes can go. This second route rests on an alternative way of understanding how we read the signs we send one another. On this view, understanding the expressions of others need not be a matter of mere correlation between outward appearances and inner feelings. Nor need it presuppose a kind of natural mechanism that allows us to read off others' expressions. Rather, if the expressions of the passions are reflections of our nature as human beings, reflections of our good, then in order to understand others we need only have a sense of our good and the ability to recognize that others share the same nature with us. And so, we might think that we revise our conception of our good in light of how others come to rethink their good. That is, our expressions stay the same, but our interpretations of them change along with our changing conception of our good. In a similar way, we might also come to revise our assessments of others' expressions. However, I am not sure whether this model accords with the way our expressions actually go. It does seem to me that our expressions do change as we revise our estimation of things, and not that we revise our interpretations of expressions with those revised estimations. And this second route affords no way of explaining our changing responses to the world.

6. CONCLUSION

So what do the expressions of the passions tell us? I have presented three possible accounts of how our emotive expressions might be external signs for Descartes, all of which present some problems. The straightforward causal account faces the standard problem of a causal theory of reference—how to single out the referent in the causal history of the sign—as well as textual problems. The common causal account can avoid the textual problems of the causal account, as well as the problems of a causal theory of reference, since the meaning of the expression is not explained by a direct causal relation. It, however, faces another problem: it cannot accommodate Descartes's account of the regulation of the passions. The source of this problem lies in its assumption that the causal relation between body and mind is fixed and determinate and an efficient causal relation requiring no further explanation. Descartes, however, does offer an explanation for these causal connections, and focussing on this explanation affords another account of the expressions of the passions. On this account the expressions signify our passions because both reflect our good as human beings. While this sort of account makes more intuitive sense, it does so by calling into question the nature of the causal relation between mind and body. The changes in expression that go along with changes of feeling seem to be best explained by a kind of mutual responsiveness of mind and body, but this model does not seem to accord with the account of mind–body interaction Descartes has available. Alternatively, the source of the significance of our expressions might come not from the soul but from our sharing a nature with those to whom we express ourselves. But this account too has its shortcomings.

That Descartes's account, whatever it might be, has problems is instructive nonetheless. For one, it is interesting that he devotes so much attention to the expressions of the passions. Descartes recognizes that the way in which our feelings are made manifest is an important part of our passionate lives. Yet the persistence of the problems brings out the difficulty for a dualist like Descartes to account for this very human function. Descartes's dualism might well afford insights for understanding both the natural world and the nature of thought, but in so far as it does not have a clear way of bridging these two realms, it runs into trouble in trying to capture the most commonplace aspect of experience as human beings.

Simon Fraser University

4

The First Condemnation of Descartes's *Œuvres*: Some Unpublished Documents from the Vatican Archives

JEAN-ROBERT ARMOGATHE AND VINCENT CARRAUD

It is well known that some of Descartes's Latin writings were placed on the Catholic Church's Index of Prohibited Books in 1663. The condemnation decree has been published many times in the modern era, in particular by Francisque Bouillier, and then (in a corrected version) by Georges Monchamp.[1] The circumstances around the condemnation have been closely studied by Monchamp, working from the archives at the University of Louvain.[2] The opening of the historic archives of the Archives of the Congregation for the Doctrine of Faith (ACDF) has now made possible the discovery of the Church's secret dossier on the condemnation,[3] which in turn allows us to illuminate the motives and circumstances surrounding it.

I. FROM MAY TO AUGUST 1662: THE DEBATES AT LOUVAIN

As Monchamp has shown, it was the University of Louvain that provided the occasional cause for the steps taken in Rome.[4] To be more

[1] Fr. Bouillier, *Histoire de la philosophie cartésienne*, 2 vols. (3rd edn. Paris, 1868), i. 466–7; Monchamp, *Histoire du cartésianisme en Belgique* (Brussels, 1886; henceforth, 'Monchamp'), 389–91. Monchamp published the 'nearly literal transcription' by Plempius.

[2] Henry Alphonse De Vocht, *Inventaire des archives de l'Université de Louvain, 1426–1797, aux Archives générale du Royaume à Bruxelles* (Louvain: Uystpruyst, 1927), no. 70, vol. 24 [3 Jan. 1661–May 6, 1667]). These archives were temporarily inaccessible in 2001–2; we had to content ourselves with reproducing the texts of the documents provided by Monchamp (with the exception of a document also transcribed by L. Ceyssens).

[3] Our thanks to Marta Fattori (Rome) for her invaluable assistance in this research, and to Theo Verbeek (Utrecht), to whom we are grateful for several corrections and clarifications.

[4] Following Monchamp, we reproduce in document 1 the deliberations of the Faculty of Arts at Louvain between 3 July and 28 Aug. 1662.

precise, the Faculty of Arts and the Faculty of Medicine were favorably inclined toward the 'new doctrine', while the Faculty of Theology, always more submissive to Rome on matters of orthodoxy, complained about the University's procrastination in condemning Cartesian teachings.

The medical doctor Plempius offers his own version of events, which the archival documents confirm. However, he provides us with a precious piece of information, one that has no documentary evidence, but which may turn out to be correct. He places the origin of the whole affair in May 1662.

In the year 1662, on May 10, the most eminent and distinguished F. Cardinal of the Holy Roman Church A., with the highest authority, sent letters from Rome to our Illustrious Master and Teacher C. L., Doctor of Theology from Louvain, in which he included these things in passing: 'I am astonished at how the errors of Cartesian philosophy lurk about there [in Louvain]; for they proceed from crude ignorance,' and then remarks that these lead to atheism.[5]

Monchamp has deciphered the initials in this piece with certainty: they belong to Cardinal F[rancesco] A[lbizzi] and to an Augustinian, a doctor from Louvain (originally from Ypres), C[hrétien] L[upus] (de Wulf).[6] De Wulf had just returned to Louvain after five years in Rome, and he was responsible for communicating the Cardinal's anxious warning about the Cartesian philosophy to his colleagues back home.[7] The internuncio Girolamo de Vecchi, who was probably alerted to the situation through the same channels, appears on the scene at the end of June with a letter to the Faculty of Arts, as noted by Plempius

---

[5] Vopiscus Fortunatus Plempius, *Fundamenta medicinae*, 4th edn. (Louvain, 1664), introduction; reproduced in Monchamp, p. 335, and Lucien Ceyssens, *Sources relatives à l'histoire du jansénisme. Sources des années 1661–1672* [henceforth, 'Ceyssens'], (Brussels and Rome, 1966), 86–7.

[6] David Aurelius Perini, oesa, *Bibliographia Augustiniana* (Florence, 1935), iii. 20–1.

[7] In a letter in which Jérôme de Vecchi explains to Cardinal-nephew Fabio Chigi all about his efforts to introduce de Wulf into the Theology faculty at Louvain (16, Dec. 1662), he describes the Augustinian cleric in these terms: '[de Wulf] must be estimated as a notable acquisition for the interests of the Holy Seat (where the scars from the past sores of Jansenism are almost fresh); you can't find a subject not only as learned, but also who gives as much and is as faithful to the Holy See, and is as inclined to its interests as this Father.' See also L. Ceyssens, 'Chrétien Lupus. Sa période janséniste (1640–1660)', *Augustiniana* 15 (1965), 294–314, 629–60; 16 (1966), 264–312.

(document 2).[8] The faculty met on 3 July.[9] A response to the letter of the nuncio was the first order of the day (document 1).

On 4 and 5 July, a committee met to draft a response, which was then submitted to the faculty (document 3). The faculty decided to have it brought to the nuncio in Brussels by two of its professors, Jean-Ulrich Randaxhe and Lambert Vincent. The two envoys returned from Brussels to read to the faculty, on July 10, a new letter from the nuncio, dated July 7 (document 4). On 29 July, the nuncio wrote to Cardinal Sforza Pallavicini[10] in Rome in order to fill him in on his activities and to lay out the situation (document 5). This unpublished document is very important, for in it the nuncio explains the motives for the steps he has taken against Cartesian doctrine. For him, the problem lies in the freedom of teaching, an unfettered freedom of opinion that can ruin the truths of faith. As proof of this, he cites the behavior of Arnold Geulincx, who is (according to him) the source of the menace:

Perhaps the first in Louvain to have started to foment this novelty was a certain professor Gulinx [*sic*] who was very well regarded in Philosophy there. A short while ago with that freedom of thought of his, he apostated himself from his faith in a despicable way, even though he was a Deacon, taking shelter for himself at the University of Leiden, where he obtained a professorship. I tried to change his mind, promising him a pardon and promising to find him something in Italy, but because he had gotten himself married, and to his own niece, it was all in vain. This case has again induced me to make the resolution to write to the above-mentioned college in order to do away with such rising discord, hoping, in a word, to see it swept under the rug.

The nuncio provides some new information about Geulincx, about whom we lack almost any biographical data.[11] Born in Anvers in 1625,

---

[8] Plempius puts the date at 1 July, 1662; in fact, it was 28 June.

[9] The details of the academic meetings, which are covered by Monchamp (pp. 342 ff.), are found in the *Acta venerandae facultatis artium studii generalis oppidi Lovaniensis ab anno 1661* (Brussels: Nat. Arch. of Belgium).

[10] A professor of philosophy (and, later, of theology) at the Collegio Romano, the Jesuit Pietro Sforza Pallavicino (1607–67) was among the censors of Jansenius' *Augustinus* (as well as of the writings of Barcos in 1647). Author of a large *History of the Council of Trent (Istoria del Concilio di Trento*, Rome, 1656–7, 2 vols. in-f°, new edn. by M. Scotti, Turin, 1962), he was named Cardinal *in petto* by Alexander VII in 1657; the nomination was made public in 1659.

[11] 'There are only a few sources on the life of Geulincx', writes J.-F. Battail, in J.-P. Schobinger (ed.), *Die Philosophie des 17. Jahrhunderts*, 2 vols. (Basle, 1993), i. 379. The main information we have comes from the preface to the *Logica* (Leiden, 1662) and the *Mémoires pour servir à l'histoire littéraire des dix-sept provinces des Pays-Bas* of Jean-Noël Paquot (Louvain, 1768), vol. 13.

and having studied philosophy under Guillaume Philippi at the Collège du Lys in Louvain, Geulincx was appointed to teach there in September 1646. In a speech in December 1652, he places himself on the side of the innovators. He was suspected of heresy in 1656, but his anti-Jansenism saved him.[12] He left Louvain for Leiden in 1658, at the same time as his conversion to Protestantism, under circumstances that, for historians, remain mysterious.[13] Bouillier sees him as the first martyr for Cartesianism,[14] but there is no explicit evidence to suggest that Geulincx was in fact a Cartesian. (He mentions Descartes for the first time in his *Saturnalia* of 1665.[15]) The Abbé Jean-Noël Paquot speaks of financial problems, something that Geulincx himself seems to confirm in the preface to his *Logica*: 'until recently, brought to your academy [Leiden] by the ruin of my affairs'.[16] The nuncio's letter introduces some new information: Geulincx, who was a deacon, and thus bound by the rules of celibacy, married his niece (or cousin[17]). This might have led someone (whom Plempius calls 'a pathetic deserter of our faith') to defect to the Reformed religion and flee to Leiden, despite the attempt at 'recovery' led by de Vecchi.

On 19 August, the Cardinal-nephew informed the nuncio all about Pope Alexander VII's interest in the affair at Louvain (document 6). The Faculty of Arts issued a decree on 28 August, which it sent to the nuncio accompanied by a letter (documents 8.1 and 8.2). But as of 27 August, the nuncio had denounced to the rector of the University

---

[12] See the letter of Thomas Stapleton, professor at Louvain, to Ferdinand Niphus, administrative assistant to the nuncio at Brussels (Royal Library at Brussels, MS 3831–3833, f°. 304, cited in L. Ceyssens, *La fin de la première période du jansénisme, Sources des années 1654–1660* (Brussels and Rome, 1963), i. 474): 'Professor Julinx, depositus, offert purgationem suam in materia haereseos, coram Illma D.V., quem admittere non abs re esset, ut simul, ad confusionem aliorum, jansenismum detestaretur.'

[13] See, for example, Cornelia-Louise Thijssen-Schoute, *Nederlands Cartesianisme* (Amsterdam: Noord-Hollandse Uitgeversmaatschaapij, 1954), 152. Herman Jean de Vleeschauwer speaks of a 'resignation in good and due form in 1658', but says nothing more; see *More seu ordine geometrico demonstratus* (Pretoria: Communications of the University of South Africa, 1961), 38.

[14] *Histoire de la philosophie Cartésienne*, i. 302.

[15] This is so even if the first five *Disputationes physicae*, which reveal a dependence on Cartesian physics, date to 1663–4.

[16] It comes up later in Geulincx's preface to his *Logica*, as well: 'my deplorable affairs and failing fortune, which, for the five years I have been living here, are nothing at all, except for the hate of evil people, calumnies, haughtiness, contempt and rage'.

[17] Bernard Rousset mentions Geulincx's application (refused) to be allowed to marry his cousin Suzanne Strickers, but does not indicate any sources; see *Geulincx entre Descartes et Spinoza* (Paris, 1999), 23.

some medical theses that were being defended on 29 August, among whose *impertinentia* were various Cartesian innovations (document 7). The University's vice-rector, Jacobus Pontanus, responded to him on 31 August (document 9), while the Faculty of Theology condemned these *disputationes* on 7 September (document 10). On 9 September, the nuncio passed this decree on to Cardinal Sforza Pallavicini (document 11), while the University, on 19 September, demanded a close examination of Descartes's philosophy and the resubmission before the Rector of the suspect opinions (document 12). Finally, on 30 September, the Cardinal-nephew, Fabio Chigi, complimented the nuncio on his work and asked him to continue keeping Rome informed about this affair (document 13).

2. FROM SEPTEMBER 1662 TO NOVEMBER 1663: THE CONGREGATIONS IN ROME

We have seen how on 9 September, right after the condemnation pronounced by the Faculty of Theology, the nuncio sent Cardinal Sforza Pallavicini in Rome a copy of the decree issued by the Faculty of Arts on 28 August (document 11). It was this communication, which was read to the Congregation of the Holy Office on 15 October, that set in motion the procedure of condemnation, as we can see in the unpublished oral proceedings found in the Vatican's archives (document 14).

The two censures that have been discovered inform us of the names and status of the two qualificators: the Discalced Carmelite Giovanni Agostino della Natività (Tartaglia) and a member of the Congregation of Somascha, Stefano Spinula. The first received the *Meditations on First Philosophy* and the *Specimina*, the Latin version of the *Discourse and Essays*, while the examination of the *Principles of Philosophy* and the *Passions of the Soul* fell to the latter. It probably took a year before the censures were prepared; one of them (Spinula's) does not bear a date, while the letter accompanying Tartaglia's is dated 28 September 1663. We will look at these two unpublished documents in greater detail below.

On Wednesday, 10 October 1663, the Congregation of the Holy Office, meeting in Rome at the Dominican convent of Santa Maria sopra Minerva in the presence of four cardinals, listened as the two censures on the works of René Descartes were read. The Congregation of the Holy Office decided to condemn the four works until they were corrected and sent the sentence on to the Congregation of the Index (document 15).[18] On 20 November the Congregation of the Index issued a decree against several works, extending the prohibition (in the same terms) to other writings of Descartes: *Comments on a Certain Broadsheet, Letter to Father Dinet, Letter to Gisbertus Voetius*, and the collection titled *Opera philosophica (editio secunda ab auctore recognita)*. It is this decree by the Index that was best known in Europe, in particular through the transcription provided by Plempius in the new edition of his *Fundamenta medicinae*,[19] and also, notably, by the *Journal des savants* (4 January 1666) and in the *Integer cursus philosophicus* of the friar Willem van Sichen.[20] An examination of the diffusion of this mitigated condemnation, as well as the subsequent condemnations, which all refer back to the decree of 1663, must be put off for a later study. Without question, the unpublished text of the two censures is crucial for the history of Cartesianism.

3. THE TWO CENSORS

The two censors bear the title 'qualificator' and are outside experts serving the Holy Office (as opposed to 'consultores') who are present at the meetings and deliberations of the Congregation). We have been able to discover some information on Descartes's two censors.

(*a*) Johannes Augustinus a Nativitate (Giovanni Agostino Tartaglia) belonged to the Discalced (or reformed) Carmelites, of which he was the provincial *definitor*. Sienese by birth, he died in Rome in 1672. He is the author of *Discorsi sacri*.[21] In the dedication (p. 4), Tartaglia explains that, despite bouts of gout in his feet and hands (*podagra* and *chiragra*), he is preparing a *Viridarium quaestionum theologicarum*, which was to include a treatise *de gratia*. The *Imprimatur* of the *Discorsi* was given by Hyacinthus Libellus, at that time the Master of the Holy Palace (which was normal for a book published in Rome).[22] We learn from a note on

---

[18] Remember that this condemnation ('they decree that [these works] are to be prohibited until they are corrected') constitutes the lowest level of condemnation, those of the third class. It apparently does not extend either to the person nor even to the *Opera Omnia*. It means that the doctrine contained in these books put on the Index can be taught, it being left to the teacher to correct the dangerous theses.

[19] 4th edn., 1664, preface; Plempius used the Proceedings of the Faculty of Theology. This is the transcription published by Monchamp, pp. 389–91 n.

[20] Willem van Sichen, *Integer cursus philosophicus*, 2 vols. (Anvers, 1666), ii 169.

[21] Johannes Augustinus a Nativitate, *Discorsi Sacri* (Rome, 1670) (Bibl. Casanatense, Rome: BB–XIII–14).

[22] Libellus would become secretary to the Congregation of the Holy Office.

page 173 that the preparation of the book was interrupted by an attack of apoplexy. In the Bibliotheca Casanatense in Rome, there is a *Compendium de Gratia contra sententiam Jansenii,* in manuscript form (25 folios, cote ms. 1744), by Tartaglia. It is noteworthy that there Tartaglia employs an Augustinian vocabulary (*coactio*), as well as the Italian term *ponderationi,* as found in the technical Latin vocabulary of the qualificators,[23] and used at the end of the censure of Descartes. Tartaglia appears as qualificator for other writings, most often philosophical ones.

(*b*) Stephanus Spinula was a member of the Congregation of Somascha, and later became Bishop of Savona. In the preface to his *Scholastica theologia,*[24] one of his friends (Carolus Bossius) mentions the learned works that Spinula has produced for the Congregation of the Index and for the Inquisition at Rome. He is also mentioned in a strongly elogistic manner by Juan Caramuel in his *Theologia moralis fundamentalis* (Frankfurt, 1652).[25] By the time the Congregation of the Holy Office gives him the task of judging Descartes's *Principles* and the *Passions of the Soul,* he was already the author of an important book, *Novissima philosophia,*[26] in which he attacked the Jesuit theologians Oviedo, Arriaga, and Hurtado; his own preference was for the Theatine Joannes Morandus, author of a coursebook in philosophy.[27]

Thus, the two experts consulted by the Holy Office were perfectly qualified by their Scholastic upbringing to read philosophical texts. In particular, Spinula's recent work primed him to take a great interest in the *Principles.*

4. THE TEXTS OF THE CENSURES

A. The Censure of Stephanus Spinula (= ACDF, document g)

Emin.mi et Rmi. domini

Vidi libellos duos Renati desCartes; quorum alter inscribitur, *Principia Philosophiae,* alter uero *de passionibus animae.*

---

[23] In another title of the manuscript (on the reverse and the inside): 'Ponderationi in riposto alle heresie di Cornelio Giansenia vescovo'.

[24] Pavia, 1681 (Bibl. Casanatense and Bibliotheque Nationale de France).

[25] Book IV ('dialexis de non certitudine'), tab. tertia, n. 69: 'eruditissimus Dominus Stephanus Spinula Congregationis Somaschae', n. 55: 'est enim doctissimus et eruditissimus', and in various other places.

[26] Genoa, 1651 (Bibl. Angelica, Rome, cote XX.20.12). Spinula taught moral philosophy at Genoa.   [27] *Cursus philosophicus,* 3 vols. (Venice, 1643).

In quibus sunt animadversione digna:

P° Deum omnes res materiales, quae sunt, fuerunt aut erunt ab initio simul creasse; unde nullam dari generationem materialium substantiarum aut qualitatum materialium productionem de nouo. Quaecumque in materialia de nouo contingere uidentur, esse essentialiter eadem entia solum diversimode loco mota et disposita.

2° Nullam dari materiam primam, nullam formam materialem substantialem, nullasque qualitates accidentales; quodcumque enim ens, simplex esse, nec aliam compositionem habere, nisi inaequalem ex partibus. [*in the margin of the two first parts*: in libello <>]

3° Substantiam materialem in extensione actuali rei in ordine ad locum formale consistere, nec unam sine aliam reperiri posse [*in the margin*: pag. 36, n. 8, 9]

4° Terram moueri motu circulari et esse unum ex planetis; solem vero fixum et immotum consistere. [*in the margin*: pag. 42, n. 21, 22]

5° Substantiarum corporearum universitatem nullis finibus circumscribi, nullo loco terminari [*in the margin*: pag. 28 in fine and pag. 72, n. 29]: et omnes mundos possibiles de facto existere.

In altero vero libello *de passionibus animae* haec habentur:

P° Passiones omnes animae, amorem, iram, spem, odium etc. sicut etiam plurimas cognitiones nouas non esse affectiones productas ab anima, quae sint actus vitales etc. sed tantum esse varios motus spirituum ad has vel illas partes corporis, per quos motus formata anima sensit illos affectus, quos experimur. [*in the margin*: pag. ab art. 126 et deinceps]

2° Ut plurimum hos affectus seu spirituum motus oriri ab obiectis externis quandoque vero ab anima. [*in the margin*: pag. 28, art. 51] Et hinc luctam illam, quae est inter carnem et spiritum consistere in eo, quod contrarii motus spirituum excitantur ab anima et ab objectis externis. [*en marge*: pag 24, art. 47]

3° nullum motum corporalem membrorum oriri ab anima [*in the margin*: pag. 10, art. 16]; quin erroneum esse credere animam dare motum et calorem corpori. [*in the margin*: pag. 3, art. 5]

4° animas hominum in seipsis formatas non esse aeque nobiles et fortes. [*in the margin*: pag. 77, art. 161]

5° posse animam facile acquirere imperium absolutissimum in omnes suas passiones. [*in the margin*: pag 27, art. 50]

Haec sunt quae in praefatis libellis ponderatione digna mihi videntur, facile enim ex eorum doctrinis conclusiones contra fidem catholicam deduci possunt.

Ita sentio saluo semper J[udicio vestro]

D. Stephanus Spinula, congr. Somasch.

To the most eminent and reverend Lord,

I have seen two books[28] by René Descartes, one of which is entitled *Principles of Philosophy*, the other *On the Passions of the Soul*. There are some noteworthy things in them:

First, that God from the beginning created, at one and the same time, all the material beings that now exist, have existed, and will exist. From this it follows that there is no generation of material substances or new production of material qualities.[29] Whatever appears to happen anew among material things is essentially the same things simply being moved and arranged in different places.[30]

Second, that there is no prime matter,[31] nor any material substantial form,[32] nor any accidental qualities;[33] for whatever is a being[34] is simple

---

[28] Judging from the page citations, the qualificators used the Amsterdam edition of the *Opera Philosophica* (Elzevier, 1650).

[29] *Principles of Philosophy* II. 36, 42; III. 45, 46.   [30] *Ibid*. II. 23, 36.

[31] This element concides in part with the censure given by Monchamp, p. 205 (catalogue of the propositions proscribed by the Company of Jesus in 1657, prop. 5). In his *Novissima philosophia*, Spinola writes: 'it is commonly thought to be evident that there is prime matter, although contrary to the ancients, there is no lack of moderns who reject it' (p. 154).

[32] This element coincides in part with the censure of the Faculty of Theology of Louvain (below, document 10, first point of the censure of the first thesis).

[33] These three theses are obviously Cartesian, but the vocabulary is scarcely present in the *Principles*, except in IV. 198, which is the only article in which Descartes uses 'substantial forms'.

[34] *Principles of Philosophy* III. 46; the vocabulary of essentiality and entity, however, is not Cartesian but is Spinula's. In his *Novissima philosophia* (p. 572), Spinula rejects the usual definition of substance ('ens per se existens independenter a subject', 'entity in itself, existing independently of the subject'). In this case, he says, we are dealing with an inadequate definition, since there are, on the one hand, material substantial forms which depend on a subject, and, on the other hand, the union of the soul and the body, which is called a 'modus substantialis', a 'substantial mode'. Thus he proposes to define substance as an 'ens per se', an 'entity in itself', and an accident as an 'entis ens', an 'entity of an entity'.

and has no compositeness other than the inequality arising from its parts.[35] [*in the margin of these first two points:*'in the book <>[36]]

Third, that material substance formally consists in the actual extension of a thing with respect to place, nor can one be found without the other. [*in the margin:* pg. 36, n. 8, 9][37]

Fourth, that the earth moves with a circular motion[38] and is one of the planets;[39] and that the sun is fixed and immobile.[40] [*in the margin:* pg. 42, n. 21, 22][41]

Fifth, that the universe of corporeal substances has no limits and is delimited by no place[42] [*in the margin:* pg. 28 in fine[43] *and* pg. 72, n. 29[44]]; and that all possible worlds in fact exist.[45]

---

[35] *Principles of Philosophy* III. 47 f. 'Composition', however, doesn't pertain to the *Principles*. Spinula had written in his *Novissima philosophia*, p. 186 (difficulties raised by 'certain ingenious recents'): 'Can there be a simple body, that is some corporeal substance which has no substantial parts but is the very most simple substance? I am an adherent of the affirmative view, since there is no convincing reason to the contrary. Moreover, when we take account the omnipotence of God, all things which don't involve confusions (*implicantia*) should be attributed to God. However you should know this one thing, that such a body must be produced immediately by God: since, indeed, it cannot be produced, then it must be created.'

[36] There is a sign and a word here that we have not been able to decipher.

[37] These aren't Descartes's concepts, but it isn't astonishing that Spinula has formulated this proposition on the basis of *Principles* II. 9, which is grounded indeed in II. 8. However, Descartes says that one should not make a real distinction between corporeal substance and extension, and not that substance *consists* in the actual extension of the thing: extension is the principal attribute of corporeal substance. More relevant would be a reference to art. 10, which reprises I. 53.

[38] *Principles of Philosophy* III. 26 in particular. But see from earlier *ibid.* I. 71, where Descartes accounts for many prejudices. It is this last reference which appears to us to be given in the margin of proposition 5: 'pg. 28 in fine'.

[39] *Principles of Philosophy* III. 27 in particular.

[40] *Ibid.* III. 13. Spinula, in his *Novissima philosophia* (p. 376) stands against certain ancient astronomers and against Copernicus, who affirm the mobility of the Earth ('it is clearly holy as a matter of faith that the Earth is immobile and that the heavens and stars move':); he adds: 'and most recently there exists a decree about this matter from the Holy Congregation against Copernicus and his followers, determining the immobility of the Earth and the motion of the stars'. He brings forward diverse proofs for geocentrism and in concluding, and refers to Libert Froidment (Libertus Fromondus), 'who above all others has written elegantly and with subtlety on this matter [in his *Meteorologica*]'.

[41] It appears that this reference, placed in the margin at the level of the fourth censured proposition, corresponds in fact to the first part of the fifth; see below.

[42] *Principles of Philosophy* II. 21. This passage was already cited by the Faculty of Theology of Louvain (see below, document 10, thesis 1, point 3). See also *Principles* III. 29.

[43] On our view, this reference should reverse places with the previous one.

[44] *Principles of Philosophy* III. 29.

[45] Spinula must be deducing this from *Principles of Philosophy* II. 21 and III. 29. However, it is nonetheless inconsistent with II.22, where Descartes insists that 'there cannot be a plurality of worlds'. Thus, perhaps, the 'in fact', which signals the deduction.

In the other book, *On the Passions of the Soul*,[46] are found the following:

First, that all passions of the soul, love, hate, hope, hatred, etc., like most new cognitions [*cognitiones*],[47] are not affections produced by the soul, which are vital acts [*actus vitales*],[48] etc., but rather are only various motions[49] of the spirits towards this or that part of the body, through which motions the informed soul [*formata anima*][50] perceives those affections that we experience. [*in the margin*: pg. from art. 126 and following][51]

Second, that usually the origin of these affections or motions of the spirits lies as much in external objects as in the soul. [*in the margin*: pg. 28, art. 51][52] And hence that the struggle that exists between the flesh and the spirit consists in the fact that contrary motions of the spirits are excited both by the soul and by external objects. [*in the margin*: pg. 24, art. 47][53]

---

[46] The page citations refer directly to the facsimile of the Latin first edition (1650), *Passiones animae*, ed. J.-R. Armogathe and G. Belgioioso (Lecce: Conte, 1997).

[47] Art. 17 could justify the usage of 'cognitiones', and art. 20 furnishes examples of new cogitations whether forged by the imagination or purely intellectual, which depend principally on the will. But in this case, these thoughts are formed by the soul ('per animam formantur', title of art. 20). This is why it seems to us that with these 'new cognitions', Spinula has rather in view the novelty constitutive of admiration and the primordial role of the latter; cf. art. 58.

[48] Recall here the commonly received scholastic position (the vegetative and sensitive soul), whence the use of 'vital acts', something not at all Cartesian, and the 'etc.'.

[49] 'Various motions' is found literally in art. 97. But Spinula evokes here the very definition of the passions, which occur 'through some motion of the spirits', art. 27, then 37, 51, etc.

[50] To the best of our knowledge, this expression is not Cartesian. One finds it again below, prop. 4.

[51] Here we are dealing with art. 126 and following. The 'that which we experience', which recalls, perhaps, the 'experimenta' of the title of art. 97, makes us begin this collection of articles with art. 97. Art. 126 is thus one example among others, the most developed, of the passionate effects of the motion of the spirits. However that may be, this first point constitutes rather a summary of the *Passions* taken together, which define the passions as mental states derived from corporeal motions. One could also refer here to *Principles of Philosophy* IV. 198.

[52] Résumé of art. 51.

[53] Exact résumé of art. 47. Spinula clearly sees that the conflict that Plato and his successors hold to be internal to the soul reduces to a conflict between the two 'sources' of the passions, the soul and external objects. Thus the corporeal motions of the animal spirits. The qualificator appears to approve what Descartes denounces as an 'error', the struggle between the lower and higher part of the soul (the sensitive and rational souls, *caro* and *spiritus* in the biblical vocabulary; see below), but not its Cartesian explanation. Bringing together arts. 51 and 47 to make this point makes evident sense.

Third, that no corporeal motion of bodily members arises from the soul [*in the margin*: pg. 10, art. 16];[54] indeed, it is erroneous to believe that the soul gives motion and heat to the body [*in the margin*: pg. 3, art. 5].[55]

Fourth, that the informed souls of men [i.e. souls placed in men as forms] considered in themselves are not formed equally noble and strong. [*in margin*: pg. 77, art. 161][56]

Fifth, that the soul can easily acquire an absolute power over all its passions. [*in margin*: pg. 27, art. 50][57]

These are the things that in the aforementioned book seem to me worth considering, for conclusions contrary to the Catholic faith can easily be deduced from their doctrines.[58]

And so I always declare myself to be in accordance with your prudent judgement.

Revd. Stephanus Spinula, Congregation of Somascha.

B. 28 September 1663, Letter of Joannes Augustinus a Nativitate Tartaglia to the Cardinal Sforza Pallavicini (= ACDF, document f)

Illmo. et Revmo. Sre.

---

[54] Title of art 16: 'How every member can be moved . . . without the work of the soul.' See also art. 5: 'men have persuaded themselves wrongly . . . that all motions of our bodies depend on the soul.' But Spinula is wrong to move from 'every member ' and 'all motions' to 'no motion'. Even though Descartes denounces as an error the belief that *all* motions of the body depend on the soul, he certainly does not say that *no* motion depends on it. This misinterpretation is obviously important, and has very high stakes.

[55] This proposition *a fortiori* literally recalls the title of art. 5 ('That it is an error to believe that the soul gives motion and heat to the body'). Once again, the qualificator brings forward that which Descartes denounces as an error.

[56] An almost literal citation of art. 161. In Descartes' text, the censured proposition constitutes a concession ('even though . . . it is easy to believe, even if . . . it might be credible'): to take it in an absolute way as Spinula does approaches misinterpretation—see art. 50, from which the thesis censured follows.

[57] An almost literal citation of the last phrase of the first part. Descartes says it even of the weakest souls, from which, perhaps, the 'easily'. It seems that the qualificator's reasoning here presupposes the 'etsi', the 'even if' in art. 161 (p. 71, l. 4), misunderstood in the censure of the previous proposition in order to construct an opposition between propositions 4 and 5: the souls of men are not equally noble and strong; *however*, a soul, however weak, can easily etc.

[58] Note that Spinula does not say that Descartes has himself reached conclusions that are contrary to the Catholic faith, but only that such conclusions can be derived from the censured propositions.

Mando qui allegata a Vs. Illma. la censura dei due libri domini Renati del Cartes quali mi furono consegnati per vederli, e darne il mio parere. Dei trattati che fà delle Meteore e delle materie Matematiche, non ne fo mentione perche sono fuori della censura Teologica. Ho avvertito nell autore ingegno sottile, e inventivo di nuove speculazioni, come anco l'eleganza dello stile non ordinaria, la modestia con la quale soggetta quanto scrive alla censura dei Teologi e riverisco in tutto i meriti di questo scrittore. Però con ogni riverenza per obedire a chi mi ha comandato, e con ogni ingenuità, dichiaro il mio sentimento intorno alla di lui dottrina, e qui baciandogli humil.^te le sacre vestie gli auguro dal cielo ogni felicità. Dal nostro convento della Scala, li 28 7bre 1663.

di VS. Illme, et Revme.

Devotissimo servo,

Tartaglia, fr. Gio. Agostino d.^a Natività carmelitano scalzo

Most Illustrious and Reverent Lord,

I hereby send the attached to Your Illustriousness, the censure of the two books of Mr René Descartes which were given to me to examine and to give my views on. I have not made mention of the two tracts on meteors and on mathematical material, since these stand outside of theological censure. I have observed in this author a subtle intelligence, as inventive in new speculations as he is also out of the ordinary in the elegance of his style, and in the modesty with respect to all the subjects about which he writes under control of the theological censors,[59] I admire as a whole the merits of this writer. However, with all reverence to obey he who had ordered me, and with all candor, I declare my views concerning his doctrine, and here, kissing with humility your sacred robe, I wish you all happiness from heaven. For our convent of La Scala, 28 September 1663.

Of Your Illustrious and Reverend Lordship the most devoted servant,

Tartaglia, Brother Giovanni Agostino della Natività, Discalced Carmelite

C. The Censure of Joannes Augustinus a Nativitate Tartaglia (= ACDF, document h)

In libris D. Renati Des Cartes, quorum alter inscribitur *Meditationes de prima philosophia*, alter *Specimina Philosophiae, seu Dissertatio de Methodo recte regendae rationis, et veritatis in scientiis investigandae.*

---

[59] No doubt a reference to the Letter to the Faculty of Theology of the University of Paris that precedes the *Meditations*.

Ingenii acumen, et eloquii nitorem summopere laudo; propositiones tamen, quas docendo interserit, non omnes approbo; quaedam enim catholicae fidei, et sacrae doctrinae principiis non satis consonant.

Meditatione 4a pag 28 ait *Neque enim opus est in me in utramque partem ferri posse ut sim liber, sed contra quo magis in unam propendeo, sive quia rationem veri, et boni in ea evidenter intelligo, sive quia Deus intima cogitationis meae ita disponit, tanto liberius illam eligo; nec sane divina gratia, nec naturalis cognitio unquam imminuunt libertatem, sed potius augent, et corroborant; Indifferentia autem illa quam experior, cum nulla me ratio in unam partem magis quam in alteram impellit, est infimus gradus libertatis, et nullam in ea perfectionem, sed tantummodo in cognitione defectum, sive negationem quandam testatur; nam si semper quid verum et bonum sit clare viderem numquam de eo, quod esset judicandum, vel eligendum deliberarem; atque ita quamvis plane liber, numquam tamen indifferens esse possem.*

Ubi videtur tollere a nostra voluntate libertatem a necessitate, et solum ponere libertatem a coactione, quod fuse explicat p. 160, resp. 6, n. 6, ubi voluntatem Dei asserit fuisse *indifferentem ab aeterno ad omnia quae facta sunt; voluntatem tamen humanam nunquam esse indifferentem, nisi quando, quidnam sit melius, aut verius ignorat* et concludit *denique indifferentia non pertinet ad essentiam humanae libertatis,* quo loco etiam philosophice errat.

De accidentis quae insunt substantiae non loquitur coherenter ad sacrum Eucharistiae mysterium, in quo manerent species substantiae panis, id est accidentia definiuit Synodus Tridentina. Ipse enim pluries negat accidentia realia; et praesertim pag. 161 et 162, resp. 6, n. 7 ubi ait: *omnino repugnat dari accidentia realia, quia quicquid est reale, potest separatim ab omni alio subjecto existere, quicquid autem ita separatim potest existere, est substantia, non accidens.* Et paucis interiectis *nihil enim aliud est fieri naturaliter, quam fieri per potentiam Dei ordinariam, quae nullo modo differt ab ejus potentia extraordinaria; nec aliud quicquam ponit in rebus: adeo ut si omne id, quod naturaliter sine subjecto esse potest, sit substantia, quicquid etiam per quantumvis extraordinariam Dei potentiam potest esse sine subjecto, substantia est dicendum.*

Ubi etiam alium errorem astruit, quod potentia Dei extraordinaria non ponit quidquam aliud in rebus, quod non ponat potentia Dei ordinaria, cum certum sit poni entia supernaturalia, siue quoad modum, siue quoad entitatem, et plura miracula fieri per potentiam Dei extraordinariam, quae sunt entia realia, et per potentiam ordinariam non ponuntur.

Eodem n° 7 admittit in corpore superficiem, quam dicit remanere post consecrationem, quod fusius explicat pag. 136.137.138.139; et sentit superficies esse substantiam conflatam ex corpusculis aeris, et uaporum, qui latent intra poros corporis, licet satis obscure rem explicet, et in illa fieri contactum, et sensationem, nec aliud percipi sensibus nisi superficiem; quod tamen in Philosophia vacillat. Tota autem doctrina authoris eo loco parum coheret cum definitione Concilii Tridentini, sess. 13, can. 2 et 4.

Meditatione 3a, pag. 15 usque ad 25: comminiscitur quandam ideam nobis insitam, ueluti characterem a Deo impressum, quae idea repraesentet ens infinitum, ex qua idea cognoscitur evidenter Deum existere; negat tamen demonstrari Deum a posteriori per effectus creaturarum etc., quae doctrina continet plures errores in Philosophia, et repugnat Scripturis clamantibus quod *invisibilia Dei per ea quae facta sunt intellecta conspiciuntur; sempiterna quoque eius virtus et diuinitas.* Hanc ideam uiri indocti, et rudes non experiunt; docti, et philosophi non utuntur; nec potest dignosci An sit idea ipsius Dei nisi praecognito quid sit, et An sit Deus, ut egregie opponitur in objectionibus pag. 47 usque ad 52 et aliis sequentibus. Quas refert ipse author, sed minime sufficienter dissoluit.

Meditatione 4a pag. 25 usque ad 30. *de vero, et falso* tradit plura principiis Philosophiae et Theologiae repugnantia. Inter alia docet non posse intelligi euidenter uerum, nisi cognoscatur euidenter Deum esse, qui sit maxima ueritas, et non possit nostram mentem decipere; ex quo sequitur in Atheo nullam demonstrationem existere, nullam mathematicam, seu Philosophicam scientiam, quae est cognitio euidens rei per eam, ante assensum fidei, quo creditur Deum existere, non esse iudicium euidens de credibilitate objecti; Atheos non esse culpabiles, si peccant, cum non habeant iudicium practicum euidens de malitia objecti, nec Deum prouidisse hominum saluti, cum non inseruerit notitias euidentes, siue speculatiuas, sive practicas, quibus ipsum inquirere per uestigia creaturarum, et culpam euitare, atque ad ipsius cognitionem nos disponere possemus.

De fide etiam diuina pag. 78 in resp. ad 2as Objectiones, ait: *Etsi fides dicatur esse de obscuris, non tamen illud, propter quod ipsam amplectimur est obscurum, sed omni naturali luce illustrius,* ex paucis interjectis subdit *Iam uero, etsi fides uulgo dicatur esse de obscuris, hoc tamen intelligitur tantum de re, sive de materia circa quam versatur, non autem quod ratio formalis, propter quam rebus fidei assentimur sit obscura;* quod deinde prosequitur, satis obscure fidei euidentiam explicans; asserit tamen lumen gratiae interius mouentis ad fidem esse euidens; quod definitione fidei, quod sit *argumentum non apparentium*, parum coheret; et communi doctrinae Theologorum quod fides sit libera, non euidenti necessitate coacta saltem de facto in iis communiter, qui credunt.

Prima propositio fundamentalis, quam statuit, quod haec sola cognitio sit indubitata, et euidens, scilicet ego sum qui cogito, et ab ipsa velut a fonte, a qua omnis euidentia deriuetur, est implexa innumeris difficultatibus, quas Autor sibi opponit in objectionibus. Sed dum extricare se contendit, magis implicat. Non enim satis explicat quid sit illud ego qui cogito, An seiunctus a corpore, vel corpori immixtus; quomodo sit euidens; si cogito, quod existo; cum unum ab alio inferatur, et supponat aliam notitiam euidentem, uel quod causa efficiens debeat cohexistere suo effectui, uel quod actus non possit existere sine subjecto suo, id est cogitatio sine cogitante; et alia absurda consequuntur etiam periculosa in fide VS. Quod omnis fidei certitudo innitatur huic primo principio: ego sum cogitans, et sic non sit firmior assensus fidei, quam hic assensus naturalis, de quo plura dubitari possunt.

In Meditatione 5a et 6a plura occurrunt nec inuicem coherentia, nec subsistentia ut de essentiis rerum materialium quod sint ab aeterno, quod *omnis veritas et certitudo scientiae ab una veri Dei cognitione dependeat, adeo ut priusquam illum nossem, nihil de ulla alia re perfecte scire potuerim*; de distinctione reali mentis a corpore, quam ratione satis infirma probat, quomodo naturae iudicium aliquando erret, ubi in Deum authorem erroris deceptionem reuocare uidetur.

In Libro qui inscribitur *Dissertatio de methodo*, plura repetit ex iis, quae in *Meditationes* asseruerat, et consequenter exposita iisdem difficultatibus.

Prosequitur per plura capita de essentia luminis, et pag. 68 et 69 explicat modum quo res corporeae videntur negans omnes species visibiles, et comparat uidentem coeco ex motu scipionis, a quo regitur dignoscentis corpora, quae in uia occurrunt, quod a Philosophia omnino alienum est.

Ex eis infero utrumque librum continere doctrinam parum tutam; ingeniosam quidem ac nouam; sed sacrae doctrinae non satis consonantem; Philosophia repugnantem, et ad finem ad quem dirigitur, scilicet notitiam ueritatis, prorsus inutilem.

Ego Frater Joannes Augustinus a Natiuitate Carmelita Discalceatus, sic censeo, saluo semper meliori judicio.

In the books of René Descartes, one of which is entitled *Meditations on First Philosophy*,[60] the other *Specimen of Philosophy, or Discourse on the Method of rightly conducting Reason and of investigating Truth in the Sciences*.[61]

I applaud the acumen of his mind and the great brilliance of his eloquence. Nonetheless, I do not approve of all the propositions that he sets out to teach;[62] for some of them are not sufficiently compatible with the Catholic faith and the principles of sacred doctrine.

Meditation 4 p. 28 says: 'In order to be free, there is no need for me to be inclined both ways; on the contrary, the more I incline in one direction—either because I clearly understand that reasons of truth and goodness point that way, or because of a divinely produced disposition of my inmost thoughts—the freer is my choice. Neither divine grace nor natural knowledge ever diminishes freedom; on the contrary, they increase and strengthen it. But the indifference I feel when there is no reason pushing me in one direction rather than another is the lowest grade of freedom; it is evidence not of any perfection of freedom, but rather of a defect in knowledge or a kind of negation. For if I always saw clearly what was true and good, I should never have to deliberate about the right judgement or choice; in that case, although I should be wholly free, it would be impossible for me ever to be in a state of indifference.'[63]

Whence it appears that any freedom from necessity is removed from our will, and is replaced simply by a freedom from constraint,[64] which

---

[60] As we have already noted, we are dealing with the edition of 1650 of the *Meditations* (qualified as the 'tertia editio'), in three parts: the second part contains Objections 5 and 7, and the third part the *Epistola ad Voetium*. Tartaglia only cites the first part, in which the fourth and sixth Objections follow upon one another. That it was this edition that was used has a certain importance, as will be seen below.

[61] This is the title of all the Latin editions of the *Discourse* from 1650 on.

[62] Tartaglia thus doesn't disapprove of the fundamental theses of Descartes as much as he does of certain auxiliary propositions, though important, to which he returns.

[63] AT vii. 57–8; the translation is from CSM ii. 40. Since this translation gives the pagination of AT, it will not be cited separately. In what follows, the translations of Descartes' writings will be taken from this translation. The choice of this quotation, which explains the second definition of freedom, immediately reveals the interest of the censor in the Cartesian rejection of the freedom of indifference. One remarks from this first quotation that the style of Tartaglia's censure is very different from that of Spinula. While Spinula summarizes the Cartesian theses in short propositions, Tartaglia cites them rather at length, and then concludes by making explicit the Cartesian error. He uses the Replies several times to clarify the *Meditations* and to assure himself of the correctness of his judgment.

[64] 'a nulla vi externa' (AT vii. 57, and again on 58, 'ab aliqua vi externa . . . coactus'). The absence of a feeling of an external determination suffices for the definition of free will. The

he explains at length in section six of the Sixth Replies, p. 160, where he asserts that the will of God has been 'indifferent from eternity with respect to everything that has been done';[65] 'nevertheless the human will is never indifferent, except when one does not know which of two alternatives is better or more true',[66] and he concludes that 'therefore indifference is not a part of the essence of human freedom',[67] whereby he errs philosophically.[68]

What he says about accidents[69] that inhere in substance is not compatible with the sacred mystery of the Eucharist, in which the outward appearances [*species*] of the substance of the bread remain, that is, the accidents defined by the Council of Trent.[70] For he denies, many times, that there are real accidents,[71] and especially in section seven of the Sixth Replies, pp. 161 and 162, where he says that 'it is completely contradictory that there should be real accidents, since whatever is real can exist separately from

censor correctly interprets Cartesian freedom as compatible with an internal necessity—that of the light of the understanding or of divine grace. Descartes doesn't speak of *necessitas* but of *propensio* (AT vii. 59). Does Tartagilia find in *Meditations* IV the Jansenist heresy? (Remember the third proposition condemned by the Bull *Cum occasione:* 'To merit, or demerit, in the state of fallen nature we must be free from all external constraint, but not from interior necessity.' For Jansenius, in fact, the virtuous act is free in the sense that it is exempt from all constraint, but not in the sense that it would be exempt from all necessity.) It is, indeed, possible: as we have said, Tartaglia is the author of a *Compendium de Gratia contra sententiam Jansenii.* He would not be the only one to see Jansenism here: Montchamp, p. 98 n. remarks that Cardinal Francesco Albizzi, whose anti-Cartesianism was at the origin of this affair, as we have seen, was the person who drafted the Bull *In eminenti Ecclesiae,* condemning Jansenius' *Augustinus* twenty years later. It remains to be noted that Tartaglia's censure presents itself as being purely philosophical.

[65] AT vii. 431–2.

[66] AT vii. 432–3. The page contained between these two previous citations is where Descartes presents, in the *Meditations,* the doctrine of the creation of the eternal truths, relating it in the terms of the letters to Mersenne of April and May 1630. The censor thus read this page, strictly framed by these very quotations, with great care. It is particularly interesting that he said nothing about them, and that he finds nothing to respond to with respect to the Cartesian thesis of divine indifference, literally cited.

[67] AT vii. 433. Once again Tartaglia finds nothing to complain about in the important thesis expressed between the previous two quotations, in which Descartes explicitly refuses the doctrine of the univocity of Being, in contrast to most of his contemporaries.

[68] Note that, for Tartaglia, Descartes is making a philosophical, and not a theological, mistake in refusing to grant to human beings freedom of indifference.

[69] Passing on to the Cartesian doctrine of the Eucharist, Tartaglia continues to read the Sixth Replies.

[70] The Council of Trent doesn't use the concept of an accident: see Pierre Cally, *Durand commenté . . .* (Caen, 1700), 75, and Jean-Robert Armogathe, *Theologia cartesiana. L'explication physique de l'Eucharistie ches Descartes et dom Desgabets* (The Hague, Nijhoff, 1977), 32, and Descartes himself, Fourth Replies, AT vii. 252.   [71] See AT vii. 434.

any other subject; yet anything that can exist separately in this way is a substance, not an accident.'[72] And a little further on he adds, 'for to occur 'naturally' is nothing other than to occur through the ordinary power of God, which in no way differs from his extraordinary power—the effect on the real world is exactly the same. Hence if everything which can naturally exist without a subject is a substance, anything that can exist without a substance even through the power of God, however extraordinary, should also be termed a substance.'[73] Whereby he adds yet another error, namely, that the extraordinary power of God cannot introduce into things anything that is not already there through God's ordinary power. For it is certain that there are supernatural things—modes as well as entities—and many miracles, which are all real things, that come about through God's extraordinary power, and not his ordinary power.[74]

Also in the same seventh section [of the Sixth Replies], he allows that there is a surface in a body that, he says, remains after consecration,[75] which is more fully explained on pgs. 136, 137, 138, 139.[76] And he believes that the surface is a substance produced from the corpuscles

---

[72] Ibid. [73] AT vii. 435.

[74] This disagreement is subsidiary to the question of real accidents. Descartes considers the concept contradictory, since what is real, being able to exist separately from every other subject, is a substance (though the definition of that which can exist without a subject), and not an accident. But one can object that real accidents cannot be separated from their subject naturally through the ordinary power of God, that is, in the common scheme of natural created beings, and that to understand the real distinction between real accidents and their substance, one must appeal to the extraordinary power of God, who alone can make real accidents exist separately, that is, really. Now, Descartes shows that the recourse to the extraordinary power of God doesn't at all modify the definition of substance, and thus that with or without extraordinary power, a real accident remains thinkable only as a substance. Put otherwise, the extraordinary power of God creates nothing new (*nihil novi*: see document 10) in things which will change their ontological status; whatever can exist without a subject is a substance, whether that be done naturally, that is, through the ordinary power of God, or by his extraordinary power, that is, supernaturally. Tartaglia is not interested here in the whole of this reasoning, but he critiques the thesis in accordance with which the extraordinary power of God places nothing in things which is not placed there by natural power.

[75] Descartes doesn't say this literally in the Sixth Replies; the remaining '*in* a body' falls within the ambiguity that Descartes wants to avoid in not talking precisely about the surface which is a part of the body (*pars corporis*), but only of that which is a mode, the terminus of a body (*extremum corporis*), that is, the external place (*Principles* II. 15) or the surface intermediate between a body and its surroundings (AT vii. 251), or, in accordance with the scholastics, the surface of the surrounding body (AT vii. 433). Tartaglia then returns to the Fourth Replies—the absence of the Sixth Objections and Replies in the edition used make these passages that much closer: AT vii. 255 says it literally.

[76] AT vii. 248–56.

of air and vapors that are found between the pores of a body[77]—as he so obscurely explains the matter—and that this is where contact and sensation occur; nor is anything perceived by the senses except the surface,[78] which nonetheless is an unsound view in philosophy.[79] Moreover, all of these doctrines of the author on this matter are hardly compatible with the Council of Trent's definition, as found in the proceedings of Session 13, can. 2 and 4.[80]

In the Third Meditation,[81] pp. 15 to 25 he contrives a certain idea innate in us,[82] like a character stamped by God,[83] which represents an infinite being,[84] and from which the existence of God is evidently known.[85] Nevertheless, he denies that the existence of God can be demonstrated *a posteriori*, through creaturely effects,[86] etc., which doctrine contains additional philosophical errors[87] and is inconsistent with Scripture's claim that 'God's invisible attributes, that is, His everlasting power and divinity, have been revealed to the eye of reason through those things that *He* has made'.[88] Unlearned and uncultivated men do not grasp this idea; learned

---

[77] AT vii. 249–50.   [78] AT vii, 249, 251, 434.

[79] Again, the Eucharistic critique is, in the first instance, a philosophical one, that is, physical. It is focused only on the denial of real accidents. Thus the doctrine that sensation is only produced by contact, that is to say, by the surface alone (Fourth Replies) is that which permits Descartes to show that real accidents have become a useless hypothesis (Sixth Replies). The incompatability with the Council of Trent that Tartaglia sees here on this strict point is secondary. The criticism of the censor is not theological.

[80] DS (Denzinger–Schönmetzer) 1652 and 1654. The reference comes from Descartes himself, AT vii, 251. Tartaglia is unaware of many elements of Descartes' Eucharistic doctrine, and seems to be unaware of the censure that the Jesuit Honoré Fabri, then Theologian of the Holy Penitentiary, had written on these matters in 1660 (BM Chartres, MS 366, pp. 26–8; texts in G. Sortais, *Le cartésianisme chez les Jésuits français* . . . (Paris, 1929), 51, n. 2). Our documents undermine the information given in Adrien Baillet (*Vie* (Paris, 1691), ii. 529), which attributes to Honoré Fabri the origin of the condemnation of 1663.

[81] After this crucial double objection, Tartaglia follows in order the Third and Fourth Meditations, then more briefly the Fifth and Sixth, throughout continuing to make use of the Objections. Tartaglia doesn't refer explicitly to matters taken up in the Second Meditation. It is remarkable that nothing concerns the First Meditation.

[82] e.g. AT vii, 45, 51. Tartaglia now enters into the proof for the existence of God from the idea of the infinite.   [83] AT vii. 51.

[84] AT vii. 45.

[85] AT vii. 45. It is Tartaglia who adds the word 'evidently' here.   [86] AT vii. 48.

[87] Note the same insistence on Descartes' errors *in philosophia*, before noting his incompatibility with revelation.

[88] *Romans* I. 20. This passage of Scripture, however, was already cited in the Dedicatory Letter to the Sorbonne (AT vii. 2), but the edition the censor used (Elzevier, 1650) doesn't include this letter (nor the 'Cum [privilegio et] approbatione doctorum'—might this have influenced the qualificators?). The letter from Tartaglia to Cardinal Pallavicini which introduces the censors, given above, however, allows us to suppose that Tartaglia knew the letter.

and philosophical men do not use it.[89] Nor can it be determined whether the idea is of God himself unless it is first known what God is, and whether he exists,[90] a point well put in the Objections, pp. 47–52.[91] The author himself addresses this point, but with only minimal adequacy.

In the Fourth Meditation, 'On Truth and Falsity', pp. 25–30, he deals with many things incompatible with the principles of philosophy and theology.[92] Among other things, he teaches that what is true cannot be clearly understood unless it is clearly known that God exists,[93] which is the highest truth, and that He cannot deceive our minds.[94] From which it follows[95] that for an atheist there can be no demonstration, no mathematical or philosophical knowledge (*scientia*)[96] (which is the evident cognition (*cognitio*) of a thing through itself); that before any assent of faith, through which one believes that God exists,[97] there is no evident judgement concerning the worthiness of something to be believed.[98] [It also follows then that] atheists are thus not guilty if they sin, since they lack an evident practical judgement concerning the evil of an object,[99] and that God has not provided for human welfare, since [on Descartes's view] He could not have employed evident notions—either speculative or practical—through which we can seek Him through the marks [He placed in] creatures, avoid guilt, and dispose ourselves toward knowledge of him.[100]

On divine faith, in the Second Replies, p. 78 he says 'although it is said that our faith concerns matters which are obscure, the reasons for embracing the faith are not obscure but on the contrary are clearer than any natural light',[101] and a little further on he adds, 'although it is commonly said that faith concerns matters which are obscure, this refers solely to the thing or subject matter to which our faith relates; it does not imply that the formal reason which leads us to assent to matters of faith is obscure',[102] which explains the evidence of faith

---

[89] It is not, for that, held to be false.

[90] First Replies, AT vii. 107–8. Tartaglia is here Thomist (*Summa Theologiae, an sit* (q. 2) before *quid sit* (q. 3)) against a Descartes who is Scotist (see, e.g. *Ord.* I, d. 3 & sect. 17).

[91] First Objections, AT vii. 96 ff.

[92] Philosophy and theology are put on the same level here.

[93] Second Replies, AT vii. 140.   [94] AT vii. 53, 62, 69, etc.

[95] All that follows about divine faith in this paragraph comes from the Second Objections and Replies.   [96] Second Replies, AT vii. 141, 125.

[97] The relation between knowledge (*scientia*) and the assent of faith here is not Cartesian.

[98] The vocabulary here is not Cartesian.   [99] See Second Objections, AT vii. 126–7.

[100] He seems to have deduced all of this from point 5.

[101] AT vii. 147.   [102] AT vii. 148.

rather obscurely. He nevertheless claims that the light of interior moving grace is evident to faith. This is hardly compatible with the definition of faith, which is 'a mark that is not evident',[103] and with the common doctrine of theologians that faith is free[104] and not constrained by the necessity of that which is evident,[105] at least among those who do in fact believe.

The first fundamental proposition that he establishes is that there is only one indubitable and evident cognition, namely, 'I, who think, am'. It is like a fountain from which all things evident derive. It is, however, plagued by innumerable difficulties, which are presented to him in the Objections. But the more he struggles to extricate himself, the more he is entangled. For he does not sufficiently explain what is that 'I' that thinks, nor whether it is joined to a body or mingled with a body; nor how it is evident that if I think, I therefore exist—since one is inferred from the other and supposes some other evident notion, either that an efficient cause must coexist with its effect,[106] or that an act cannot take place except in its subject (that is, there cannot be a thought without a thinker).[107] There are other absurd consequences of this doctrine, even some that threaten the faith (see above); for example, that the certainty of faith rests upon this first principle: I am thinking, and thus that there is no firmer assent involved in faith than this natural assent, about which many doubts can be raised.

In the Fifth and Sixth Meditations, there are many things that either fail to cohere with one another or are insupportable, such as the claim about the essences of material things that exist eternally;[108] the view that 'the certainty and truth of all knowledge depends uniquely on my knowledge of the one true God, to such an extent that I was incapable of perfect knowledge about anything else until I knew him';[109] what he

---

[103] *Hebrews* 11.1.

[104] For the theologians, see, for example, St Thomas, ST IIa–IIae q2 resp and ad 2; and the Council of Trent, Decree on Justification, Denzinger–Schönmetzer 1525, can. 5. Descartes doesn't deny that faith is free, indeed he says the contrary. We find here the difficulties posed by the Cartesian definition of freedom.

[105] As is the case with the faith of demons: see St Thomas, *ST* IIa–IIae q5 a. 2 ad 1 et 2.

[106] First Replies, AT vii. 108.

[107] Tartaglia seeks to characterize the kind of certainty found in the inference of the existence of the self from the act of thinking. This reasoning is an inference which presupposes something else as evident: either that the efficient cause can coexist with its effect, or that the act of thinking cannot exist without a subject which thinks, and thus that a subject exists. In brief, Tartaglia has, doubtless, suspected that the existence of the *ego* gives rise to a syllogism, as have others. (Second Replies, AT vii. 140–1.)   [108] AT vii. 64.

[109] AT vii. 71.

says concerning the real distinction between mind and body, which he proves by rather weak reasons;[110] and what he says about how natural judgement sometimes errs,[111] whereby he appears to attribute deception to God and make him the author of error.[112]

In the book that is entitled *Discourse on Method*, he repeats many of the claims that he makes in the *Meditations*, and consequently faces the same difficulties.

He pursues, through many chapters, the question of the essence of light,[113] and on pp. 68 and 69 explains how corporeal things are seen, while denying that there are any visible species,[114] and he compares this to a blind man seeing by means of the motion of his staff, through which he detects differences between bodies that come in his way,[115] something completely foreign to philosophy.

From these things, I conclude that the book does not contain much safe doctrine. It is indeed ingenious and novel, but it is not sufficiently compatible with holy doctrine. It is repugnant to philosophy and useless for the end it serves, that is, the knowledge of truth. Therefore, I, Brother Johannes Augustinus of the Nativity, Discalced Carmelite, give my opinion, as always under the provision of a more authorized judgement.

5. GENERAL COMMENTS ON THE CONDEMNATION OF 1663

The dossier discovered in the archives at Rome is important for two reasons: on the one hand, for the information that it provides us on the chain of events leading up to Descartes's works being placed on the Index, and on the other hand for the content of the censures produced by the two qualificators.

The documents cohere perfectly with what we know from Plempius's summary and from the work of Georges Monchamp in the archives at Louvain. It was the discomfort of Cardinal Albizzi, who was well informed by Chrétien Lupus (de Wulf), that eventually attracted the attention of the internuncio, ever on the alert since Geulincx's departure from Louvain. Pope Alexander VII Chigi was, at the same time, both hostile to Jansenism and opposed to moral laxism.

---

[110] AT vii. 77–8.   [111] AT vii. 76.   [112] AT vii. 77.
[113] In the *Dioptrics*, Discourses I and II.   [114] *Dioptrics*, Discourse I, AT vi. 586.
[115] Discourse I, AT vi. 585–6.

He surrounded himself with rigorous theologians, such as the Cistercian and future Cardinal Bona, the Jesuit Cardinal Sforza Pallavicini, his future biographer, and curialists such as Michelangelo Ricci and Agostino Favoriti; at the end of his pontificate, he would condemn two series of laxist propositions. The chronological progression, bracketed by the meetings of the faculties at Louvain and the nuncio's letters, demonstrates the extreme agitation of some parties, but also the tactical positions taken. Girolamo de Vecchi, the provisional abbé of Monreale, in Sicily, was internuncio from 1 March 1656, to 4 April 1665. He had to confront formidable Jansenist quarrels,[116] and had every reason in the world to manage as quickly as possible the doctrinal problems raised by the innovators in the arts and medical faculties at Louvain. Above all, we can see how the Faculty of Arts dragged its feet. It insisted on its faithfulness, but was slow in its decisions and spent the summer discussing the matter in committees and deputations without issuing the preventative measures demanded by the nuncio. The faculty was content, in the end, to denounce 'the inordinate zeal for the Cartesian doctrine', as it wrote to the nuncio, but this did not commit it to very much. The Faculty of Theology chose to intervene much later, and we have seen that the nuncio was anxious for the University to take the steps that the faculties themselves were so slow to put in place. The censures that were finally issued, by both the Faculty of Arts and the Faculty of Theology, contain many fine sentiments and the professors' assurances that they supported the real condemnations of Descartes's doctrines. As Monchamp has remarked, the decree by the Faculty of Arts, for which the nuncio waited so long, did not really meet the demands that he had made. The decree has two parts (document 8.2), one that condemns rationalist and anti-Christian works, and another that takes note of how widely disseminated Descartes's works are. If the faculty regards anti-Christian rationalism with great pain, it expresses no particular sentiment on the dissemination question, and does not rule out the promotion of Cartesians (something that the nuncio had demanded), but only those who would sustain philosophical opinions that are inconsistent with the faith. Thus, far from seeing in the Faculty of Arts' decree (as Victor Cousin does[117]) a condemnation of Cartesianism, an attentive reader will find therein a deaf and stubborn resistance to the nuncio's

---

[116] See Monchamp, 339–41 et L. Ceyssens i, xix–xx.

[117] *Fragments philosophiques pour servir à l'histoire de la philosophie, Oeuvres* (Brussels, 1841), ii. 182.

injunctions (as well as to the campaign led by Plempius). For the most part, the faculty simply duplicates the decree (which alone has the force of law) from a letter to the nuncio that is very severe towards the Cartesians, all the while skillfully recognizing that it cannot prevent 'a disordered zeal for the doctrines of Descartes' in the teaching of 'subjects at the University that are not a part of this faculty [i.e. medical subjects]'. The contrast between the tone of the letter and the essence of the decree did not escape the notice of the nuncio, who sent the dossier to Rome. The University, on September 19, sought to avoid any personal censure of particular professors and confined itself to generalities. While the nuncio may have received encouragement and compliments from Rome (documents 6 and 13), his letters to the professors at Louvain evince a certain irritation; he was forced to backpedal before the Faculty of Arts and tone down his criticisms in his letter of 7 July 1662 (document 4).

The procedure at Rome, which the Congregation of the Holy Office opened on 15 October (document 14), began with the nomination of qualificators from outside the Congregation, experts who would be given the task of censuring the works in question. Several months later, these experts—Tartaglia and Spinula—presented their conclusions. These two censures are the work of knowledgeable theologians who read the texts without any presuppositions; Tartaglia did not try to hide how interesting he found the *Meditations* to read:

I have observed in this author a subtle intelligence, as inventive in new speculations as he is also out of the ordinary in the elegance of his style, and in the modesty with respect to all the subjects about which he writes to the theological censors. I admire as a whole the merits of this writer.

Their two censure texts reveal no familiarity with any previous censures—either those by the theologians consulted by Plempius and published in his *Fundamenta medicinae*, or that by Thomas Compton Carleton in his *Philosophia universa*, or even that of Honoré Fabri, among others that are unknown to us. As in other philosophical censures,[118] we see the two Roman experts reading texts and giving their advice, without caring about what other authorities may think (such as

[118] Thomas Compton Carleton, *Philosophia universa* (Anvers, 1649), 246. See Marta Fattori, ' "Vafer Baconus": la storia della censura del *De augmentis scientiarum*', *Nouvelles de la République des Lettres* 2 (2000), 97–130.

the philosophers and theologians at Louvain (document 100)). Far from reproducing already formulated censures,[119] they read the four works that were confided to them with a fresh eye.

Spinula, the philosopher, concentrated on the second and third parts of the *Principles*. He evidently took note of article 36 in Part Two, a crucial element, and saw how articles 45–47 of Part Three constituted a treatise on method in Cartesian cosmology, which he regarded as novel. In particular, the importance of article 47 did not escape his keen notice. He saw perfectly well how Descartes sought to explain the actual state of the world without employing prime matter, substantial forms, or real accidents, and based simply on the arrangement of unequal parts of one and the same divisible matter of terrestrial bodies.[120] While his reading of the second part of the *Principles* focuses directly on the Cartesian thesis of the indefiniteness of the world, he is not afraid to draw a conclusion about the existence of other possible worlds, in explicit opposition to Descartes's intentions. In his censure of the *Passions of the Soul*, he is troubled essentially by the author's mechanicism. Here, too, he concentrates on a passage that is, in effect, decisive: the joint between the first and second parts, and he twice picks up what Descartes has denounced as errors and turns them back upon him. If his reading is not totally free of misinterpretation, it is nonetheless extremely interesting. In the last proposition, the physicist in him gives way to the theologian as he censures the possibility raised by Descartes that one can completely master the passions.

Tartaglia concentrates above all on the *Meditations*, including the Objections and Replies, which he read attentively. He isolates two crucial doctrines whose problematic nature he carefully delineates: first, the Cartesian rejection of freedom of indifference (in Meditation Four and the Sixth Replies); and second, the denial of real accidents and its consequences for the physical doctrine of the Eucharist (Meditation Six and the Fourth Replies). After these two touchstones, both theologically very sensitive but about which he declares himself to be making principally a philosophical judgement, Tartaglia follows the order of the

---

[119] On the other censures, see Trevor McClaughlin, 'Censorship and Defenders of the Cartesian Faith in Mid-Seventeenth Century France', *Journal of the History of Ideas* 40 (1979), 563–81.

[120] See Vincent Carraud,' "La matière assume successivement toutes les formes": Note sur le concept d'ordre et sur une proposition thomiste de la cosmogonie cartésienne', *Revue de métaphysique et de morale* 1 (2000), 57–79.

Meditations from the Third Meditation onward, while continuing to address in turn certain arguments from the First and Second Objections. The qualificator clearly approves of the objections raised by Caterus and Mersenne. As for the Second Meditation, it does not receive any independent treatment. And it is remarkable that he has nothing whatsoever to say about the First Meditation. It is in this third part of the censure that the qualificator shows his originality, and most of his criticisms have a guiding thread: the proper Cartesian notion of the evident (Second, Fifth and Sixth Meditations) approached in a fourfold way: (*a*) the evidence of the existence of God (Third Meditation); (*b*) the subordination of the evidence of truth to the evidence of the existence of God (Fourth Meditation); (*c*) divine faith (Second Replies); and (*d*) the problematic status of the Cogito as evident (Second Meditation).

In both cases, one cannot help but be struck by the essentially *philosophical* character of the censures. It is no mean virtue to be able to read the works of one's greatest contemporary thinker, to have to do it, by profession, without what Descartes calls 'prejudices', and to do it with complete integrity.

École pratique des hautes études (Sciences religieuses, Sorbonne)
(Jean-Robert Armogathe)
Université de Caen (Vincent Carraud)

[translated by Steven Nadler and Daniel Garber]

DOCUMENTS

The dossier of the condemnation that we have found in the historical archives of the Roman Congregation for the Doctrine of the Faith (ACDF)[121] is titled:

'Censura in duos libros[122] D. Renati des Cartes

Primus inscribitur: *Meditationes de prima philosophia*

2ndus inscribitur: *Specimina Philosophiae, seu Dissertatio de Methodo recte regendeae rationis, et veritatis in scientiis inuestigandae*

---

[121] Res doctrinales, Censura librorum 1663 ('French cote' L 7102) #9.
[122] The 1650 edition of the *Opera philosophica*.

Decretum S. Connis sub die 10 Octobris 1663. Statuens quod prohibeantur libri, donec corriguntur, ad quem effectum mittetur decretum ad S. Cong.m Indicis.'

This dossier contains, in order:

(*a*) The letter from Girolamo de Vecchi to Cardinal Pallavicini of
       9 September, 1662 (1 fo., r, autograph signature).

(*b*) The letter from de Vecchi to Cardinal Pallavicini of 29 July, 1662
       (1 fo., r/v, autograph signature).

(*c*) A copy of the letter from the nuncio to the University of Louvain
       of 28 June, 1662 (1 fo., r/v).

(*d*) A copy of the decree of the Faculty of Arts at Louvain of 29 August,
       1662 (1 fo., r/v).

(*e*) A copy of the letter of Jacobus Pontanus to the nuncio of 31 August,
       1662 (1 fo., r).

(*f*) The letter of Tartaglia of 28 September, 1663, accompanying the
       censure (1 fo., r).

(*g*) The censure of Spinula (1 fo., r/v).

(*h*) The censure of Tartaglia (2 fo., 4 pp.).

We have tried to reconstitute here, from these sources, all the events
that led to the censure of 1663. We have numbered the items in order,
indicating at the end the classification provided by Monchamp (Roman
numerals) or by the ACDF (letters). The first document, from the deliberations of the Faculty of Arts, allows us to construct the chronology of
the subsequent items.

Document 1 (= Monchamp V, pp. 615–17), 1662, deliberations of the Faculty of Arts of Louvain (*Liber decimus quartus Actorum Venerandae Facultatis Artium, studi generalis oppidi lovaniensis ab anno 1661*, fos. 64 et sv.)

Indicta est deputatio 3ª Julii 1662
1°an placeat audiri litteras Illustrissimi Domini Internuncii directas
ad Facultatem Artium, contra doctrinam Cartesii,[123] et quid iis
respondendum?

---

[123] See document 2 (letter of 28 June 1662).

Conclusum est ad I^{um} committi DD. Deputatis, cum assumendis maxime professoribus ut concipiant responsum mittendum ad Illustrissimum Dominum Internuncium.[124]

Die 4ª Julii 1662, indicta deputatio in majori numero in horam octavam, sub juramento, in qua proposita sunt sequentia:
1°quid placeat fieri quoad litteras Internuncii?
Ad Ium concipiendus est libellus a Domino Dictatore ad Internuncium et aliquos esse mittendos ad ipsum qui . . . cum ipso . . . agent et rogarunt DD. Randaxhe et Vincent ut dignentur illud onus suscipere.

Die 5ª Julii 1662, indicta est deputatio in medium nono, in qua fuit lectus conceptus formatus a Domino Dictatore et remissus ad Facultatem.

Eadem die [*5 July*], indicta est congregatio Facultatis in h. 9, sub juramento, et fuerunt proposita sequentia:
DD. Deputatos censuisse aliquos deputatos mittendos esse Bruxellas, ratione litterarum Internuncii.
Conclusum est ad Ium placere resolutionem DD. Deputatorum, mittendos esse DD. Randaxhe et Vincent cum litteris Facultatis ad Illustrissimum Internuncium quarum hic tenor fuit:
[*see below, document 3*]

Die 10a Julii indicta est congregatio Facultatis sub juramento in horam octavam et fuerunt proposita sequentia:

quid placeat fieri sub litteris Illustrissimi Domini Internuncii relatis per DD. Deputatos, quarum tenor est hic:
[*see below, document 4*]

Ad secundum, committi DD. Regentibus[125] et senioribus professoribus.

Die 14 Augusti, indicta est deputatio in majore numero sub juramento, in horam octavam, in qua nunciatum est a DD. Decanis Illustrissimum Dominum Internuncium venisse ad hanc civitatem, pridieque fuisse salutatum ex parte Universitatis, an placeat etiam ut salutetur ex parte Facultatis, item quid placeat ipsi responderi quoad illud decretum quod petit fieri in postremis suis litteris, casu quo aliquem de Facultate desuper interroget.

---

[124] See document 3.
[125] The Regents were the presidents of pedagogies, the colleges of the university.

Resolutum est, cum ipse salutatus fuerit ex parte Universitatis, non esse necesse ipsum denuo salutari. Verum si veniat die . . . ad Scholam Artium prout DD. Porcensibus ipsum ad Artium Facultatem invitantibus, se venturum promisit, eum esse per D. Dictatorem in Vico statim absoluto actu salutandum, ipsique gratias agendas pro honore exhibito.[126] Quoad decretum ab ipso petitum, conclusum est esse formandam aliquam ordinationem ex parte Facultatis, qua obligetur quilibet professor ad (?) quandocunque in explicatione aliqua materia occurret in qua erit occasio agendi de aliqua ex propositionibus periculosis aut male sonantibus, illudque referendum esse ad Facultatem.

Eadem die [*16 August*], indicta est congregatio Facultatis in medium nonae, sub juramento . . . in qua proposita sunt sequentia:

DD. Deputatos in majore numero nuper resolvisse esse formandum ordinationem etc. prout supra, quoad decretum petitum ab Illustrissimo Domino Internuncio.

Conclusum est ad Ium committi Deputatis ut forment aliquem conceptum illius ordinationis et ille formatus referatur ad Facultatem.

Die 28 Augusti, indicta est deputatio[127] in majore numero convocatis DD. Professoribus ad concipiendam ordinationem petitam ab Illustrissimo D. Internuncio, quam formatam judicarunt esse praelegendam Facultati.

Eadem die [*28 August*], indicta est congregatio Facultatis, sub juramento, in medium duodecimo, in qua lectus est conceptus DD. Deputatorum quoad ordinationem petitam ab Illustrissimo Domino Internuncio et petitum quid placeat circa illam fieri.

Resolutum est illam ordinationem placere, eamque publicandam in scholis per Dominos Professores, copiamque illius mittendam esse ad Illustrissimum Dominum Internuncium, adjecta epistola.

[*see below documents 8. 1 and 8. 2*]

---

[126] It must be understood that the nuncio had arrived on the 13th in Louvain, and was greeted by the University. He was invited to attend on Aug. 15 a public activity of a student of the Pedagogy of Porc. The Faculty of Arts avoided their responsibility to greet him, arguing that in so far as he was greeted by the University, he had been greeted by all of the Faculties together. The secretary of the Faculty (the *dictator*) contented himself with greeting him at the end of the activity, beneath the portico (*in Vico*), and to thank him for the honor which he had brought to the Faculty. As for the decree which the nuncio demanded, it was drafted in very general terms, not mentioning Descartes explicitly.

[127] The letter of the nuncio to the Rector of Aug. 27 (document 7) probably motivated this extraordinary meeting and the vote on the decree.

Document 2 (= ACDF c), 28 June 1662, letter from the nuncio de Vecchi to the Faculty of Arts of Louvain

Doctissimi Viri

Gravi dolore intelleximus facultate Vra. etiamnum serpere profanas uoces atque errores Renati Carthesii et Christianae Juventuti tradi Philosophiam noxiam, quae maiori postmodum labore debebit dedisci. Louaniensis Academiae antiqua laus est quod nouitates non recipiat, quam laudem absit ut Vestrum aliqui euacuent, aliqui euacuari patiantur. Philosophia Vra. debet esse germane Christiana, recta semita, clauis et lumen ad veram Theologiam, id est, legitimum intellectum ac expositionem sacrarum litterarum atque sanctorum Ecclesiae Patrum, quos omnes a Democrito et Epicuro, adeoque et ab eorum resuscitatore[128] Renato Carthesio certum et clarum est penitus abhorrere; certum et clarum est ab eiusdem dogmatibus abhorrere capitales quosdam Fidei Catholicae articulos. Unde et apud S. Sedem male olet ille, nollemque Vos ibidem eiusdem faetoris esse participes aut suspectos. An Maiores Vestri ignoravere veram Philosophiam quousque nouus hic dogmatistes per cenosos Epicuri ac Democriti cineres quibusdam Vestrum aperiret oculos! Quo haec tendant uidetis, et quandoque audistis a Facultate Theologica, cui oportebat plene obeditum; quocirca serio hortamur ut periculosissimis hisce nouitatibus ex integro abdicatis, tradatur denuo uetusta Philosophia quae Academia V.ra tot praestantissimos in omni facultate Doctores peperit, deduxitque ad hodiernum splendorem et dignitatem. Etiam publicas Conclusiones quae quasi sub exercitii fuco coeperunt, non sine iactura Nominis V.ri spargere hanc scabiem, fieri optamus forma antiqua, quae quidem sicut ex obligatione muneris nostri duximus Vobis significanda, ita confidimus Vos non solum sanis hisce consiliis obtemperaturos, sed etiam decreto aliquo praecauturos ut imposterum a promotionibus arceantur qui eiusmodi dogmata sectari comperientur.

Datum Bruxellis 28. Junii. 1662

Vestrum studiosissimus

Hier. Ab. Mtis Regalis

---

[128] It appears that the nuncio echos the accusation made by Plempius against Descartes, with a play on words, ' Renatus Democritus', *Fundamenta medicinae*, 3rd edn. (Louvain, 1654), 376 (the parallel between Democritus and Descartes is found in the appendix: *Doctorum aliquot virorum iudicia de Philosophia Cartesiana*, in a letter from Plempius dated 21 Dec. 1652).

Document 3 (= Monchamp I, pp. 611–12), 5 July 1662, letter from the Faculty of Arts of Louvain to the nuncio de Vecchi

Illustrissime et reverendissime Domine

Triste fuit et durum audire doctrinam nostram traduci tanquam christianae juventuti noxiam,[129] eo magis quod uti majores nostri, ita et nos toti solliciti simus ut *sicut oculi ancillae in manibus dominae suae*,[130] ita oculus philosophiae nostrae ad doctrinam sacram, velut dominam attente respiciat, et jugiter illam suscipiat; quin imo jam per quadriennium integrum, junctis professorum omnium viribus et animis desudatum est, ut ea quae sacrae et superiori scientiae non subservirent, velut lolium et tribulos fatigantes extirparemus iisque (quod multorum et primariorum pridem votum fuit) substitueremus exactam librorum De Anima pertractationem, quibus juventus in sui ipsius et ingenitae nobilitatis notitia amplius proficeret et propinquius principiis christian-is admoveretur: proinde conatibus his et scopo nobis praefixo e diametro adversum foret, si periculosa et male olentia Chartesii, vel cujuscumque alterius dogmata, etiam sub exercitii fuco, juvenum animis instillarentur, quibus et omnibus optamus impressum, quam quoslibet fidei catholicae articulos, quam sanctos ecclesiae patres veneremur, et cujuscumque graveolentiae apud Sanctam Sedem, cui toti devoti sumus, etiam suspicionem detestemur. Quae omnia ut compertiora sint simulque sinistris informationibus plenius satisfiat, censuimus deputan-dos e corpore nostro qui has perferrent. Hos ut patienter audire Illustrissima Dominatio Vestra dignetur, nobisque et suum et apostolicum affectuum conservare, enixe rogamus, et id sperantes manemus,

Illustrissimae Vestrae Gratiae,
observantissimi famuli,
Decanus et Facultas Artium,
Studii generalis oppidi lovaniensis.

Lovanii, 5 julii 1662

---

[129] The drafters take up the same terms as the beginning of the letter of the nuncio (document 2).

[130] Citation of Psalm 122, 2. The image of the servant (*philosophia*) and her mistress (*theologia*) serves as a reminder of the expression 'philosophia, ancilla theologiae' (Roland de Crémone, *Summa* l. I, prol., q. 2, a. 2).

[*address:*]
Illustrissimo ac reverendissimo domino,
Domino Hieronymo Vecchiis Montis regalis abbati
apud Belgas pronuntio apostolico,
Bruxellis

Document 4 (= Monchamp II, pp. 612–13), 7 July 1662, letter from the nuncio de Vecchi to the Faculty of Arts of Louvain

Doctissimi viri,

Dum super dogmatibus Carthesii periculosis litteras[131] ad Facultatem philosophicam scripsimus, non vestram Artium Facultatem notare intendimus, vel ullum ejus membrum, tanquam sinistrae alicujus doctrinae suspectum, sed quia audimus nonnullos Lovanii majori quam par est erga Carthesium zelo philosophari, qui, quamvis extra Facultatem vestram constituti,[132] possent tamen juventuti christianae, seu catholicae ejus eruditioni officere, hinc nostras ad vos dirigendas censuimus, quibus propinquius dictae juventutis et christianae philosophiae germana integritas incumbit, tum ut messem vestram ab inimicis zizaniis pergeretis immunem servare, tum ut prurientem aliorum scabiem sanare, iisque philosophiae vestrae sinceritatem communicare satageretis: proinde mens nostra fuit Facultatis vestrae manum velut medicam huic malo adhibere, et ne inficiatur grex vester, plane confidimus vos constanter advigilaturos, imo uti scripsimus,[133] decreto aliquo et Facultatis vestrae authoritate praecauturos, ut a pro-motionibus arceantur, qui contra sanam et catholicam professorum vestrorum eruditionem praefati Cartesii noxia dogmata sectari comperientur. Vobis demum salutaria quaeque animitus apprecamur.

Vestrum studiosissimus,
Hieronymus, abbas Montis Regalis.
Bruxellis, 7ª Julii 1662

[*address:*]
Doctissimis viris Facultatis Artium almae Universitatis lovaniensis,
Lovanii

---

[131] Document 2.
[132] De Vecchi is addressing the Faculty of Medicine, and adopts a medical vocabulary (*scabies, sanare, medica* . . .).   [133] In document 2.

Document 5 (= ACDF b), 29 July 1662, letter from the nuncio de Vecchi to Cardinal Pallavicini

Da qualche anno in qua s'era cominciata a' insinuar nelle scuole di Louanio la Filosofia di Renato Cartesio, abbracciando molti le di lui opinioni, e gia si uedeuano stampate in varie Tesi che dalli studenti andauano publicam.^te difendendosi. Onde considerando io quanto repugnasse una simile Dottrina a più fondamenti della fede et alli principii della Teologia, alla quale è specialm.^te ordinato la Studio della filosofia in quest'Università, ne scrissi al Collegio de' Filosofi l'acclusa lett.^a da quali essendomi star' inviati due deputati, dopo hauer discussa la materia restorno meco d'accordo di pigliar in rimedio del Decreto da me suggeritoli in essa Lettera con risolut.^ne di formarlo quando tra'poco dovranno esaminarsi i Promouendi.

Il primo che forse cominciasse in Louanio a fomentar queste nouità fu un tale Gulinx professore iui assai stimato in Filosofia, il quale con queste sue libertà d'opinioni ha poco fà benche Diacono apostato miserab.^te dalla fede ricouerandosi nell'Università di Leida, doue ha ottenuto una Catedra. Io feci officii per ridurlo, promettendoli il perdono e di trovarli qualche conditione in Italia, ma per essersi maritato anco colla propria nepote, è stato il tutto in uano. Questo caso ancora mi ha stimolato a risolvermi di scriuere al Collegio sudetto per l'estirpatione di tal nascente zizania, sperando di vederla in breue sotto casa. Ho stimato moi debito il dar del tutto conto all'E.V. alla quale profondissim.^te vesto inchinandomi.

Brusselles, 29. luglio 1662

Document 6 (= Ceyssens, pp. 96–7), 19 August 1662, Rome, from Flavio Chigi, Cardinal-nephew, to Jérôme de Vecchi, nuncio at Bruxelles

Le diligenze che Vostra Signoria significa d'haver usate per impedire che in Lovanio non s'insegni la perniciosa filosofia del Cartesio, rimostrano il zelo e l'attentione con che Ella invigila esattamente al buon servitio della santa Sede. Nostro Signore se n'è compiaciuto grademente e le ne ha date benigne lodi.

Si persuade la Santità Sua che, secondo gli avvertimenti prudenti di V.S., i capi dell'Università faranno le parti loro in proibire si scandalosi insegnamenti. Tuttavia sarà bene che Ella proseguisca a invigilarvi con inviare avviso quà se altro di nuovo occorrerà.

Document 7 (= Monchamp VI, pp. 617–18), 27 August 1662, letter from the nuncio de Vecchi to the Rector of the University of Louvain

Magnifice Domine,

Hortatus nuper fui Vener. Facultatem Artium, ut conaretur epicureis dogmatibus cartesianae philosophiae obsistere, et antiquam aristotelicam doctrinam tueri. Et ipsi quidem hortationem nostram plane libenter amplexi ita se facturos promiserunt. Licet autem monitum hoc pro omnibus generaliter, ac praesertim pro medicis, sufficere putaverim; en tamen prodeunt theses cum impertinentibus,[134] 29° Augusti, mane propugnandae in schola medica (earumque exemplar penes me est), in quibus non agnoscuntur in corporibus, nisi 'motus, quies, situs, figura et magnitudo'. Quod videtur sacrosanctum altaris mysterium subverti. 'Argumenta quae brutis animam asserunt, non esse probabilia. Dubium esse an bruta vivant. Nihil sub coelo esse novi, seposita anima rationali:[135]–videlicet prout intelligi puto ab Authore—nullas animas, nullas qualitates de novo produci, quia nullae sint. Omitto *laudes*, quae Cartesio attribuuntur. Cum itaque gliscenti huic malo remedium opponi oporteat, sedulo commendo Dominationi Vestrae, ut statim adhibito Theologorum aliorumque prudentium virorum[136] consilio discutiat memoratas theses; et si quae propositiones cartesianis erroribus obnoxiae in iis reperiantur, vel Theses ipsas proscribere velit in totum, vel mandare ut saltem propositiones quae Cartesii novitatem continent seu sapiunt, expungantur, aut alio modo suaviori, prout prudentiae vestrae magis expedire videbitur, (provideas). Quocirca rem totam judicio vestro plane committo, absque alio responso, cum tempus disputationum proximum longiorem moram non recipiat. Praestabit in hoc Dominatio Vestra et alma Universitas rem Sanctissimo

---

[134] The *Impertinentia* were propositions unrelated to the principal subject of the dispute (hence their name), whose often paradoxical character brought out the originality and vivacity of the candidate.

[135] See document 10: Monchamp (p. 365) is thus right to see a lapse into ' nullas animas' instead of 'nullas formas'.

[136] The addition of *viri prudentes* to the theologians brings Plempius to mind.

Domino Nostro pergratam, quem de vestra vigilantia operaque edocebo.[137]

Documents 8.1 and 8.2 (Monchamp III and IV, a copy of IV in ACDF, item d)

Document 8.1: 28 August 1662, letter from the Faculty of Arts to the nuncio de Vecchi

Illustrissime ac reverendissime Domine,

Quandoquidem Illustrissima Vestra Gratia manum Facultatis nostrae veluti medicam contra periculosa quaedam Carthesii dogmata requisiverit, pro ea quam semper de sana doctrina habuimus sollicitudine, duximus nullatenus differendum esse quin tam justo viri tanti desiderio prompte satisfaceremus. Ecce hic, Vir Illustrissime, decretum Facultatis nostrae, quo omnibus et singulis e coetu nostro ac praesertim philosophiae professoribus injungimus, ut juventutem nobis subditam serio praemoneant, et efficacibus argumentis contra talium dogmatum fundamenta praemuniant, optantes ex animo ut etiam suppositis extra Facultatem nostram constitutis eadem qua nostris authoritate inordinatum erga Carthesii doctrinam zelum prohibere possemus. Deum optimum maximum rogaturi ut Illustrissimam ac Reverendissimam Dominationem Vestram diu inter romanae cathedrae assertores reipublicae christianae praelucere concedat.

Illustrissimae ac Reverendissimae Dominationis Vestrae,
Humillimi famuli, decanus et Facultas Artium,
Studii generalis oppidi lovaniensis.

Document 8.2 (= Monchamp IV, pp. 614–15; we follow the copy in ACDF document d), 28 August 1662, decree of the Faculty of Arts

Veneranda Artium Facultas Studii Generalis Oppidi Lovaniensis mature considerans quantum boni publici intersit ut juventutis christianae philosophia sacrae doctrinae debite conformetur et nullatenus ei adversetur, necnon dolenter videns iam ex diversis partibus illorum authorum in publicum prodire libros qui ita proprii ingenii ductum et corruptae

---

[137] The letter of the Cardinal-nephew of 19 Aug. (document 6) shows well the interest that Pope Alexander VII took in this matter.

naturae lumen extollunt ut illud lumini catholicae fidei anteponant et ex eius instinctu dogmata cudant nova, Christianae Philosophiae adversa. Hinc est quod praefata Artium Facultas pro integritate fidei catholicae et alumnorum suorum syncera eruditione sollicita serio hortari atque mandare duxerit prout per praesentes hortatur et mandat omnibus et singulis e numero suo, et praesertim philosophiae professoribus ut, ne incauta juventus eiusmodi noxia dogmata legendo forte vel audiendo imbibat, eandem juventutem ex occasione sedulo et frequenter, ubi visum fuerit praemoneant, et fortibus rationibus in eam rem allatis praemuneant, uti ab illis documentis quam diligentissime caveat. Porro cum Renati Carthesii scripta multorum nunc manibus terantur; noverit quoque praedicta juventus, quod etsi author ille in multa quae naturae experimenta concernunt non infoeliciter videatur incidisse, nihilominus quaedam in illis reperiantur sanae et avitae dictae facultatis Artium doctrinae non satis consona. Proinde mandamus omnibus et singulis Philosophiae Professoribus nostris, ut juventutem super illis proprius et specialius instruant, ubi et quando opportunum videbitur, et data occas^{ne} discipulis suis inculcent nullos a Facultate Artium Lovaniensi ad promotionem in Artibus admitti nisi praevio juramento, quo iurent se in qualibet controversia philosophica illam sententiam quae stat pro fide catholica amplexuros. In quorum fidem haec sigillo nostro et secretarii nostri signatura communiri volvimus

Datum Lovanii, die 29. Augusti 1662
De mandato Dominorum meorum
Signatum: P. Lenoir, Secret. cum sigillo eiusdem facultatis in panerubro

Document 9 (ACDF, document e), 31 August 1662, Vice-Rector Jacques Pontanus[138] to the nuncio Jérôme de Vecchi

Ill^{me} Domine,

Litterae Vestrae datae 27. mensis currentis in absentia Magnifici D. Rectoris ab Oppido, mihi tanquam ViceRectori traditae sunt die 29. eiusdem mensis circa meridiem, et postquam in scholis medicorum

---

[138] It is the Vice-Rector who responds, since they are between two Rectorats (which last for six months), that of André Laurent (end of February to end of August) and that of Nicolas Meys (elected 31 Aug. 1662 to the end of February 1663): see Monchamp, p. 355. See the notice on Pontanus in the *Biographie nationale de Belgique*, vi. 317

defensae essent theses istae quas Illma D. V. petebat supprimi vel
expurgari ab erroribus Carthesianis antequam defenderentur. Litteras
Ill^{mae} D.V. communicavi quamprimum Deputatis Universitatis, quibus
theses istae vehementer displicuerunt, et contra eiusmodi dogmata
Carthesiana serio agendum censuerunt. Ex eorundem assensu requisivi
Facultatem Theologicam ut dictas theses mature examinet, et quae
perniciosa nec toleranda censuerit, ea Magnifico D. Rectori exhibeat, ut
ipse authoritate sua et mediis opportunis eadem et alia eiusdem farinae
ex scholis academicis eliminet et proscribat. Inquam rem Theologos
nostros aliosqui plures diligenter allaboraturos confido. Quid autem hac
in parte praestitum fuerit, intimabitur postea Ill^{mae} D. V.rae. Interea
Deum precabimur ut eandem Ill^{mam} D.V. diutissime servet incolumen.
Lovanio, die ultima Augusti 1662

Document 10 (= Monchamp VII, a better text is in Ceyssens, pp. 98–101 following F.U.L., vol. 388, f°s 380–382[139]), 7 September 1662, deliberation of the Faculty of Theology of Louvain

Convocata fuit facultas ad domum decani,[140] ut ferret judicium super
quibusdam thesibus[141] et *Impertinentibus* in scholis medicorum 29 die
Augusti proxime praeteriti propugnatis; quod facere rogabatur a
M. D. Rectore per speciales litteras Ill^{mi} D. Internuntii desuper interpel-
lato.[142] Post rem serio examinatam et plures sessiones desuper habitas,
dederunt Eximii Domini suum judicium atque illud per manus decani
M. D. Rectori transmiserunt, cuius hic est tenor:
Thesis: Numquid qui de medicina aut philosophia nunc usque (unicum
si excipias Renatum de Cartes) scripserunt, grues dici merito possunt,
cum gruum instar se mutuo sint insequuti ? *Disput.* 7, *Impert.* 1.
Censura: temeraria percunctatio, qua toti antiquitati insultatur, profanae
novitati applauditur, et Cartesius, non paucis alioqui erroribus sanitati

---

[139] See also *Quaedam recentiorum philosophorum ac praesertim Cartesii propositiones damnatae ac prohibitae* (Paris, 1705), 14–15 and Roger Ariew, 'Quelques condamnations du cartésianisme: 1662–1706', introductory essay in *Bulletin Cartésien* XXII, *Archives de philosophie* 57 (1994), 1.

[140] André Laurent (see Nicholas of Vernutz (Vernulaeus), updated by Christian van Langend-onck, *Academia lovaniensis*, 1667 edition, p. 16 and Valerius Andreas, *Fasti academici . . .* (Louvain, 1650), 145).

[141] At issue here are the theses of the physician Guillaume Philippi (see Monchamp, pp. 351–70).   [142] See above, document 7.

fidei christianae dissonis obnoxius, immerito extollitur; quorum errorum specimen subinseritur:

1° per substantiam nihil aliud intelligere possumus, quam rem quae ita existit ut nulla alia re indigeat ad existendum. Et quidem substantia, quae nulla plane re indigeat, unica tantum potest intelligi nempe Deus. Alias vero omnes nonnisi ope concursus Dei existere posse percipimus . . . Possunt autem substantia corporea et mens, sive substantia cogitans creata, sub hoc communi conceptu intelligi, quod sint res quae solo Dei concursu egent ad existendum. Parte I *Princip. Philos.*, nos 51 et 52.

Ex quo consequens est quod praeter animam rationalem non detur ulla forma substantialis nequidem in brutis et plantis, quod etiam variis locis innuit.[143]

2° Omnino repugnat dari accidentia realia, quia quidquid est reale potest separatim ab omni alio subjecto existere, quidquid autem ita separatim potest existere est substantia non accidens. Nec refert quod dicatur, accidentia realiter non naturaliter sed tantum per divinam potentiam a subjectis suis sejungi posse; nihil enim aliud est fieri naturaliter, quam fieri per potentiam Dei ordinariam, quae nullo modo differt ab eius potentia extraordinaria, nec aliud quidquam ponit in rebus; adeo ut si omne id quod naturaliter sine subjecto esse potest sit substantia, quidquid etiam per quantumvis extraordinariam Dei potentiam potest esse extra subjectum,[144] substantia est dicendum. *Respons. ad object.* 6, post *Meditationes*, n°7.[145]

Ex quo consequens est non remanere accidentia panis et vini sine subjecto in eucharistia.

3° Extensio corporis est attributum ejus essentiam naturamque constituens. In *Meditationibus, seu notis*, pag. 172.[146]

4° Cognoscimus praeterea hunc mundum, sive substantiae corporeae universitatem, nullos extentionis suae fines habere. In *Princip. Philos.*, parte II, n°21.[147]

---

[143] See, for example, section 3 of the Sixth Replies. This censure concides in part with that of Spinula on the *Principles*, point 2. For an explanation of this 'consequens', presented in a non-Cartesian vocabulary, see Monchamp, p. 358.

[144] Descartes: *sine subjecto*.

[145] Sixth Replies, AT vii. 434–5. This censure coincides with that of Tartaglia, for the same reasons.

[146] Sixth Replies, n. 10, AT vii. 442. The text given by the *Quaedam recentiorum philosophorum* adds: 'et parte 1. Princip. Philosoph. Num. 53', which is in fact a faithful summary of AT viii. 1.25.

[147] AT viii. 1.52. This point coincides with the censure of Spinula, point 5 on the *Principles*.

5° Hinc etiam colligi facile potest [. . .]. Atque omnino si mundi essent infiniti, non posse non illos omnes ex una et eadem materia constare, nec proinde plures sed unum tantum esse posse, etc. Ibid., n°22.[148]

Thesis: per certam motus, quietis, situs, figurae, magnitudinis, partium modificationem, medicamentorum omnium virtutes, corporis pariter actiones optime et clare et distincte explicantur. Numquid igitur merito qualitates eorumdem ut frustraneas expungimus et tamquam poetica (ut vere sunt) commenta explodimus? *Disput.* 1, *impert.* 1.

Censura: positio haec continet doctrinam temerariam, exoticam et in fide perniciosam; censuram autem intolerabilem.[149]

Thesis: certior ac evidentior est animae seu mentis nostrae existentia quam corporis. *Disput.* 11, *impert.* 1.

Censura: male dicitur, quod existentia animae sit certior quam existentia corporis, cum haec tam sit certa de fide quam illa.

Thesis: argumenta in brutis animam asserentia (sepositis sacris) non convincunt, imo nec probabilia sunt. *Disput.* 12, *impert.* 1.

Censura: falsa, insulsa, praesumptuosa, ac toti reverendae antiquitati injuriosa positio.

Thesis: anima nostra non dicitur esse in pede, aut si mavis, in capite, imo nec in ulla corporis parte. *Disput.* 13, *impert.* 3.

Censura: positio erronea et veritati catholicae fidei inimica, conciliis Viennensi ac novissimo Lateranensi adversa, quibus definitur, quod anima rationalis seu intellectiva sit forma corporis humani vere, per se et essentialiter; et oppositum deinceps asserentes, defendentes seu pertinaciter tenere praesumentes tamquam haeretici censendi decernuntur.

Thesis: sanius vivunt (si proprie vivant) animalia bruta quam homines. *Disput.* 15, *impert.* 2.

Censura: in dubium revocare, an animalia bruta proprie vivant, scripturis sacris est dissentaneum.

Thesis: nihil, seposita anima rationali, sub coelo novi. *Disput.* 16, *impert.* 2.

---

[148] AT viii. 1. 52. Spinula, point 5 on the *Principles*, draws a completely different conclusion from this article, where Louvain seems to see a limitation on the power of God (Monchamp, p. 360).

[149] This very vigorous, indeed emphatic, condemnation is essential for understanding the origin of the affair. The denial of sensitive qualities (*qualités sensibles*) aroused the attacks of Plempius, and explains the nuncio's efforts against the 'new teaching'.

Censura: assertio, ob binam significationem vocis *novi*,[150] captiosa; ac praeterea sive vox illa nominaliter usurpetur, sive verbaliter, principiis fidei dissentanea.

Thesis: auctoritas in scientiis naturalibus pons asinorum vere dici potest et debet.

Censura: assertio insolenter superciliosa, docentibus contumeliosa, discentibus insuper perniciosa.

Thesis: mortalitas hominis in ipsius ignorantia consistit. *Disput*. 19, *impert*. 2.

Censura: assertio novitia, falsa, erronea, Scripturis, Conciliis et Patribus dissona.

Ipsum denique Thesium corpus tot spurcitiis atque illecebrosis foeditatibus respersum est, ut neutiquam illae potuerunt absque praesentissimo multorum scandalo publice exponi; et in confertissimo omnigenorum auditorum confluxu evulgari ac cunctis promiscue adventantibus distribui.

Document 11 (= ACDF a), 9 September 1662, letter of the nuncio de Vecchi to cardinal Pallavicini

Con mia lett.ᵃ delli 29. Luglio[151] diedi raguaglio a V. E. di quanto haueuo operato nell'Università di Lovanio per impedir i progressi che vanno facendo nelle scuole de' filosofi e medici le nuove opinioni di Renato Cartesio, e come haueuo proposto al Collegio de' Filosofi (che chiamano Facoltà dell'Arti) di uoler con Decreto speciale mettere qualche rimedio a questo male et obligar li Promouendi alli Gradi nella loro Disciplina, di professar qualla Filosofia communem.ᵗᵉ ricevuta da' Teologi. Doppo uarii congressi hà la Facoltà sudetta formato l'accluso decreto, quale ho stimato mio debito trasmettere à V. E. Anco l'Università medesima spero debba corroborar questa presente ordinat.ⁿᵉ con altro decreto che comprenda generalmente tutti dell'Accademia, come me ne rinouano l'intentione colla qui aggiunta risposta[152] resami dal Vice Rettore in occas.ⁿᵉ di certe Tesi del Dottor

---

[150] On this play on words, since '*novi*' can be taken as a substantive (in this case, the thesis, denying real accidents or new substantial forms conforms to the Cartesian doctrine of the Eucharist: see the censure of Tartaglia) or as a verb (the thesis is then skeptical, and at least provisionally Cartesian, in another sense): see Monchamp, pp. 364–5. The nuncio didn't see the play on words on *novi*; see document 7.

[151] Document 5.   [152] Document 8.1.

Dorlicx[153] Professor Primario di Medicina, quali haueuo detto che uietasse di publicare. Se altro accaderà in questa materia non lassaro di participarlo hum.te a V.E. a cui
profondim.te intanto resto inchinandomi,
Brussellis 9. Sett.bre 1662

Document 12 (= Monchamp VIII, pp. 621–2), 19 September 1662, Acts of the University of Louvain

Die martis 19° septembris, indicta est deputatio extraordinaria in majori numero in qua lectae sunt litterae Ill^mi D^ni Internuncii die 29° Augusti supra registratae,[154] super thesibus in Facultate medica defendendis, atque post modum per Facultatem Sacrae Theologiae juxta tenorem dictarum litterarum, attamen post defensionem earumdem thesium examinatis, ad quas supramentionatae Facultatis sacrae resolutio hic quoque lecta est; eaque audita, ponebat Magnificus D^nus an D^ni judicarent aliquas ex dictis propositionibus seu thesibus posse (servata pace inter omnes) defendi seu manu teneri.

Conclusum est rogandos esse D^nos Professores aliarum Facultatum qui examinent philosophiam Carthesii; et si quid inveniant sanae doctrinae contrarium, deferant ad Magnificum rectorem ut illud possit eliminari; major autem pars judicat adhaerendum esse antiquae doctrinae, ab hac et aliis catholicis universitatibus hactenus receptae, donec aliter a superioribus fuerit ordinatum; cavendum tamen ne professor ullus nominetur in edictis quae fortasse continget evulgari; monendas etiam esse singulas Facultates ut in posterum a scurrilibus impertinentibus abstineant.

Document 13 (= Ceyssens, p. 101; ASV, Nunziatura Fiandra, t. 143, f°18ᵛ), 30 September 1662, the Cardinal-nephew Flavio Chigi to Jérôme de Vecchi, nuncio at Bruxelles

Nel decreto fatto dalla facoltà filosofica di Lovanio acciò in quelle scuole non s'insegnino sentenze pernitiose, come in specie quelle del Cartesio, si riconosce il buon frutto degli zelanti uffitii di Vostra Signoria in ordine all'impedire ogni abuso che fusse sopra di ciò potuto

---

[153] Pierre Dorlicx, born in Zonhoven at the end of the sixteenth century, *licencié* in medicine in 1625, physician of the city of Diest until 1638, the year when he obtained his doctorate and became professor of anatomy and surgery at Louvain.   [154] See document 7.

introdursi, persuadendosi Sua Beatitudine che in tal materia non sia hora per sentirsi altra novità.

Document 14 (ACDF, Acta S.O.—Decreta S.O. 1662, f °185ᵛ), 15 October 1662

Feria IVa 15 octobris 1662.

Lectis litteris internuntii Belgii datis 9. septembr. Quibus mittit exemplar decreti facti ab Artium facultate Lovanii contra libros Renati Cartesii, et propositiones in eis contentas. Decretum ut mittantur per manus omnium qualificatorum libri dicti Cartesii, ut diligentius a R. P. D. Assessore et ab ipsis videantur.

Document 15 (ACDF, Acta S.O.—Decreta S.O. 1663, 1101, f °186ᵛ), 10 October 1663

Index decretorum, 1663 established by Joannes Lupus, notary of the Holy Office

Feria iiii Die X. octobris 1663

Fuit Cong Sancti Officii in Conventus S. Maria supra Minervam coram Emis. et Rmis DD. S.R.E.[155] Cardinalibus Ginetto,[156] Corrado,[157] Albitio[158] et Pallavicino[159] Generalibus Inquisitoribus, praesentibus RR.PP.DD. Assessore, et Commissario Gnal. Sancti Officii, nec non R.D. Petro Seripta,[160] Procuratore fiscali S. Officii, in qua proposita fuerunt causae infrapositae, quas in notam sumpsit idem D. Assessor et mihi Notario tradidit, uidelicet: . . .

Relatis censuris P. Tartaglia Ord. Carm. Disc. et P. Spinula, Somaschi, ad libros Renati de Cartes, quorum unus inscribitur, Meditationes de prima philosophia; alter, Specimen Philosophiae; alter, Principia Philosophiae; alter, de Passionibus animae, decreverunt quod prohibeantur donec corrigantur, et ad hunc effectum mittetur decretum ad Sacram Congregationem Indicis.

---

[155] Eminentissimis et Reverendissimis Dominis Sanctae Romanae Ecclesiae.

[156] Prefect of the Holy Office.

[157] Giacomo Corradi, created cardinal by Innocent III in 1652, died in 1666.

[158] Francesco Albizzi, born in 1593, created cardinal by Innocent III in 1654, died in 1684.

[159] Pietro Sforza Pallavicini, born 1607, created cardinal *in petto* by Alexander VII in 1657, publicly recognized as cardinal in 1659, died 1667.

[160] Pierre Seripta, Fiscal Procurator of the Holy Office.

5

Justice and Law in Hobbes

MICHAEL J. GREEN

Justice is one of the most important moral concepts for Hobbes and the most mature statement of his moral philosophy is presented in chapters 13–15 of *Leviathan*. Nonetheless, Hobbes makes three claims about justice in these chapters that are in tension with one another.

1. There is no such thing as justice or injustice in the state of nature.

   To this war of every man against every man, this also is consequent; that nothing can be unjust. The notions of right and wrong, justice and injustice have there no place. Where there is no common power, there is no law: where no law, no injustice.[1]

2. Injustice is, by definition, breaking a valid covenant.

   the definition of INJUSTICE, is no other than the *not performance of covenant.* And whatsoever is not unjust, is *just.*[2]

3. There are valid, obligatory covenants in the state of nature.

   Covenants entered into by fear, in the condition of mere nature, are obligatory.[3]

The first and second points together imply that there are no valid covenants in the state of nature. That contradicts the third point. The second and third points together imply that there is such a thing as justice and injustice in the state of nature. That contradicts the first point.

Hobbes is committed to the second and third points as they stand. He is committed to saying that injustice consists in breaking a valid covenant because he calls it a definition and he was notoriously insistent on the importance of definitions.[4] He is committed to saying that there can be valid covenants in the state of nature because his theory holds that

---

[1] *EW* iii. 115.   [2] Ibid. 130.   [3] Ibid. 126.
[4] See, for example, ibid. 121; ibid. 31; ibid. 52.

the sovereign is established by covenants made in the state of nature. If there could not be any valid covenants in the state of nature, the theory would fail. If Hobbes is committed to these positions, the first point cannot be taken at face value. How, then, should it be understood?

There are two passages that seem to make the first point; I will refer to them as the first and second problem passages. I have already presented part of the *first problem passage*; here it is in its entirety.

> To this war of every man against every man, this also is consequent; that nothing can be unjust. The notions of right and wrong, justice and injustice have there no place. Where there is no common power, there is no law: where no law, no injustice. Force, and fraud, are in war the two cardinal virtues. Justice, and injustice are none of the faculties neither of the body, nor mind. If they were, they might be in a man that were alone in the world, as well as his senses, and passions. They are qualities, that relate to men in society, not in solitude. It is consequent also to the same condition, that there be no propriety, no dominion, no mine and thine distinct; but only that to be every man's, that he can get; and for so long, as he can keep it.[5]

The striking sentence, 'Where there is no common power, there is no law: where no law, no injustice', was not included in the Latin edition published in 1668, seventeen years after the English edition.[6] However, the same claim was repeated, with greater elaboration, in the *second problem passage* and was not deleted in the Latin edition.

> But because covenants of mutual trust, where there is a fear of not performance on either part, (as hath been said in the former chapter,) are invalid; though the original of justice be the making of covenants; yet injustice actually there can be none, till the cause of such fear be taken away; which while men are in the natural condition of war, cannot be done. Therefore before the names of just, and unjust can have place, there must be some coercive power, to compel men equally to the performance of their covenants, by the terror of some punishment, greater than the benefit they expect by the breach of their covenant; and to make good that propriety, which by mutual contract men acquire, in recompense of the universal right they abandon: and such power there is none before the erection of a commonwealth. And this is also to be gathered out of the ordinary definition

---

[5] *EW* iii. 115.

[6] Thomas Hobbes, *Leviathan: With Selected Variants from the Latin Edition of 1668*, ed. Edwin Curley [hereafter *Leviathan, Latin Variants*] (1651; Indianapolis: Hackett, 1994), 74, n. 10. There is some uncertainty as to whether the Latin edition reflects Hobbes's mature thoughts of the 1660s, the formative ones of the 1640s, or a combination of the two. See Edwin Curley's introductory note, 'Purposes and Features of this Edition', ibid., pp. lxxiii–lxxiv.

of justice in the Schools: for they say, that *justice is the constant will of giving to every man his own*. And therefore where there is no *own*, that is, no propriety, there is no injustice; and where there is no coercive power erected, that is, where there is no commonwealth, there is no propriety; all men having right to all things: therefore where there is no commonwealth, there nothing is unjust. So that the nature of justice, consisteth in keeping of valid covenants: but the validity of covenants begins not but with the constitution of a civil power, sufficient to compel men to keep them: and then it is also that propriety begins.[7]

What is at issue is whether justice is possible only among those governed by laws and a common power. Hobbes's understanding of law is fairly straightforward: 'law, properly, is the word of him that by right hath command over others.'[8] By a 'common power,' Hobbes clearly means a person, institution, or deity with the authority to issue laws and the ability to ensure the safety of those who accept limits on what they can do to protect themselves. There are two kinds of power and law that Hobbes might have had in mind: on the one hand, the civil sovereign and civil law, on the other, God and the law of nature.[9]

What Hobbes means by 'justice', however, is significantly less clear as he seems to accept three different definitions. I will call Hobbes's explicit definition of justice the *Contractual definition*. This defines injustice as the 'not performance of covenant'.[10] Hobbes pairs this definition of injustice with two different statements about what justice consists in: on the one hand, 'whatsoever is not unjust' and, on the other, 'keeping of valid covenants'.[11] If justice consists in any behavior that is not unjust, then every act that does not breach a covenant will be just even if there are no laws, common powers, or valid covenants. If justice involves keeping valid covenants, however, then it might be the case that laws and

[7] *EW* iii. 131. The former chapter referred to is ibid. 124.

[8] Ibid. 147. The Latin edition reads 'law, properly, is the word of one who commands, whether orally or in writing, in such a way that everyone who is bound to obey knows that it is his word' (Hobbes, *Leviathan, Latin Variants*, 100, n. 17). See also ibid. 251.

[9] I am assuming that if the laws of nature are literally laws, as opposed to mere dictates of reason, then they must be commanded by God (*EW* iii. 147). If Hobbes holds, as he sometimes claims, that the laws of nature are literally laws only when they are commanded by the civil sovereign (ibid. 253), then the second option collapses into the first.

[10] Ibid. 130. I will assume that he means the non-performance of a valid covenant.

[11] Ibid. 130. ('the definition of INJUSTICE, is no other than the *not performance of covenant*. And whatsoever is not unjust, is *just*'); ibid. 131 ('justice consisteth in keeping of valid covenants').

common powers are necessary for justice, provided they are necessary conditions of valid covenants. The ambiguity is annoying but, for the purposes of this essay, it need not be resolved. The Contractual definition's account of the possibility of injustice gives rise to the problem even if the account of the possibility of justice is obscure.

What causes confusion is that Hobbes argues for the Contractual definition by appealing to two other definitions of justice. According to what I will call the *Scholastic definition*, 'justice is the constant will of giving to every man his own' and injustice consists in not giving a man his own.[12] According to what I will call the *Sine Jure definition*, injustice is action '*Sine Jure*' [without right], that is, 'action or omission without *jus*, or right'.[13] The key to solving the problem lies in the relationships among these definitions.

I will argue that the distinction between the Contractual and Scholastic definitions solves the puzzle with which I began. The Scholastic definition of justice (justice is giving to every man his own) is narrower than the Contractual definition (injustice is the not performance of covenant). Hobbes argues that all failures to give each his own are ultimately instances of breaking a covenant. But one can break a covenant without failing to give someone his own. This gap between the Contractual and Scholastic definitions helps to resolve the initial problem. I will argue that Hobbes's claim that injustice is impossible in the absence of law and coercive power applies to injustice as defined by the Scholastic definition, but not to injustice as defined by the Contractual definition. On this interpretation, points 1–3 are consistent.

The *Sine Jure* definition of justice (injustice is action without right) is broader than the Contractual definition (injustice is the not performance of covenant): every broken covenant involves acting without right but not all actions without right violate covenants. The difference between these definitions suggests that Hobbes tacitly accepted an Aristotelian distinction between general and particular justice where general justice consists in obeying every law of nature and particular justice consists in obeying the one law of nature concerning covenants. The *Sine Jure* definition concerns what general and particular justice have in common, such that they are both instances of justice. Hobbes

---

[12] EW iii. 131.
[13] Ibid. 118 ('*Sine Jure*'); 'Elements of Law,' *EW* iv. 82 ('action or omission without *jus*').

may have held that general justice is impossible in the absence of law and a common power, but this does not undermine the solution to the problem as general justice is distinct from particular justice.

THE CONTRACTUAL DEFINITION AND COMMON POWERS

The first problem passage asserts that there is no such thing as justice and injustice without law and a common power; the second problem passage gives an argument for that conclusion. This argument holds that covenants are 'the original' of justice and injustice but there is no justice or injustice until 'the fear of not performance' is taken away by a power that compels performance. A covenant is a kind of contract in which at least one party is trusted to do his part in the future.[14] While the third law of nature requires keeping covenants, covenants are invalid if one party has a 'reasonable suspicion' that the other party will not do his part.[15] If you and I agree to exchange a barrel for a bucket and I reasonably fear that you won't give me the bucket, our agreement is void and I am not obliged to give you the barrel. Of course, 'nothing is more easily broken than a man's word' and only 'fear of some evil consequence' could motivate keeping covenants.[16] If there is no common power to instill such fear, everyone can reasonably suspect that others will break their covenants and all covenants are thus invalid. Perversely, our agreement could be void even if both of us mean to do our parts: if you know that I reasonably fear you won't do your part, then you can reasonably fear that I won't do mine, even if you know that you would otherwise have done your part. A common power can remove at least reasonable suspicions by threatening to punish covenant-breakers. The covenants of those with 'a common power set over them both, with right and force sufficient to compel performance' are thus not generally void as those in the state of nature are, although they may be rendered invalid for some other, more particular, reason.[17] We can each assume the other will do his part, if only to avoid punishment, thus our covenant will be valid and each will be obligated to do his part. Injustice consists in violating a valid covenant

---

[14] *EW* iii. 121. [15] Ibid. 130, 124. [16] Ibid. 118.
[17] *EW* 124.

and, since a common power is a necessary condition of valid covenants, a common power is a necessary condition of the possibility of injustice.

What common power does Hobbes have in mind? The second problem passage clearly refers to the civil sovereign and that would fit with the strategy of discussing the evils of the state of nature in order to show that a civil sovereign is needed. Nonetheless, there are two problems with saying that justice depends on the civil sovereign and his laws. The first is a textual problem. If having a civil sovereign is a necessary condition of making valid covenants, then there are no valid covenants in the state of nature but, as I will show a little later, Hobbes explicitly claims that there can be valid covenants in the state of nature. The second problem is analytical. The sovereign's powers are derived from covenants made in the state of nature. The sovereign's possession of these powers thus cannot be a necessary condition of valid covenants. Hobbes may assert that the sovereign makes it much easier to have valid covenants but he cannot claim that the sovereign is necessary.

God is a second possible common power. God is a power over all human beings, even in the state of nature, and a possible enforcer of the laws of nature. Perhaps when the first problem passage asks us to consider what the world would be like without laws or a common power, Hobbes meant to ask us to consider how it would be without God or his laws of nature. The introduction of the laws of nature in the next chapter, one might think, introduces God as their maker. Without God, human beings have neither law nor morality and are at war; with God, they have laws and the power to enforce them such that they might construct a commonwealth and live in peace. Thus, one might think, the first point, that there is no justice or injustice in the state of nature, is ambiguous. If we consider the state of nature without any laws at all, there is no such thing as justice and injustice; taken this way, the first point is true. If we consider the state of nature with the laws of nature, but without civil laws, however, there might be such a thing as justice or injustice as God will enforce covenants; taken this way, the first point is false.[18]

The apparent similarity of the two problem passages presents a textual difficulty for this interpretation. The second problem passage asserts

---

[18] I am paraphrasing A. P. Martinich's ingenious suggestion that there is a distinction between 'primary' and 'secondary' states of nature. See A. P. Martinich, *The Two Gods of Leviathan* (Cambridge: Cambridge University Press, 1992), 75–7.

that there is no such thing as justice without the civil sovereign. This would have to be dismissed or at least distinguished from the putative assertion in the first problem passage that God's sovereignty is sufficient to make justice possible, even in the state of nature. Nonetheless, Hobbes does seem to give God a role in enforcing covenants. He compares the fear of God with the fear of one's fellow man and argues that although fear of one's fellow man is 'commonly the greater fear', it is not sufficient to get men to perform their covenants in the state of nature. This leads him to conclude that 'nothing can strengthen a covenant of peace agreed on, against the temptations of avarice, ambition, lust, or other strong desire, but the fear of that invisible power, which they every one worship as God.'[19]

This characterization of God's role is disappointing. First, it is unclear. If fear of one's fellow man is a greater fear than fear of God, it should be at least as effective in motivating people to perform their covenants.[20] Second, God's enforcement of the laws of nature would threaten the argument for the civil sovereign. If the fear of God were sufficient to motivate people to keep their covenants, then it would be sufficient to motivate compliance with all of the laws of nature and there would be no need for the civil sovereign. God is omnipotent and omniscient; what could a mere human sovereign add?[21] Hobbes might well have thought that the laws of nature are divine commands, but his account of God's role in enforcing them is muddled and seems half-hearted.

---

[19] *EW* iii. 128.

[20] On Martinich's reconstruction, the argument is that people do not fear God as much as a human sovereign because God is more remote and they irrationally ignore remote threats no matter how great. Nonetheless, their fear of God is sufficient to get them to establish a civil sovereign who will, in turn, ensure that they keep God's commands as expressed in the laws of nature (Martinich, *The Two Gods of Leviathan*, 98–9; see also pp. 80, 159–60). Perhaps that is what Hobbes meant, but it is disappointingly *ad hoc*. Why would the fear of God motivate me to help create an absolute monarchy but not motivate me to pay the grocer? The suggestion that the social contract is motivated by a fear of God fits poorly with Hobbes's own description, according to which it is motivated by the fear of others in the state of nature or fear of a conqueror (*EW* iii. 185).

[21] Suppose, with Martinich, that Hobbes held that 'the root of all obligation is God's omnipotence, because irresistible power directed to an object literally binds, ties or constrains that object to a certain course of action' (Martinich, *The Two Gods of Leviathan*, 100). God's omnipotent power would literally constrain all human beings to comply with His will as expressed by the laws of nature and there would be no problem with conflict in the state of nature.

Not only is Hobbes's position unclearly stated and poorly motivated, it stands at odds with his more developed arguments. Immediately after repeating the claim that all covenants in the state of nature are invalid, Hobbes presents a long argument with the opposite conclusion: his famous reply to the Fool. The Fool agrees that covenants exist and that the 'breach of them may be called injustice, and the observance of them justice', but he suspects that injustice, so understood, may 'sometimes stand with that reason which dictateth to every man his own good'.[22] Hobbes argues in reply that there are good self-interested reasons for keeping one's covenants. In the state of nature, Hobbes claims, defensive confederacies are necessary for self-preservation and the Fool, by breaking his covenants, would not be admitted into one.[23] Perhaps this argument does not show that one has overwhelming self-interested reasons for keeping every covenant but it is at least good enough to show that there are self-interested reasons for keeping some of one's covenants, even in the state of nature. That is enough to show that fear of a higher power is not necessary to motivate people to perform their covenants.

Covenants are made invalid by the 'fear of not performance', so for there to be valid covenants in the absence of a common power it has to be possible that at least one party to a covenant made in the state of nature does not reasonably fear that the other will not do his part.[24] That condition is clearly met. If I wonder whether you will do your part in our covenant, the refutation of the Fool offers me some reassurance. It shows that you have strong self-interested reasons for keeping up your end and that ought to calm my suspicions.[25] The argument against the Fool assumes there is no

---

[22] *EW* iii. 132.

[23] Ibid. 133. Thus, there is a reason for being on good terms with others in the state of nature. For a different view, see Martinich, *The Two Gods of Leviathan*, 80.

[24] Perhaps you are thinking that there is another invalidating condition: one party discovers that keeping the covenant will cost him his life. Such a person would not be obligated to perform his covenant as it was originally formulated, but he would be obligated to compensate the other party for the value of the covenant (*EW* iii. 126).

[25] In fact, the problem with the argument against the Fool is that, like the claim that God enforces covenants, its conclusion appears to be too strong: if self-interest always favored keeping one's covenants, then there would be no impediment to laying down the right of nature and taking other steps towards peace even in the absence of a civil sovereign. For discussion of this problem, see Jean Hampton, *Hobbes and the Social Contract Tradition* (Cambridge: Cambridge University Press, 1986), 64–6, 72; Gregory Kavka, *Hobbesian Moral and Political Theory* (Princeton: Princeton University Press, 1986), 147–56; and David Gauthier, 'Hobbes's

civil sovereign and that fear of God plays no role. It thus shows that valid covenants are possible in the absence of either of the two possible common powers. Another way that performance is assured is if it has already happened. If you have already done your part, I cannot fear that you will not do it. Hobbes is usually clear about this. In the argument against the Fool, he emphasizes that, 'the question is not of promises mutual, where there is no security of performance on either side; . . . but either where one of the parties has performed already; or where there is a power to make him perform.'[26] At one point, Hobbes suggests that first performance in the state of nature is always irrational, as anyone doing his part first would 'betray himself to his enemy; contrary to the right (he can never abandon) of defending his life'.[27] But his own examples show that this is exaggerated. The pirates who set a captive free on the condition that he return to pay his ransom do not put themselves in any special danger.[28] Nor do conquerors always put themselves at risk if they withhold 'the present stroke of death' in return for promises of obedience.[29] Hobbes argues that the covenants in both cases are valid and the victims are obliged to pay ransom and obey their conquerors. He does not even consider the possibility that the pirates or conquerors were irrational to perform their part in these bargains first. So there can be such a thing as a valid covenant in the state of nature and injustice, as it is defined by the Contractual definition, can exist in the absence of law and a common power.

THE SCHOLASTIC DEFINITION AND PROPRIETARY RIGHTS

If a common power is not necessary for valid covenants, then the two problem passages, which say that without a common power and law there is no such thing as justice and injustice, cannot be accepted at face value. Fortunately, they can be understood as making a narrower point that is

Social Contract', in G. A. J. Rogers and Alan Ryan (eds.), *Perspectives on Thomas Hobbes* (Oxford: Clarendon Press, 1988), 126–33.

[26] *EW* iii. 133. The premise of the argument in the second problem passage appears to be carefully worded to avoid cases in which one party has already performed his part since it narrows the discussion to 'covenants of *mutual* trust where there is a fear of not performance *on either part*' (ibid. 131, emphasis added). The conclusion of the passage, however, is much broader: that no covenants are valid, not just that covenants of mutual trust are invalid.

[27] Ibid. 124.   [28] Ibid. 126.   [29] Ibid. 188.

consistent with Hobbes's other positions: that there is no such thing as what I will call *proprietary rights* in the state of nature and thus there is no such thing as justice as understood in the Scholastic definition (justice is giving to every man his own). This is compatible with there being valid covenants in the state of nature and thus justice and injustice as defined by the Contractual definition (injustice is the not performance of covenant).

In each problem passage, Hobbes illustrates the claim that there is no such thing as justice and injustice in the state of nature by saying there is no such thing as propriety in the state of nature. By 'propriety', Hobbes means, among other things, what we would call property rights and rights to personal security: '[o]f things held in propriety, those that are dearest to a man are his own life, and limbs; and in the next degree (in most men,) those that concern conjugal affection; and after them riches and means of living.'[30] What these cases have in common is that they involve exclusive rights to things such as life, wife, and land. My property right to my watch, for example, is a right that I alone control the watch such that all others have a duty to leave the watch alone. As Hobbes put it, 'the propriety which a subject hath in his lands, consisteth in a right to exclude all other subjects from the use of them.'[31] My right to physical safety has the same feature: it excludes everyone else from, say, beating on my body without good cause. I will call rights with this exclusive feature *proprietary rights*.

Hobbes clearly holds that there are no proprietary rights in the state of nature. For example, he writes in the second problem passage that, 'where there is no coercive power erected, that is, where there is no commonwealth, there is no propriety; all men having right to all things.'[32] The standard story about safety in the state of nature explains why this is so. Everyone has what Hobbes calls the Right of Nature, that is, the right to do anything he believes will help to preserve his life. As the danger and uncertainty of one's surroundings increase, so does the range of things that might be necessary for self-preservation. Since Hobbes believes that anything may be needed for self-preservation in the dangerous and uncertain state of nature, he holds that the Right of Nature gives everyone in such circumstances the right to all things including the use of

---

[30] *EW* iii. 329.

[31] Ibid. 235 24.7. See also ibid. 165.

[32] Ibid. 131. See also ibid. 233, 313. The statement of the position is particularly crisp in *De Cive* (*EW* ii, 100).

other people's bodies.[33] Thus others will have a right to anything I might possess in the state of nature, including my body, because the Right of Nature gives them the right to all things in these circumstances. It is therefore impossible for me to have exclusive rights to anything in the state of nature.

In the second problem passage, Hobbes mixes this argument about the absence of proprietary rights in the state of nature with a similar argument about the absence of valid covenants. The second problem passage immediately follows the Contractual definition of justice (injustice is the not performance of covenant). In it, Hobbes argues that covenants are invalid without a common power and concludes that without a common power there cannot be such a thing as either justice or 'that propriety, which by mutual contract men acquire'. He then gives the Scholastic definition of justice (justice is giving to every man his own), notes that there are no proprietary rights in the state of nature, and concludes that there is nothing unjust in the state of nature. The passage ends with the repetition of the Contractual definition of justice and an assertion that a civil sovereign is necessary for both the validity of covenants and for proprietary rights. In other words, he writes as if the two definitions were equivalent and as if covenants were in the same position as proprietary rights.

This is a mistake as the Scholastic definition is narrower than the Contractual definition. Specifically, there can be valid covenants, and hence injustice according to the Contractual definition, even if there are no proprietary rights, and hence no such thing as injustice according to the Scholastic definition. This is the case in the state of nature. I have explained why valid covenants are possible in the state of nature and why there are no proprietary rights in the state of nature. These might seem to be contradictory positions because covenants and other agreements are often used to create proprietary rights. But while covenants serve this function in a commonwealth, they cannot do so in the state of nature. This follows from Hobbes's account of the Right of Nature and covenants. In the state of nature, Hobbes claims, the Right of Nature entails a right to all things. The right involved is what would now be called a liberty: having a right to all things means that there is nothing wrong with taking anything that might help to preserve one's life but it does not mean that

---

[33] *EW* iii. 116–17.

anyone has a duty to allow one to have what one needs or otherwise
provide aid. Covenants, for Hobbes, involve laying down part of one's
right to all things: in our covenant to exchange the barrel for the bucket,
I agree to lay down my right to the barrel provided you lay down your
right to the bucket. Covenants do not create new rights where none had
existed before but rather they involve subtracting some of each party's
right to all things. To lay down a right is to give up a bit of one's moral
liberty and thereby to gain obligations; your laying down the right to the
bucket makes it the case that it would be wrong of you to take it. What
I gain from our covenant is not an additional right to the bucket but, at
most, the subtraction of one competitor's rights to it.[34] Since this is so,
covenants in the state of nature do not create proprietary rights. Even if
you give up your right to the bucket, others will retain their rights and
I will not have a proprietary right to it. I will have as much right to the
bucket as others do and it will thus not be my own. In such a case, the two
definitions have different implications. According to the Contractual
definition, our covenant means that you are obliged to let me have the
bucket and that it would be unjust of you not to do so. However, it would
not be unjust of you to take the bucket according to the Scholastic
definition: it isn't my own bucket, so if you were to take it you would not
fail to give me my own and you would not do anything unjust.

One might object that it is logically possible to gain proprietary rights
by making covenants with everyone in the state of nature. Some of
Hobbes's contemporaries had, in fact, proposed that various means of
gaining property rights, such as first occupancy, had been established by
a pre-political agreement.[35] While Hobbes does not confront this view

---

[34] *EW* iii. 118.

[35] Hugo Grotius and Richard Selden both held such a view. They believed that all things
had once been owned in common but that private property had since become fully legitimate.
They reasoned that this transition was possible only if the common owners, that is, everyone,
had agreed to it. See Hugo Grotius, *De Jure Belli ac Pacis Libri Tres*, trans. Francis
W. Kelsey, et al., vol. 2 (1646; Oxford: Clarendon Press, 1925), 189–90 [II. ii. ii. 5], and John
Selden, 1584–1654, *Of the Dominion, or Ownership, of the Sea*, trans. Marchamont Nedham
[1620–1678] (London: Printed by William Du-Gard, 1652), 21–3 [I. ii]. Hobbes may have had
this view in mind in the second problem passage as both works were published before
Leviathan (1651): the first edition of *De Jure Belli ac Pacis* was published in 1625 and Selden's
work was first published in Latin as *Mare Clausum* in 1635. Perhaps Hobbes's idea was that the
kind of covenant Grotius and Selden imagined would be invalid. However, his claim that all
covenants in the state of nature are invalid is much broader than this and more than he would
have needed to dispute such a view.

directly, he would probably deny that such a covenant could be sincerely made. One cannot lay down one's right to things that might be necessary for self-preservation and, given the danger and uncertainty of the state of nature, almost anything might be necessary. Even a more modest covenant—say, a covenant simply to establish my right to the bucket and no more—would be problematic. Hobbes might reasonably ask whether such a covenant could be valid, that is, free from worries about non-performance. How could I know everyone well enough to be confident that they will keep their covenants and respect my rights? While one might be able to keep tabs on the members of a small group like a defensive confederacy, it is impossible to do so for everyone. This means we cannot appeal to the refutation of the Fool to establish the validity of this universal covenant by showing that everyone will have strong self-interested reasons for abiding by it. Given these points, covenants in the state of nature cannot establish proprietary rights and the way is open for Hobbes to say both that there are valid covenants in the state of nature and also that there are no proprietary rights in the state of nature.

The absence of proprietary rights is independent of whether there are valid covenants in the state of nature. The presence of proprietary rights, however, depends on a covenant since the sovereign makes proprietary rights possible and the sovereign's powers are based on a covenant. The sovereign does two things to make proprietary rights possible. First, the sovereign reduces the scope of the Right of Nature by imposing peace and order. In the commonwealth, no one needs a right to all things in order to stay alive, hence, no one has such a right.[36] This contraction of the right to all things is a necessary, but not sufficient, condition for proprietary rights: it makes it possible for me to be the only one with a right to the bucket but it does not create a mechanism for gaining such a right. The second thing the sovereign does is provide the means by which proprietary rights are generated. The sovereign does this by stipulating laws that all subjects are obliged to obey. For example, the civil laws may give you the proprietary right to a bucket that includes the power to transfer this proprietary right to me by means of a covenant. In such a case every other subject's obligation to respect my right to the bucket would have a contractual basis, even though only

[36] *EW* iii. 276.

you would voluntarily transfer the right to the bucket to me. All subjects are required to respect my right because they are parties to the covenant that establishes the sovereign and binds them to obey the civil laws. Thus the possibility of anything being a man's own depends on the existence of a civil sovereign. But the civil sovereign's powers depend on a covenant: that is why everyone in the commonwealth is obligated to obey the same rules governing the acquisition and transfer of property rights. This means that the Contractual definition (injustice is the not performance of covenant) accounts for the possibility of proprietary rights, and hence justice on the Scholastic definition (justice is giving to every man his own).

This gives us a clear sense in which justice depends on law. First, justice as defined by the Scholastic definition depends on law.

The distribution of the materials of this nourishment, is the constitution of *mine*, and *thine*, and *his*; that is to say, in one word *propriety*; and belongeth in all kinds of commonwealth to the sovereign power. For where there is no commonwealth, there is (as hath been already shown) a perpetual war of every man against his neighbour; and therefore every thing is his that getteth it, and keepeth it by force; which is neither *propriety*, nor *community*; but *uncertainty*. . . . Seeing therefore the introduction of propriety is an effect of commonwealth; which can do nothing but by the person that represents it, it is the act only of the sovereign; and consist-eth in the laws, which none can make that have not the sovereign power. And this they well knew of old, who called that *Nomos*, (that is to say, *distribution*,) which we call law; and defined justice, by *distributing* to every man *his own*.[37]

Second, covenants underwrite the law. Here is Hobbes's account of the chain of reasoning about justice from *Elements of Philosophy* (1655):

if a question be propounded, as, whether such an action be just or unjust; if that unjust be resolved into fact against law, and that notion law into the command of him or them that have coercive power; and *that power be derived from the wills of men that constitute such power*, to the end they may live in peace, they may at last come to this, that the appetites of men and the passions of their minds are such, that, unless they be restrained by some power, they will always be making war

---

[37] *EW* iii. 233. See also 'A Dialogue between a Philosopher and a Student of the Common Laws of England', (*EW* vi. 29).

upon one another; which may be known to be so by any man's experience, that will but examine his own mind. And, therefore, from hence he may proceed, by compounding, to the determination of the justice or injustice of any propounded action.[38]

The italicized clause shows where the covenant that establishes the commonwealth enters the story: it is what gives the sovereign power to create the laws that make proprietary rights possible. Justice, as understood in the Scholastic definition, thus has a contractual basis.

We are also in a position to see why Hobbes might have run the Scholastic and Contractual definitions together. The Scholastic definition was widely accepted by natural lawyers as a platitude about justice.[39] Hobbes does not reject this platitude but, on the contrary, seems to accept it. In the Epistle Dedicatory of *De Cive*, he claims it as the starting point that enables him to make progress in moral philosophy where others have failed.[40] In *Leviathan*, it sometimes seems to have equal standing with the Contractual definition, as in these passages: 'justice (that is to say, performance of covenant and giving to each man his own) is a dictate of the law of nature' or 'every sovereign ought to cause justice to be taught, which (consisting in taking from no man what is his) is as much as to say, to cause men to be taught not to deprive their neighbours by violence or fraud of anything which by the sovereign authority is theirs.'[41] He even concedes that, 'The Definition is good, and yet it is Aristotle's.'[42] While he is committed to the Contractual definition as the fundamental definition of justice, Hobbes is also in a position to

---

[38] 'Elements of Philosophy', *EW* i. 73 (emphasis added).

[39] William Lucy referred to it as 'the usual definition of *justice* among the *Schoolmen*' (William Lucy [1594–1677], *Observations, censures, and confutations of notorious errours in Mr. Hobbes his Leviathan and other his bookes to which are annexed occasionall animadversions on some writings of the Socinians and such haereticks of the same opinion with him* (London: Printed by J.G. for Nath. Brooke at the Angel in Cornhill, 1663), 213). It can be found in Thomas Aquinas, *Summa Theologiae*, II-II Q58 A1; Grotius, *De Jure Belli ac Pacis Libri Tres*, 12–13 [Prolegomena §8]; and Francisco Suárez, 'On Laws and God the Lawgiver', in *Selections from Three Works of Francisco Suárez* (1612; Oxford: Clarendon Press, 1944), 28 [I. ii. 2].

[40] See the 1641 Epistle Dedicatory of *De Cive* (Thomas Hobbes, *On the Citizen*, ed. and trans. Richard Tuck and Michael Silverthorne (1647; New York: Cambridge University Press, 1998), 5–6).

[41] *EW* iii. 253, 329.

[42] 'A Dialogue between a Philosopher and a Student of the Common Laws of England', (*EW* vi. 8). The definition is usually credited to Ulpian and not Aristotle. Hobbes more accurately calls it 'the ordinary definition of justice in the Schools' (*EW* iii. 131).

accommodate the Scholastic definition. His account of proprietary rights shows that there can be such as thing as justice, as understood by the Scholastic definition, only within the commonwealth. The more fundamental Contractual definition thus explains the widely accepted Scholastic one and that helps to make the case for the Contractual definition.

This solves the initial problem. The best interpretation of the first claim, the contention that justice and injustice do not exist in the state of nature, is that justice and injustice in a certain domain, namely that of proprietary rights, do not exist in the state of nature. This is compatible with the Contractual definition's being the canonical definition of justice (the second claim) and the possibility of valid covenants in the state of nature (the third).

THE *SINE JURE* DEFINITION AND GENERAL JUSTICE

One may object that the Contractual definition (injustice is the not performance of covenant) cannot be Hobbes's fundamental definition of justice on the grounds that he argues for the Contractual definition by appealing to another definition: the *Sine Jure* definition (injustice is action without right).

Right is laid aside, either by simply renouncing it; or by transferring it to another. . . . And when a man hath in either manner abandoned, or granted away his right; then is he said to be OBLIGED, or BOUND, not to hinder those, to whom such right is granted, or abandoned, from the benefit of it: and that he *ought*, and it is his DUTY, not to make void that voluntary act of his own: and that such hindrance is INJUSTICE, and INJURY, as being *Sine Jure* [without right]; the right being before renounced, or transferred.[43]

It seems as though Hobbes is saying that the reason why it is unjust to violate a covenant is that doing so involves acting without right.[44] If so, one might think, his real view must be that justice is fundamentally defined by what one has a right to do and that the definition of injustice

---

[43] *EW* iii. 118. In the Latin edition, everything from 'And when a man . . .' to 'voluntary act of his own:' was replaced by this: 'And however he does this, he ought not to hinder the person who has the right from using the thing. For this would be to make his own act void' (Hobbes, *Leviathan, Latin Variants*, 81, n. 8).

[44] This is Martinich's preferred definition, though he puts it in terms of violating obligations (Martinich, *The Two Gods of Leviathan*, 91–2).

as 'no other than the not performance of covenant' is too narrow: violations of covenants are only one way of acting without right. If the *Sine Jure* definition (injustice is action without right) is Hobbes's definition of justice and Hobbes holds that what one has a right to do is spelled out by laws—either the laws of nature in the state of nature or civil laws in a commonwealth—then justice depends on laws and the common powers that make them.

The first possible source of laws that define what one has a right to do is the civil sovereign. There is some textual evidence that this is Hobbes's view. He claims several times that the civil laws define what justice and injustice consist in. For example, he defines civil law as rules 'for the distinction of right and wrong' and argues for this definition on the grounds that it is self-evident, 'that laws are the rules of just, and unjust; nothing being reputed unjust, that is not contrary to some law'.[45] This accords with an early definition of a just man: 'all these words, *he that in his actions observeth the laws of his country*, make but one name, equivalent to this one word, *just*'.[46] This kind of claim is repeated in subsequent summaries and defenses of his theory. In the course of battling with Bishop Bramhall (1668), he writes that,

the civil laws are the rules of good and evil, just and unjust, honest and dishonest. Truly, I see no other rules they have. The Scriptures themselves were made law to us here, by the authority of the commonwealth, and are therefore part of the law civil. If they were laws in their own nature, then were they laws over all the world, and men were obliged to obey them in America, as soon as they should be shown there, though without a miracle, by a friar. What is unjust, but the transgression of a law? *Law* therefore was before unjust: and the law was made known by sovereign power before it was a law: therefore *sovereign power* was antecedent both to *law* and *injustice*. Who then made unjust but sovereign kings or sovereign assemblies?[47]

The point also appears in the *Dialogue* on the common law (1681).

Seeing then that a Just Action . . . is that which is not against the Law; it is Manifest that before there was a Law, there could be no Injustice, and therefore Laws are in their Nature Antecedent to Justice and Injustice.[48]

---

[45] *EW* iii. 251.   [46] Ibid. 21.

[47] 'An Answer to Bishop Bramhall's Book, Called "The Catching of the Leviathan"' (*EW* iv. 369).

[48] 'A Dialogue between a Philosopher and a Student of the Common Laws of England' (*EW* vi. 29).

Nonetheless, Hobbes cannot hold that civil laws are necessary preconditions of justice. First, there are the problems mentioned earlier: Hobbes claims that there are valid covenants in the state of nature and that the sovereign's powers are derived from a covenant made in the state of nature. Given his claim that breaking covenants is unjust, he is committed to the possibility of injustice without civil laws. Second, the suggestion that the civil laws define justice and what one has a right to do conflicts with Hobbes's position regarding what he calls 'the true liberty of a subject', namely, those 'things which, though commanded by the sovereign', a subject 'may without injustice refuse to do'.[49] The sovereign's authority is based on a covenant in which the subjects lay down their rights to govern themselves and authorize the sovereign to act on their behalf. But no one can lay down the right to defend himself against imminent threats and therefore everyone retains the right to try to escape if, for example, the sovereign attempts to kill him.[50] This means that justice and injustice are not simply defined by the sovereign's commands: if they were, it would be unjust to run away when the sovereign commands me to stop and accept my punishment. Third, the laws of nature prohibit one from acting in ways that are inimical to self-preservation. Those who violate the laws of nature thus act without right, even if they are not governed by a civil sovereign.[51] That means that justice as it is defined in the *Sine Jure* definition (injustice is action without right) cannot depend on civil law.

This brings us to the other way that laws might limit rights. Since the laws of nature can deprive one of the right to act, perhaps justice depends on the laws of nature. There is textual evidence for this view as well. Hobbes holds that it would be 'a thing unjust' to keep a vow to break a law of nature: breaking a law of nature is said to be unjust even if

---

[49] *EW* iii. 203.

[50] Ibid. 204–5.

[51] For the view that only covenants, and not the laws of nature, restrict rights see D. D. Raphael, 'Hobbes on Justice', in G. A. J. Rogers and Alan Ryan (eds.), *Perspectives on Thomas Hobbes*, (Oxford: Clarendon Press, 1988), 156–7. The Laws of Nature, however, seem to limit what one has a right to do, prior to any covenant. For example, anyone can perform a covenant first but no one has a right to do so since that would be to 'betray himself to his enemy, contrary to the right (he can never abandon) of defending his life and means of living' (*EW* iii. 124). In addition, sovereigns have no right to break the laws of nature even though they do not covenant to obey them (ibid. 178, 199, 263, 297, 304, 322, 342).

doing so involves keeping a covenant.[52] He also claims that the justice of men and actions depend on their conformity to reason.[53] Since reason discovers all of the laws of nature, and not merely the law concerning covenants, this implies that justice consists in obeying all of the laws of nature.[54] Finally, Hobbes says of the laws of nature that, 'he that fulfilleth the law, is just.'[55] Being a just person seems to involve fulfilling all nineteen laws of nature and not merely the third law, which forbids breaking covenants. This would conflict with the Contractual definition, which limits injustice to violations of covenants, but it makes sense on the *Sine Jure* definition, which holds that injustice is action without right. The laws of nature forbid certain acts, such that one has no right to do them, injustice is action without right, therefore it is unjust to break any law of nature.

However, Hobbes generally lists justice as one virtue or law of nature among others, as opposed to characterizing it as the whole of virtue or the sum of the laws of nature.[56] Furthermore, he needs such a distinction for two of his more developed positions on the laws of nature. First, the Contractual definition of justice (injustice is the not performance of covenant), Hobbes's explicit definition, depends on such a distinction. To see this, suppose that you have been generous towards me and that I am insufferably ungrateful in return, such that you repent your previous good will towards me. Suppose also that I do this not because I think it has any bearing on my prospects for survival but because I find it amusing to watch you gnash your teeth in anger and regret. My action would not be unjust according to the Contractual definition since I would not be breaking a covenant and, according to that definition, nothing other

---

[52] *EW* iii. 125.

[53] 'The names of just and unjust' signify 'conformity or inconformity to reason' (ibid. 131).

[54] 'A law of nature is a precept, or general rule, found out by reason' (ibid. 116).

[55] Ibid. 145.

[56] 'Justice therefore, . . . that is to say, keeping of covenant, is a rule of reason, by which we are forbidden to do any thing destructive to our life; . . . and consequently a law of nature' (*EW* iii. 134). 'The laws of nature are immutable and eternal; for injustice, ingratitude, arrogance, pride, iniquity, acception of persons, and the rest, can never be made lawful' (ibid. 145). 'For the laws of nature (as justice, equity, modesty, mercy, and (in sum) doing to others, as we would be done to) . . . are contrary to our natural passions that carry us to partiality, pride, revenge and the like' (ibid. 153).

than the non-performance of covenant is unjust. But I would be unjust according to the *Sine Jure* definition since I would have broken the fourth law of nature. I could not claim that I was exercising my right of nature as it only gives me the right to anything that I think would aid self-preservation and, by hypothesis, I had no such thought. Hobbes, properly, kept the two cases apart.

as justice dependeth on antecedent covenant; so does GRATITUDE depend on antecedent grace; that is to say, antecedent free-gift: and is the fourth law of nature . . . The breach of this law, is called ingratitude; and hath the same relation to grace, that injustice hath to obligation by covenant.[57]

If injustice involved breaking any law of nature, the passage would say that ingratitude bears the same relationship to justice as keeping covenants does, namely, breaking a law of nature.

Hobbes also holds that sovereigns can break the laws of nature in dealing with their subjects, but insists that they would not thereby commit injustice. For example, when King David killed the innocent Uriah, he violated the law of nature and sinned against God, but his sin was iniquity and not injustice.[58] Sovereigns cannot be unjust to their subjects because the subjects authorize all of the sovereign's actions in the covenant that establishes the commonwealth. This means that the sovereign's actions are, for the purposes of moral accounting, the subjects' own actions. Assuming that no one can act unjustly towards himself, it follows that the sovereign cannot be unjust to his subjects.[59] However, the sovereign's rights are limited by the laws of nature.[60] Thus David was unjust according to the *Sine Jure* definition (injustice is action without right) but, since he violated no covenant with Uriah, he was not unjust according to the Contractual definition (injustice is the not performance of covenant). Therefore, Hobbes's denial that David was unjust suggests that the *Sine Jure* definition is not the fundamental definition of justice.

There is a puzzle here. The Contractual definition is considerably narrower than the *Sine Jure* definition but they are both concerned with justice. How are they related to one another? I believe that they

---

[57] *EW* iii. 138.   [58] Ibid. 199.   [59] Ibid. 163, 199.

[60] The sovereign 'never wanteth a right to anything (otherwise than as he himself is the subject of God, and bound thereby to observe the law of nature)' (ibid. 199).

correspond to what broadly Aristotelian theories called general and particular justice. General justice, in these theories, amounts to doing the right thing while general injustice consists in wrongdoing.[61] In Aristotle, justice in the general sense consists in virtues that are 'related to another' while Aquinas held that it 'directs man in his relations with other men'; every virtue and law contributes to the common good, so every virtue and law concerns behavior related to the good of others, thus every virtue or law counts as an instance of general justice.[62] Particular justice, on the other hand, is characterized as a distinctive virtue. It is also a virtue that concerns other people, but in a more direct way. According to Aristotle, particular justice is concerned with fairness in the distribution of goods and honors and in interactions with particular other people.[63] According to Aquinas, particular justice is the virtue that is directed immediately at the good of others, as opposed to the other virtues which promote the good of others indirectly, by improving the common good.[64] Suárez claims that the particular meaning of *iustitia* is 'a special virtue which renders to another that which is due'.[65] Aristotle and Aquinas both hold that particular justice is divided into distributive and commutative parts: the former concerns the distribution of goods such as honor or wealth, the latter concerns transactions among individuals, such as buying, selling, theft, murder, and so on.[66]

Hobbes's remarks about justice fit the Aristotelian pattern. The passages that put forward the *Sine Jure* definition of justice (injustice is action without right), namely, those that claim the just person follows all of the laws of nature or conforms with reason, match the Aristotelian claim that general justice consists in all of the virtues and obedience to laws in general. On the other hand, the Contractual definition of justice (injustice is the not performance of covenant) is an account of particular justice. First, it defines a specific kind of moral requirement governing one's relationships with others and is therefore distinct from other laws and virtues such as those concerning gratitude. Second, Hobbes used the

---

[61] Aristotle, *Nicomachean Ethics*, book V, ch. 1 (henceforth, *NE*); Aquinas, *Summa Theologica*, II–II Q58 A5 (henceforth, *ST*).

[62] Aristotle, *NE*, book V, ch. 1; Aquinas, *ST*, II–II Qu 58 A5.

[63] Aristotle, *NE*, book V, ch. 2.   [64] Aquinas, *ST*, II Q58 A5.

[65] Suárez, 'On Laws and God the Lawgiver', 30 [I. ii. 4].

[66] Aristotle, *NE*, book V, ch. 2 §§12–13; Aquinas, *ST*, ii–ii Q58 A5.

Contractual definition to revise the earlier accounts of particular justice.
He assimilates commutative justice entirely to the Contractual definition, arguing that justice consists in what contractors voluntarily accept
and that there are no further questions of equality or fairness in
exchanges beyond that.[67] Distributive justice, on the other hand, does
not fit the Contractual definition and is expelled: it applies to arbitrators,
is more properly called equity than justice, and belongs under a different
law of nature than the one concerning contracts and covenants.[68]
Hobbes's account is particularly close to that of Francisco Suárez.
What distinguishes general and particular justice, at least according to
Aquinas, is that the latter involves a more direct relationship between
individuals; exactly what this more direct relationship consists in is left
fairly vague in Aquinas. Suárez offers a sharper account of the more direct
relationship: it consists in interactions involving another person's rights.
According to Suárez, the strict sense of *ius* or right is

> bestowed upon a certain moral power which every man has, either over his own
> property or with respect to that which is due to him. For it is thus that the
> owner of a thing is said to have a right (*ius*) in that thing, and the labourer is
> said to have that right to his wages by reason of which he is declared worthy of
> his hire.[69]

The relationships subject to particular justice, in turn, are those in which
respect for others' *ius* or rights is involved.

> *ius* is so understood in the *Digest* in the passages (I.i.10), where justice is said to
> be the virtue that renders to every man that which belongs to him.
> Accordingly, this right to claim (*actio*), or moral power, which every man
> possesses with respect to his own property or with respect to a thing which
> in some way pertains to him, is called *ius*, and appears to be the true object of
> justice.[70]

Hobbes uses the Contractual definition of justice to give a different
account of the kind of relationship to which particular justice applies.
Justice, on the Contractual definition, does not involve respecting rights
because covenants do not generate rights. In our covenant, we both lost

---

[67] *EW* iii. 137.   [68] Ibid. 138, 142.
[69] Suárez, 'On Laws and God the Lawgiver', 30 [I. ii. 5].   [70] Ibid. 31 [I. ii. 5].

rights rather than gaining them: I laid down my right to the barrel, you laid down yours to the bucket. Instead, I gained an obligation not to take the barrel. Should I go back on the deal, I would not violate your rights but I would 'injure' you, in Hobbes's technical understanding of the term.[71] So what characterizes the relationships subject to particular justice on Hobbes's account are voluntarily assumed obligations on the part of the party who has laid down a right and the susceptibility to injury on the part of the party to whom the right has been laid down.[72] Of course, the differences between Hobbes and Suárez, however interesting they may be, are beside the point. What is important is that they were doing the same thing: sharpening the account of exactly what kind of relationship particular justice involves.

The Contractual definition (injustice is the not performance of covenant) is Hobbes's account of particular injustice. The role of the *Sine Jure* definition (injustice is action without right) is to explain why particular justice is an instance of general justice: particular injustice, like all other kinds of general injustice, involves action without right. Where Aristotle claimed that all kinds of justice, general and particular, consist in virtues that are 'related to another' and Aquinas held that justice 'directs man in his relations with other men', Hobbes held that all instances of injustice involve action without right and, presumably, that all kinds of justice involve action with right. The laws of nature forbid certain kinds of behavior, meaning one has no right to act in those ways.[73] Failure to perform one's covenant is also action without right, in so far as the relevant right has been laid down. If we take the laws of nature as a whole to correspond with general justice and the Contractual definition as defining particular justice, the *Sine Jure*

---

[71] *EW* iii. 118.

[72] There is a complication. Hobbes claims that violating the law of nature injures God (David-Uriah) (ibid. 199). This threatens to collapse the distinction between general and particular justice because it means that all violations of the law of nature are instances of particular injustice. Hobbes's answer is that violations of the laws of nature that do not involve covenants are instances of particular injustice only with respect to God and not with respect to other people. The injury is done to God because he has a right to rule and human beings have obligations to obey his commands. A second problem is that God's right to rule does not have a contractual basis. This problem can be avoided only if God's right to rule is somehow specially derived. That is what Hobbes suggests in saying that God's right to rule stems from his power, as opposed to a contract, though his account is unclear (ibid. 345).

[73] Ibid. 116.

definition would explain what the two have in common, such that they both count as definitions of the same broad thing: justice.

Admittedly, Hobbes does not use the terms 'general justice' or 'particular justice' and the distinction does not play a significant role in his theory as he is predominantly concerned with particular justice. My claim is that the apparent conflict between the two definitions dissipates if we interpret his remarks in the light of this distinction. Ingratitude is wrong because it involves a violation of general justice: it is a failure to act with right or a failure to do the right thing. But it is not an instance of particular injustice, in which another party is injured, because it is not a violation of a covenant or other contract.

Does general justice depend on law or a common power? The flat-footed answer to this question is yes. Hobbes believes the requirements of morality are spelled out by the laws of nature and, since general justice consists in the whole of morality, it follows that laws are a necessary condition for the existence of general justice. This is not a very interesting sense in which general justice depends on law, however. The interesting question concerns whether Hobbes holds that general justice depends on laws that are commands issued by a commander. In this case, the laws in question would be the laws of nature and the commander would be God. Hobbes's position on whether the laws of nature are divine commands is not clear and his discussion of justice does not settle the matter. The bulk of his account concerns particular justice while his remarks about general justice do not address this issue. If there is a case for thinking that Hobbes held that the laws of nature must be divine commands, it will have to be made on the basis of arguments about Hobbes's attitude towards the laws of nature as a whole, and not merely on the basis of his specific contentions concerning justice and covenants.

CONCLUSIONS

Hobbes did not show that justice depends on laws. In fact, his arguments undermine this contention. Furthermore, the passages claiming that justice does depend on law can be interpreted to mean something more modest: justice depends on law in certain domains, namely, those that concern proprietary rights. Thus his theory is largely consistent with his explicit definition: injustice consists in breaking covenants.

I would like to close with some remarks about the status of my interpretation. I am claiming that there is a consistent view whose major parts are all present in Hobbes's writing. Hobbes himself does not always consistently articulate this view. If I am right, he sometimes slips between the official, Contractual, definition of justice and the Scholastic definition. He also has a marked tendency to exaggerate the civil sovereign's role in making justice possible. Specifically, his claims that justice and injustice do not exist in the state of nature and that the civil sovereign defines the rules of justice are not supported by his theory. In short, I regard some of Hobbes's explicit claims as mistakes. I will try to explain why Hobbes might have made the mistakes I attribute to him in order to support my contention that these are errors rather than his considered views.

The significance of Hobbes's claims about the Scholastic definition (justice is giving to every man his own) and proprietary rights would have encouraged him to slip in the ways that I claim he did. Property rights, a subset of proprietary rights, were an important issue in the political struggle between Parliament and Charles I. Charles faced severe financial problems and attempted to raise funds without parliamentary consent; these attempts, in turn, struck many as threatening both Parliament and recognized individual liberties.[74] Hobbes tried to show how justice, as understood by the Scholastic definition, is compatible with his absolutist political views. In doing so, he opposed many generally accepted views of his day. For example, it was widely believed that property rights had been established prior to the commonwealth. The Eighth Commandment's prohibition on theft, for example, makes sense only if there is such a thing as property which can be stolen.[75]

---

[74] Clarendon, for example, argues that subjects without secure property rights would have no stake at all in political stability. Edward Hyde 1st Earl of Clarendon, *A brief view and survey of the dangerous and pernicious errors to church and state, in Mr. Hobbes's book, entitled Leviathan* (Oxon: Printed at the Theater, 1676), 54–5, 69–72, 76–9, 82–4, 163–4.

[75] Both Antony Ascham, writing anonymously as Euctactus Philodemius, and William Lucy criticized Hobbes on the grounds that property rights are based on natural law as articulated in the Ten Commandments. See Antony Ascham [d. 1650], *The Original & End of Civil Power* (London: [s.n.], 1649), 15–16, and Lucy, *Observations, censures, and confutations of notorious errours in Mr. Hobbes his Leviathan*, 160–2, 213–14. Others held that the laws of nature permit common ownership but that they also back private ownership as it had, as a matter of historical fact, been instituted. See, for example, Grotius, *De Jure Belli ac Pacis Libri Tres*, 189–90 [II. ii. ii. 5]; Selden, *Of the Dominion, or Ownership, of the Sea*, 21–3 [I. ii]; and Suárez, 'On Laws and God the Lawgiver', 277–9 [II. xiv. 17].

More importantly, there was broad agreement that subjects held property rights against sovereigns. This was the position of intellectuals such as Suárez and Jean Bodin.[76] It was also the predominant view in English politics in so far as the major disputes concerned the strength of property rights against the sovereign and not whether such rights existed at all. Some held that property rights are absolute, such that sovereigns can never take property without Parliamentary consent. The standard competing view, held by most political absolutists, was that sovereigns could take goods without parliamentary consent but only in cases of necessity.[77] Hobbes's account of the Scholastic definition and proprietary rights posed a sharp challenge to these positions. His elegant reconstruction of the Scholastic definition denies both that there are any property rights prior to the commonwealth and that subjects have property rights against the sovereign. He would have seen these as important achievements and thus might well have tended to slip from a cautious formulation such as 'justice as it is commonly conceived is impossible in the state of nature' to the more dramatic 'justice is impossible in the state of nature.'

Hobbes began working on political philosophy at least partly in response to the crises surrounding Charles I's extra-parliamentary fundraising during the 1620s and 1630s. He was involved in collecting the Forced Loan (1626–7) and dedicated his first political work, the *Elements of Law* (1640), to the Earl of Newcastle, one of Charles's hardline advisors. The dedication makes it clear that he and Newcastle hoped the book would contribute to the political debate.[78] After all, he had articulated a strikingly novel position. While most of those inclined to defend Charles's position did so on the grounds that the taxes were necessary, Hobbes believed he had shown that the sovereign need not respect property rights at all.[79] Hobbes himself attributed a great deal of

---

[76] See Suárez, 'On Laws and God the Lawgiver', 277–8 [II. xiv. 15] and Jean Bodin [1530–1596], *The Six Bookes of a Common-weale*, trans. Richard Knolles [1550?–1610] (London: [Printed by Adam Islip] impensis G. Bishop, 1606), 97.

[77] For this characterization of the contemporary political debate, I have drawn on Johann P. Sommerville, *Thomas Hobbes: Political Ideas in Historical Context* (New York: St. Martin's Press, 1992), 89–95.

[78] 'Elements of Law', (*EW* iv. xv).

[79] Richard Tuck also believes that Hobbes was drawn to political philosophy by these financial crises. He interprets Hobbes as trying to apply the lessons of epistemological skepticism to

importance to his analysis of the Scholastic definition. In the Epistle Dedicatory to *De Cive* (1641), he maintained that there is a single reason why moral philosophy had made little progress:

none of those who have dealt with this subject have employed a suitable starting point from which to teach it. For the starting point of a science cannot be set at any point we choose as in a circle. In the very shadows of doubt a thread of reason (so to speak) begins, by whose guidance we shall escape to the clearest light; that is where the starting point for teaching is; that is where we must find our illumination as we direct our course to clear away doubts. Hence whenever an author loses the thread through ignorance or breaks it through passion he is no longer delineating the tracks of science but his own erratic path.

He then identified the Scholastic definition of justice as his starting point.

And so when I turned my thoughts to the inquiry about natural justice I was alerted by the very name of justice (by which is meant a constant will to give every man *his right*) to ask first how it is that anyone ever spoke of something as *his own* rather than *another's*; and when it was clear that it did not originate in nature but in human agreement (for human beings have distributed what nature has placed in common), I was led from there to another question, namely, for whose benefit and under what necessity, when all things belonged to all men, they preferred that each man should have things that belonged to himself alone. And I saw that war and every kind of calamity must necessarily follow from community in things, as men came into violent conflict over their use; a thing all seek by nature to avoid.[80]

Hobbes claimed to have developed the main parts of his theory from beginning with the Scholastic definition of justice. This passage recounts the destructive side of the project: showing that there is no such thing as one's own without a civil sovereign. This leads naturally to Hobbes's constructive story about how the civil sovereign makes proprietary rights and hence justice on the Scholastic definition possible.

This helps to explain why he might have slipped. He began with the commonly accepted Scholastic definition and showed that it is empty in

the issue of who can decide whether a given tax is necessary. See Richard Tuck, *Philosophy and Government*, 1572–1651 (Cambridge: Cambridge University Press, 1993), 297–314.

[80] *De Cive*, Epistle Dedicatory, 1641 (Hobbes, *On the Citizen*, 5–6).

the state of nature. He then offered a positive explanation of why justice, so understood, exists in the commonwealth. The positive account involves a new definition of justice, but the fate of the Scholastic definition would have been the center of attention for both Hobbes and his readers. So it would have been natural, although strictly speaking mistaken, for him to claim that he had shown that justice is possible only in the commonwealth. By the same token, we can understand why he would say that civil laws define the rules of justice since obligations to respect proprietary rights depend on civil laws. Perhaps Hobbes should have said of the state of nature that 'justice and injustice have there a place, but one that is extremely small' instead of 'justice and injustice have there no place'. He also should have described the civil laws as 'the rules of just and unjust governing the most important rights' rather than as simply 'the rules of just and unjust'. But that was not really Hobbes's way and, for the purposes of illustrating what he saw as the incommodities of the state of nature and the importance of the civil sovereign, the differences are hardly worth noting.

ACKNOWLEDGEMENTS

Material in the essay was delivered to a seminar on Hobbes at the University of Chicago, the Chicago Political Theory Conference, and the Midwest Seminar on Early Modern Philosophy. I am especially grateful to Danielle Allen, Edwin Curley, Patrick Frierson, Daniel Garber, and Gerald Siarny for their comments.

University of Chicago

6

The Circle of Adequate Knowledge:
Notes on Reason and Intuition in Spinoza

SYLIANE MALINOWSKI–CHARLES

One of the fundamental characteristics of Spinoza's theory of knowledge, and one of the most intriguing, is the quasi-automatic character of the progress of knowledge, which Spinoza puts forward in paragraph 85 of the *Treatise on the Emendation of the Intellect*[1] and illustrates by the image of the intellect forging its own tools of perfection in paragraphs 30–2[2]. Lia Levy's recent study of Spinoza's notion of consciousness shows the complexity and richness of this problematic, which should be considered crucial for the understanding of Spinoza's theory of knowledge.[3] One can immediately grasp the importance of the automatic or 'quasi'-automatic character of the cognitive perfection of the mind in the framework of a metaphysics of necessity: it is a matter of showing that even the liberation which results from knowledge operates according to the laws

This work was elaborated with the support of an FQRSC postdoctoral fellowship at the Université de Montréal. A shorter version of this text was presented to the Association des Amis de Spinoza and the Groupe de Recherches Spinozistes, 15 Dec. 2001, at the Université de Sorbonne-Paris I. I would like to thank those in charge of these two organizations for their kind invitation, and especially Pierre-François Moreau. I would also like to extend my warmest thanks to Bruce Baugh for translating this text into English, and to James Crooks for revising the whole.

[1] G ii, 32. The numbering of paragraphs is done according to Bruder (C. H. Bruder, *Benedicti de Spinoza Opera Quae Supersunt Omnia*, 3 vols. (Leipzig: Tauchnitz, 1843–6). See C i, 37: 'They never conceived the soul (as we do here) as acting according to certain laws, like a spiritual automaton.' For an elucidation of this formula in the *TIE*, see Wim N.A. Klever, 'Quasi aliquod automa spirituale', in E. Giancotti (ed.), *Proceedings of the First International Congress on Spinoza: Spinoza nel 350° Anniversario della nascita, Urbino 4–8 ottobre 1982* (Naples: Bibliopolis, 1985), 249–57.   [2] G ii, 13–14; C i, 16–7.

[3] Lia Levy, *L'automate spirituel. La naissance de la subjectivité moderne d'après l'Éthique de Spinoza* (Assen: Van Gorcum, 2000). I share most of Levy's analyses but regret that she did not bring to the forefront the affective dimension of consciousness in Spinoza's theory, a task I attempted in my doctoral thesis ('Conscience et connaissance expérientielle: le rôle des affects dans la progression éthique', University of Ottawa, 2002; unpublished).

of nature, and in particular the laws of the understanding. There would be no point in thinking that the mind could free itself from the determinism of its own essence: its functioning, like that of all things, is mechanical; that is, it obeys the eternal and immutable laws of nature as a whole.

My interest here concerns the concrete way in which this determinism operates at the level of the human individual. More specifically, since the theme is immense and needs to be limited, I am concerned with the ways in which this determinism is actualized in *adequate* knowledge. I am thus deliberately leaving to one side the progress in the first kind of knowledge and the transition from imagination to reason, which I have dealt with elsewhere.[4] I will concentrate solely on what I call the circle of adequate knowledge, which is subsequent to the decisive transition from a mainly inadequate knowledge to a mainly adequate one. I am thus assuming an already wise man, or one already acting for the most part in accordance with right reason, although I am aware that it is all a question of the proportion between adequate and inadequate knowledge, and that the imagination is never totally left behind. The specific focus of what follows is to try to account for the dynamic of progress at the heart of adequate knowledge. This must be done on two levels: the level of the transition from the second to the third kind of knowledge, and then the level of the perfecting of intuitive knowledge. This analysis will allow me to bring to light a circularity of adequate knowledge that reinforces or strengthens itself in the mind, and allows the mind to perfect itself indefinitely. It is thus a matter of finding the 'mainspring' of this spiritual automaton that is the mind or the soul (*mens*), and we will find that this mainspring is affective in character.

BIRTH OF THE DESIRE TO KNOW BY MEANS
OF THE THIRD KIND OF KNOWLEDGE[5]

Proposition 28 of the last part of the *Ethics* states clearly and unequivocally that it is impossible to derive intuitive knowledge directly from

---

[4] See Syliane Charles, 'Le salut par les affects: le rôle de la joie comme moteur du progrès éthique chez Spinoza', *Philosophiques* 29/1 (2002), 73–87. Whereas in that article I dealt mostly with what I am leaving aside here, in this article I develop what I had merely sketched out in the earlier one.

[5] For reasons of uniformity and ease of reference, in this text I make use of the *Ethics*' division of knowledge into three kinds.

imagination: 'The striving, or desire, to know things by the third kind of knowledge cannot arise from the first kind of knowledge, but can indeed arise from the second' (E5P28).[6] We should note here that Spinoza does not exactly state that the third kind of knowledge cannot arise from the first, which nevertheless would assuredly be consistent and accurate, but that the *conatus* (striving) or *desire* to know by the third kind of knowledge can only come from the second kind of knowledge—that is, from reason, which according to the *Ethics* corresponds to the formation of 'common notions'. The conatus, effort or appetite, which in its conscious form goes by the name of *cupiditas*, or desire, is the very essence of man (E3P7 and E3P9S). Concerning the first kind of knowledge, Spinoza very clearly shows that the orientation of desire towards a particular object is never anything other than the fruit of the individual's pursuit of his own good, and is explained by the individual's belief that this object is capable of providing him with an increase in power, which he will experience as joy. Only an affective experience of the joy of adequately knowing could explain the formation of a desire to know more and better. True, one is often in error concerning what is really a source of joy and strengthening, and men do in fact find themselves alienated by their passions, transported totally outside of themselves and their own power over themselves. But the affectivity *at the heart of adequate knowledge* that guides desire towards new objects is not misleading.[7] Only a desire can generate a desire, only a power can be modified into another power, and that holds whether one is at the level of adequate or inadequate knowledge. We can thus understand E5P28 to mean that the *joy* felt during the formation of common notions, that is, the increase in the essential power of existing and in the desire to exist, explains the birth of the desire to know by the third kind of knowledge. It seems to me important to underline the necessary role of affectivity to explain the self-generation of desire. In fact, it is this same desire which, modified into joy, acquires by this very fact the power to provide itself with new objects of joy, and thus desire that which gave birth to it: adequate knowledge.

But this raises a theoretical problem. For why would we not remain at the level of rational knowledge, and why would we want to know by

---

[6] G ii, 297; C i, 609.

[7] Or more exactly, this affectivity is not interpreted erroneously. Indeed, I do not believe that affectivity is ever misleading in Spinoza, even if the judgement that derives from it can be: affectivity is the very expression of being, and is in itself necessarily true; it's just that it can be linked by the mind to inadequate causes when the mind has insufficient knowledge.

the *third* kind of knowledge, if this third kind of knowledge were unknown to us? If we did not have, starting with rational knowledge, the affective experience of the joy of intuitively knowing? It seems to me that this problem only arises, and becomes theoretically insurmountable, if one separates rational knowledge from intuitive knowledge. In other words, if one posits an essential difference between reason and intuition, one cannot understand the emergence from the midst of reason of a desire to know intuitively, rather than rationally over again. In my view, this clearly demonstrates the necessity of uniting them. Although many agree on minimizing the separation between the two, they have not exposed the full extent of the logical implications of anchoring intuition in reason. For the distinction between the two knowledges cannot be ontological: the two knowledges must logically *always* be given together, being in reality the same knowledge, but simply under two different modalities. Before turning to the explanation of my own solution to this problem, I would like briefly to recall the traditional view of intuition in the Spinoza literature.

H. G. Hubbeling, in his authoritative book on Spinoza's methodology,[8] retraces very clearly the sources of Spinoza's distinction between reason and intuition in the philosophical tradition. Platonistic in its origins, the distinction between discursive reasoning and intuition took the form of a very common distinction between *ratio* and *intellectus* in the Middle Ages. As Hubbeling clearly puts it, 'The first faculty forms general concepts out of sense data by means of abstraction, the second guides man to ideas that are free from any sense experience and gives him a direct contemplation of God.'[9] The resemblance between this statement and what Spinoza presents in the *Ethics* is patent. How could one not be struck by the similarity between Spinoza's passages about the intellectual love of God that accompanies the third kind of knowledge, and the medieval idea of a free contemplation of God? It is precisely due to this similarity of vocabulary that mystical interpretations of Spinoza have arisen,[10] and they may surely claim to have a certain basis in the texts. However, the similarity between the medieval conception of intuition and that of Spinoza may well be restricted by Spinoza's particular take

    [8] H. G. Hubbeling, *Spinoza's Methodology* (Assen:Van Gorcum & Prakke, 2nd edn., 1967).
    [9] Ibid., 17.
    [10] See for instance Jon Wetlesen, *The Sage and the Way. Spinoza's Ethics of Freedom* (Assen:Van Gorcum, 1979).

on these concepts. After all, it is well known that Spinoza appropriated terms inherited from the tradition—either Scholastic or Cartesian— and transformed them for his own purposes (e.g. substance, mode, etc.). Hubbeling reminds us in the same chapter that in contrast to the scholastic way, Spinoza is not consistent in his use of *intellectus*, and that he uses it when talking both about reason and about intuition. So the question can legitimately be asked: is Spinoza's conception of intuition exactly the same as that of the tradition, i.e. radically separate from 'reason', understood as the faculty of discursive reasoning?

Hubbeling's own explanation of the different kinds of knowledge does not provide us with a clear answer to this question, but there is a useful clue he brings to our understanding of it.[11] For him, there is in Spinoza an intrinsic problem of reconciling his deductive method, which needs general concepts as a starting point (i.e. the definitions), and his nominalism, which leads him to reject all general concepts as abstract and to criticize them as 'universal notions.'[12] Specifically, Hubbeling stresses that Spinoza speaks of reason in the *Treatise on the Improvement of the Understanding* with less respect than in the *Ethics* or in the *Short Treatise* because in the first, this kind of knowledge is said to provide us with universal notions, whereas in the two others it forms common notions, giving real knowledge.[13] Whether this is a matter of evolution or not (a thesis hard to defend, since the writing of the *Short Treatise* is considered prior to that of the *Treatise on the Improvement of the Understanding*), it is clear that Hubbeling points to a major source of differentiation in the understanding of reason in its relation to true knowledge. Furthermore, relying on Letter 12, he seems to minimize the difference between reason and intuition in Spinoza's definite conception.[14] The difference here is drawn only between imagination, i.e. knowledge of the first kind, and 'true knowledge', which in Spinoza

---

[11] It must be noted that he offers a bolder interpretation in an article published in 1986: 'The Third Way of Knowledge (Intuition) in Spinoza', *Studia Spinozana*, 2 (1986), 219–31. In this article, he clearly says that reason and intuition are not as different from one another as is commonly held, and even that 'the whole of Spinoza's philosophy is now presented in the second way. Thus, the great advantage of the third way is diminished' (p. 229). However, I have chosen to use his 1967 book instead because its main thesis has no equivalent in the more recent paper, and seems more promising to me. [12] Hubbeling, *Methodology*, 20–3.

[13] Ibid., 13–14.

[14] 'For we can conceive everything in two ways, either abstractly by means of our senses or in itself by means of reason. True knowledge is knowing things in God, *sub specie aeternitatis*' (ibid. 29).

refers to both the second and third kinds of knowledge. For Hubbeling, the confusion present in the text between the two adequate kinds of knowledge, which takes the form of a problem of reconciling knowledge by common notions (reason) with knowledge of the thing's essence (intuition), is itself nothing but a consequence of the original and crucial problem of Spinoza's methodology.[15] The deductive method considers the common notions as a sufficient source for true knowledge. However, on Hubbeling's reading, common notions are left behind in Spinoza's nominalism, which leads him to the idea of an intuition of the *particular* thing in the light of eternity. Hence, on this view, the problem of reconciling the two kinds of adequate knowledge is left open, and the texts are deemed to be ambiguous. Hubbeling is definitely right in saying that they are, despite the fact that many interpreters do not seem to have found the ambiguity to be very problematic.

Let us look more closely at the interpretation of the leaders of Spinoza scholarship in the Anglo-American and French traditions of the twentieth century, for each initiated a very different view of Spinoza's theory of knowledge.

In the Anglo-American world, it was Harry Austryn Wolfson's comprehensive interpretation of Spinoza, *The Philosophy of Spinoza* (1934),[16] that oriented all subsequent approaches to Spinoza by English-speaking scholars. His influence has been determinative, and his insistence on Spinoza's inheritance from the medieval sources, in particular, has never or seldom been put into question in this tradition. As a result of this reliance on Wolfson, Spinoza seems always to have been considered as the thinker who made a superb synthesis of the problems of the tradition, particularly those of the medieval and modern traditions, but who, after all, made *nothing but* a synthesis of them, without 'innovating' in the true sense of the term. The same holds for Spinoza's conception of knowledge, which Wolfson makes conscious efforts to reduce entirely to Saadia's,[17] despite the fact that it requires distorting the text in many respects. This violence done to Spinoza's writings is particularly evident, for example, in Wolfson's invention of three features within the second

---

[15] Hubbeling, *Methodology,* 30.

[16] H. A. Wolfson, *The Philosophy of Spinoza. Unfolding the Latent Processes of his Reasoning* (Cambridge, Mass.: Harvard University Press, 1948; 2 vols. in 1; 1st edn., 1934).

[17] Ibid. ii. 132.

kind of knowledge: (*a*) simple ideas, (*b*) common notions, and (*c*) deductions drawn from these two as in a syllogism, although he recognizes that Spinoza only explicitly mentions one, i.e. common notions.[18] It is no surprise, then, to see that Wolfson argues that Spinoza's view of reason differs greatly from that of intuition, as is the case in the philosophical tradition he merely follows.[19]

Because of Wolfson's great influence, the similarity between the two kinds of adequate knowledge has rarely been considered a valuable subject matter for Anglo-American interpreters, as if the question had been solved once and for all.[20] In the French tradition, however, which was until recently unaware of English-speaking philosophy,[21] the opposite approach was adopted. Far from being crushed under the weight of a giant and all-inclusive tradition, Spinoza was rediscovered at the end of the 1960s and considered a truly innovative thinker—often excessively, as if someone could philosophize in isolation from any history of ideas. Indeed, if he was read in regard to a tradition, it was almost exclusively Cartesianism. Just as any Anglo-American approach to Spinoza in the twentieth century was made through the lens of Wolfson and bears his mark, any French reading of Spinoza up to the end of the 1980s was made through the lens of two or three major interpreters, namely Martial Gueroult, Gilles Deleuze, and, to a lesser extent, Alexandre Matheron.[22] This multiplicity of leading interpretations, as well as the

[18] 'Under the second kind of knowledge he is going to mention only the common notions which form the basis of knowledge derived from them by the art of reasoning . . . It is these which in Propositions XLIV–XLVI Spinoza identifies with the common notions—one of the three subject-matters of the second kind of knowledge' (ibid. ii. 158).

[19] 'The common notions of Spinoza's second kind of knowledge, like the immediate premises in Aristotle's demonstrative knowledge, are ultimately in their final analysis traceable to sense-perception. They are considered to be the work of the intellect only because it is the intellect which transforms these sense-perceptions into scientific universal notions. Spinoza's third kind of knowledge, however, is of a different nature. It has no connection with sense-perception at all' (ibid. ii. 155).

[20] An important exception in this respect is Errol E. Harris, who does not draw such a sharp distinction between reason and intuition. See for example *Spinoza's Philosophy: An Outline* (New Jersey: Humanities Press, 1992), 48: '*Scientia intuitiva* is not below or less than reason, but beyond it. It is reason raised to its highest power, the intellect functioning with consummate efficiency, the ultimate grasp of reality as it is in the intellect of God.'

[21] For instance, it is only very recently that Wolfson's book was translated into French: *La philosophie de Spinoza: pour démêler l'implicite d'une argumentation*, trans. Anne-Dominique Balmès (Paris: Gallimard, 1999).

[22] See Martial Gueroult, *Spinoza*, 2 vols. (Paris: Aubier-Montaigne, 1968 and 1974); Gilles Deleuze, *Spinoza et le problème de l'expression* (Paris: Éditions de Minuit, 1968), trans. Martin

proximity of other philosophical trends in Europe (particularly German interpretations), makes it more difficult to discern one major voice speaking in French Spinoza literature, but it should be noted that these three readings do not disagree on any fundamental point of interpretation either. And in the 1990s, a new Spinoza scholarship was developed in France (under the influence of Pierre-François Moreau, Alexandre Matheron, Pierre Macherey, and others), working in intense conjunction with Spinoza societies and scholars in Europe, especially in The Netherlands and in Italy, toward a more 'empiricist' and 'ethics-directed' reading of Spinoza. The interpretation I put forward in this essay pertains to this latest trend. And in this whole French tradition, the continuity of the second with the third kind of knowledge is very commonly acknowledged (although the two are not united to the extent I wish to show they are).

Gueroult and Deleuze both theorized the continuity of the two kinds by saying that common notions lead the mind to an idea of God as the cause of everything, which accounts for the transition to the knowledge proceeding from God's essence to 'the adequate knowledge of the essence of things' (*E*2P40S2), i.e. intuitive knowledge. In addition, they both relate this transition to the question I am starting from, i.e. that of the birth of the effort to know by the third kind of knowledge in the second. Gueroult offers no detailed account of this transition from one to the other.[23] Deleuze, on the other hand, offers a more extended explanation of the relation between reason (or knowledge by common notions) and intuition, devoting a chapter of his *Expressionism in Philosophy: Spinoza* to it.[24] He explains how the idea of God effects the transition: all common notions lead to God as the universal cause of everything, but in so far as the idea of God is not itself a common notion, since it is individual, it helps the mind to transcend knowledge by

---

Joughin: *Expressionism in Philosophy: Spinoza* (New York: Zone Books, 1992); and Alexandre Matheron, *Individu et communauté chez Spinoza* (Paris: Éditions de Minuit, 1969).

[23] See Gueroult, *Spinoza, ii*, esp. 467–71: 'The effort to know through the third kind of knowledge arises from the second as well as from the third kind of knowledge (*E*5P28). It can arise from the second kind, as it is obvious that when the mind raises itself by Reason to know that all things depend on the very necessity of God's eternal nature (*E*2P44C2), it is naturally led to know these things through the cause that produces them, that is, through God, and to deduce their essence from the formal essence of those attributes of God of which the mind has an adequate idea; that is, it is led to know things through knowledge of the third kind' (471).

[24] Deleuze, *Expressionism*, 289–301.

common notions and to discover knowledge through essence.[25] Deleuze even asks himself, in a footnote, if those two kinds of knowledge should be considered one, but he gives a very nuanced—and finally timid—answer to this 'complex problem'.[26] Finally, Matheron went a step further again by acknowledging a sort of *unity* of the two kinds of knowledge in 1969. But once again, the explanation is condensed in a few pages and, particularly, in a footnote that intends to make a synthesis of those pages, but in fact adds the very elements of unity or circularity that lack development in the body of the text.[27] In sum, this idea of continuity between, or even unity of, the second and third kinds of knowledge as an explanation of the transition from the one to the other is definitely promising, but it seems to be truncated in these authors.

We have seen that this view is almost completely lacking in Anglo-American interpretations of Spinoza because of Wolfson's long-lasting influence and authority. Although traditional interpretations of Spinoza's theory of adequate knowledge do not insist on the fundamental unity of its two kinds, or even contradict it, it seems to me necessary to see reason and intuition as two angles of the same knowledge, this logical necessity simply following from the question of the transition from the second to the third kind of knowledge. It is precisely the coherence of this hypothesis that I will attempt to demonstrate in what follows.

THE 'MOMENTS' OF ADEQUATE KNOWLEDGE

As *E*2P40S1 indicates, for Spinoza, universals, transcendentals, and general notions do not correspond to anything existing; rather, they are

[25] Ibid. 299: 'The idea of God thus plays in the *Ethics* a pivotal role . . . (1) Every common notion leads us to the idea of God. As related to the common notions which express it, the idea of God itself belongs to the second kind of knowledge. It represents, in this respect, an impassive God; but the idea accompanies all the joys that flow from our power of understanding (insofar as this power proceeds through common notions). The idea of God is thus the limiting point of the second kind of knowledge. (2) But although it necessarily relates to common notions, the idea of God is not itself a common notion. So it propels us into a new element. We can come to the idea of God only through the second kind of knowledge; but in arriving at the idea we are determined to leave behind the second kind of knowledge, and enter into a new state. In the second kind of knowledge, the idea of God serves as a basis of the third; and by "basis" must be understood the true driving force, the *causa fiendi*. This idea of God will then change its content, taking on another content in the third kind of knowledge to which it determines us.'

[26] Ibid. 300 n. 34: 'To what extent are ideas of the second and third kinds the same ideas? Are they differentiated only by their function and use? The problem is a complex one . . .'.

[27] See Matheron, *Individu et communauté*, esp. 580–2, with the important n. 42.

purely fictitious constructions of the imagination. There thus can be no 'knowledge' of them in the proper meaning of the term, as they are nothings, empty objects. If one wants to avoid making the *Ethics'* knowledge by common notions into a nothingness of knowledge, that is, into a purely abstract knowledge, one must assume that this knowledge corresponds to the understanding of that which is common to everything *among finitely existing things*; or to the grasp of that in the universal which is contained in the *particular*, if one prefers to continue using this term. What matters is to see that all knowledge remains a knowledge of what exists, and that what exists always presents itself to us in the first place under a modified, finite form. The interpretation of adequate knowledge that I am proposing respects the idea that knowledge is always and above all knowledge of the particular. By that, I mean that the object of rational knowledge and that of intuitive knowledge are fundamentally the same, namely, a particular existing object in nature. Knowledge loops back on itself in passing through a knowledge of what is *involved* in the mind, namely, the infinite divine power, which allows knowledge to be determined differently (one passes from knowledge *sub duratione* to knowledge *sub specie aeternitatis*). But there no more exists an abstract, adequate knowledge than there are abstract beings. Adequate knowledge remains knowledge of a particular existing thing.

Let us take a simple example. I perceive a desk in front of me. My inadequate knowledge of this desk is a particular knowledge; it expresses the precise way in which my body is affected by it. If now I have an adequate knowledge of the desk in front of me, which I obviously continue to perceive through the imagination, this is because I see that in it which expresses common notions. Not 'general notions', refuted from the outset in the first Scholium to *E*2P40 by Spinoza's nominalist position (thus I do not suddenly see 'deskness' through the desk), but I see what is common to every body without exception, and which corresponds in particular to the finite, mediate modes of extension that are motion and rest, and to their properties—like dimension, surface, etc. (note that common notions are characterized as ideas concerning the attribute of extension).[28] Adequately conceiving this desk simply means

---

[28] See *E*2P38: 'Those things which are common to all, and which are equally in the part and in the whole, can only be conceived adequately' (G ii, 118; C i, 474); its demonstration, which is carried out only with reference to bodies; and its corollary: 'From this it follows that there are

understanding that the desk, like all things, is a particular expression of infinite power (the infinite power of being extended in this case). That means understanding its necessity through its divine cause. Thus, in my knowledge by common notions of the desk in front of me, I have a perception of the infinite power that it involves. I also have an idea of myself as being in the truth, and so of the infinite power of thinking—this point will be developed shortly. This is the 'ascending' angle of the loop.

Now, working from this perception of divine power and eternity, I come back to the particular thing, no longer as it appeared to me in a determinate time and space, with such-and-such a form, colour, height, etc., but to its essence, which is simply a degree of power. I then see this desk—inanimate though it may be—as a particular part of the whole of nature, of the infinite power of nature. This is the 'descending' angle of the loop, that which 'proceeds from an adequate idea of the formal essence of certain attributes of God to the adequate knowledge of the essence of things' (*E*2P40S2).[29] And this is intuition; we can see that the definition of intuitive science given in the second Scholium of Proposition 40 of *Ethics* II is contained in this quotation. Knowledge returns to the particular object to be known by means of grasping the infinite divine power that is expressed by it. But this remains the same knowledge, due to the Spinozistic notion of the involvement or implication of the cause in the effect, such that one cannot know the effect without simultaneously knowing the cause, as stated in the important Axiom 4.[30]

---

certain ideas, *or* notions, common to all men. For (by Lemma 2) all bodies agree in certain things, which (by P38) must be perceived adequately, *or* clearly and distinctly, by all' (G ii, 119; C i, 474). It seems that rational knowledge can be realized only on the basis of a perception concerning the attribute of extension, and knowledge of the attribute of thought follows secondarily (on the logical plane) from knowledge by common notions. Knowledge of the infinite mediate mode of the attribute of thought is simply not explicitly presented as the inevitable passage towards knowledge of the attribute of thought, and the mystery surrounding it thus remains. Note that the infinite mediate mode of thought has been characterized by Gueroult, in order to make up for the silence of Letter 64 to Schuller, as 'the universe of existing ideas that the attribute produces absolutely through the intermediary of essences generating their existences' (Gueroult, *Spinoza, i.* 318). It has been very differently characterized as 'the infinite love that God bears toward himself' by Jean-Marie Beyssade; see 'Sur le mode infini médiat dans l'attribut pensée. Du problème (lettre 64) à une solution,' *Revue philosophique de la France et de l'étranger*, 119/1 (1994), 23–6. However, I cannot try to settle this thorny question here.

[29] G ii, 122; C i, 478.

[30] *E*1Ax4, G ii, 46 (Ci. 410): 'The knowledge of an effect depends on, and involves (*involvit*), the knowledge of its cause.'

If I may schematically summarize what I am proposing before going into a more rigorous examination: one can divide reason and intuition into two 'moments' each, provided that we understand the 'moments' in question here not as moments in time, which would be meaningless, but as simultaneous and simply logically distinct steps of a knowledge that 'involves' different objects in order to return to itself, particularizing itself in the course of this logical journey.

In rational knowledge, according to the *Ethics*, my first perception is of whatever the body that is the object of my idea has in common with all other things: this is the first moment of rational knowledge. It does not yet provide a conception of the essence of the thing, but only a conception of a general characteristic, which moreover is identified in relation to extension.

The fact that I possess this true idea immediately implies an awareness of being in the truth, a doubling back on itself of knowledge in the form of certainty (see *E*2P21S, *E*2P43 and D, *KV* 2/2 and 3, *TIE* 34): 'As soon as someone knows something, he thereby knows that he knows it, and at the same time knows that he knows that he knows, and so on, to infinity' (*E*2P21S).[31] For, as theorized in paragraphs 33–35 of the *Treatise of the Emendation of the Intellect*, this awareness, this idea of an idea, this 'knowing oneself knowing', or this certainty, is nothing other than the objective essence of my mind, which finally experiences itself as it is in God, as the adequate idea of a thing, and does this in a doubling-back that is unlimited because it takes itself as an object indefinitely. This is the second moment of rational knowledge: the mind knowing itself in its own power, that is, as it discovers the infinite power that it involves. This is the 'moment' related to the attribute of thought as we can reconstruct it from the *Short Treatise* and the *Treatise on the Emendation of the Intellect*. Moreover, if one takes into account the introduction of common notions in the *Ethics*, one can say that in grasping a characteristic common to all bodies in one's true idea of a thing, the mind at the same time understands the power of expressing a certain constitutive ratio of motion and rest, and thus discovers the infinite power of the attribute of extension.

In doing so, the mind has 'the adequate idea of the essence of certain attributes of God': this is the starting point for the third kind of knowledge.

---

[31] G ii, 109; C i, 468.

The idea of the attribute of *thought* is provided to the mind by the unlimited doubling-back of its self-consciousness given with each true idea, that is, by the fact that when it fuses with its own objective essence, it experiences God's infinite power of thought. And as far as the adequate idea of *extension* given to the mind is concerned, the common notions of the *Ethics* constitute the mind's access to grasping the power of the attribute of extension, thanks to the recognition of extension's power acting in all bodies.

The mind then 'proceeds' from the infinite to the finite in returning to the particular object of its knowledge, conceived as a part of this infinite power. This is the second 'moment' of intuition: in other words, the mind has the intuition of the essence, of itself, *and* of the thing on the basis of its experience of the infinite power, this essence being simply a precise and unique degree of power.

Note that my way of characterizing the 'moments' follows the dual structure of Spinoza's expressions to designate them: as can be seen in the citations given above, it is said that the mind is conscious of itself or of being in the truth 'at the same time' that it knows a thing through reason, and it is said that intuitive knowledge 'proceeds' from a certain idea or knowledge to another. Indeed, the very idea that I am proposing concerning an ultimate complementarity between reason and intuition—at the heart of a 'circular', adequate, global knowledge of a given object—rests on the fact that the second moment of rational knowledge is identical to the first moment of intuitive knowledge, that is, that of the knowledge of the essence of (i.e. of the power proper to) the attribute of thought and the attribute of extension. Adequate knowledge of a particular thing, single despite its two angles, quite simply is that which apprehends what the mind involves: the divine power. And given that its object is a state of power, this apprehension is an affective knowledge, as will be shown in what follows.

THE MOMENTS CORRESPONDING TO AN AFFECTIVE EXPERIENCE

Now that this tentative characterization of the 'circular' journey of adequate knowledge has been carried out, I can turn to my main goal by trying to discern in this journey the affective moments that would allow me to demonstrate: (1) the birth of the desire to know by the third kind of knowledge at the heart of rational knowledge, which would explain the automatic transition from reason to intuition; (2) the birth of a desire to know adequately other objects, which this time would be produced at the heart of the third kind of knowledge, since it is clear that no one is content with intuitive knowledge of *one* thing, but that one would want to know as many things as possible by this kind of knowledge. I am seeking affective moments here because, as I explained above, only desire can generate desire. It is thus a matter of identifying, from among the elements relative to adequate knowledge (of the second or third kind), those qualified by Spinoza in affective terms or terms concerned with feeling. My intent is to conduct this study by re-examining each of the logical 'moments' in order to find the affective mainspring of the automatism of knowledge.

The first moment is the perception of a thing using common notions, or the conceiving of any true idea: this moment is purely perceptual; its object is the particular thing. Here we are at the limit between comparative imagination and reason. There is no apparent affectivity in this grasp of the object through reason.

Then follows (on the logical plane, not the temporal one) the moment of certainty, or of the mind's self-consciousness: this knowledge is an affective experience of power, as evidenced by the vocabulary of experience used on this subject in the *Treatise on the Emendation of the Intellect*, notably in the following passage from paragraph 34: 'Everyone can experience this, when he sees that he knows what Peter is, and also knows that he knows, and again, knows that he knows that he knows, etc.'[32] Or by the vocabulary of feeling in paragraph 35: 'certainty is nothing but the objective essence itself, i.e. the mode by which we are aware of [*sentimus*, 'we feel'] the formal essence is certainty itself.'[33] This experience is that of an *increase* in the power of thought, which the mind can experience only joyously: this moment is thus eminently 'affective'. As for the *object* of this knowledge at its 'second' moment, it is a certain type of power, an infinite power which in the *Ethics* is grasped in extension through the common notions, as much as in thought through self-consciousness. In

---

[32] *TIE* 34, G ii, 14; C i, 18.

[33] *TIE* 35, G ii, 15; C i, 18. Curley's translation does not reflect the affective dimension evident in the Latin.

sum, this 'moment' is the apprehension of the power involved both in our mind and in the particular body. One could further adduce as proof of the affective character of this knowledge the fact that a secondary form of it corresponds to the *amor erga Deum*, the mind's love towards God which accompanies its self-consciousness,[34] which clearly shows, if further evidence were needed, that the knowledge given to the mind here is a joy.[35]

Moment 'three', that of the knowledge of the attributes, from which the formal essence of the particular thing is deduced, can be identified with the preceding moment, or else can be seen as its immediate logical consequence. In that case, what one deduces from the affective grasp of the infinite divine power is its property of eternity. The third moment thus could correspond, through knowledge of the power of thought and of the power to express a certain proportion of motion and rest, to the understanding of the *necessity* for substance to exist and to modify itself through an infinity of forms (including the particular form that one finds in the fourth moment in deducing it logically, almost arithmetically, from its eternal possibility of coming into existence). The necessity for substance to exist in a determinate form is none other than a particular mode's eternal possibility of existing, an eternal possibility that constitutes its own eternity (one can already catch a glimpse here of the fourth moment, the descent back down to the particular).[36] This eternity corresponds to the eternal possibility of an existing essence, in the sense that, by existing, it detaches itself from the pure abstractness of the arithmetical infinity of possible essences—like a blank wall on which a particular essence detaches itself by its transition to existence, says Spinoza (*KV* 2/20 Adn 3,8), or again like rectangles which, once

---

[34] 'He who understands himself and his affects clearly and distinctly loves God, and does so the more, the more he understands himself and his affects' (*E*5P15, G ii, 290; C i, 603). See also *E*5P14.

[35] I leave to one side the question of '*acquiescientia (Mentis, sui, in se ipso . . .)*', which by itself would require a separate study.

[36] An excellent explanation of the meaning of the eternal essence of a particular body can be found in an article by A. Matheron, 'La vie éternelle et le corps selon Spinoza', *Revue philosophique de la France et de l'étranger*, 119/1 (1994), 27–40. See esp. pp. 38–9: 'To conceive the essence of a thing under the aspect of eternity, consequently, is to conceive the thing itself, as a real being, on the basis of God's essence: it is to conceive it through God and to understand that, from the mere fact that it is conceived by God, it must necessarily exist at some time or other . . . Thus, to the degree that we *are* this eternal idea, we ourselves are, for all eternity, the knowledge of the third kind of the essence of our body and of our mind that God forms.'

they have been drawn inside a circle, are distinguished from the infinity of other rectangles one could draw (E2P28S). The 'third' moment, the first moment of intuition, is thus quite obviously the moment of an experience of power, which one can furthermore understand as the experience of an essential property of infinite power: its eternity, that is, the necessity of its existence.

As for the last moment, that of the understanding of the inclusion of a particular essence in this infinite essence and its properties, this is also the moment of an idea of power, not infinite this time, but finite: one puts the eternal essence of the particular thing, in so far as this has been actualized, back into the midst of this infinity of possibilities. This understanding, the *Short Treatise* affirms, is an awareness and an enjoyment of the thing itself: 'We call that clear knowledge which comes not from being convinced by reasons, but from being aware of and enjoying the thing itself. This goes far beyond the others.'[37] It corresponds to knowledge of the thing *sub specie aeternitatis*, it being understood that knowledge of eternity is necessarily implied in the apprehension of the particular thing as a finite mode of infinite and eternal substance.

Is it possible that this affective understanding, inasmuch as it is the idea of a certain power, is logically also the feeling or *experience* of eternity that Spinoza refers to in the Scholium of Proposition 23 through the expression 'we feel and know by experience that we are eternal'?[38] I think so, and in fact I can see no decisive reason for denying it. Let us briefly examine the terms of the affirmation contained in this Scholium: the 'we' refers to all men; the verbs designate a sensation or a feeling (*sentimus*) and an experience undergone (*experimur*: we have an experience of, we experiment); 'that we are eternal' refers indeed to individual eternity, not to abstract substantial eternity. Faced with the choice between the sensation and feeling as the referent of '*sentimus*', I would have to choose the affective referent of 'feeling', which is the only one which conforms to the fact that it is not the body which feels, but the mind. Evidence for this is found in the following quotation, and in particular the connection made between 'feeling' and memory:[39] 'Though we do not recollect that we existed before the body, we nevertheless *feel* that our mind, insofar as

---

[37] *KV* 2/2, no. 2, G i, 55; C i, 99.

[38] 'Sentimus, experimurque, nos aeternos esse' (*E*5P23S, G ii, 296; C i, 607–8).

[39] The following sentence affirms this: 'For the mind feels those things that it conceives in understanding no less than those that it has in the memory' (G ii, 296; C i, 608).

it involves the essence of the body under a species of eternity (*quatenus Corporis essentiam sub specie aeternitatis involvit*), is eternal.'[40] This last sentence allows us to see clearly that the mind feels its eternity in so far as the eternity of its body is *involved* (*quatenus . . . involvit*) in its own essence: in other words, the eternity felt by the mind is both its own eternity and that of the body, but this sensation of self is mediated by the eternity included, involved, in the essence itself. There is thus a mediation here that is similar to the circular schema I am proposing for the mind's movement through the divine power that it *involves* in order to know adequately a particular thing, of which the ascending side of the circle is called 'reason' and the descending side 'intuition'.

It is difficult to conceive of any other experience of one's eternity than that which could be provided by the affective moments at the heart of adequate knowledge identified above. My reading of experiential affectivity and eternity in Spinoza, largely and generally inspired by the works of Pierre-François Moreau[41] and Chantal Jaquet,[42] here radically departs from them in that it sees in the experience of eternity a necessarily *adequate* structure of knowledge. Neither of them are willing to grant this, since, according to them, experience in Spinoza's works is always linked to inadequate knowledge, is always 'vague' (*experientia vaga*). But it is certain that for one thing, there exist active affects for Spinoza, and that for another, Spinoza refers to an affect (and incidentally identifies it with an experience) in the Scholium of a proposition which, by its very position after *E*5P20S, concerns adequate knowledge (in the Scholium to Proposition 23 of *Ethics* V). Moreover, I have clearly identified the affective moments at the heart of the circle of adequate knowledge that would be excellent candidates for corresponding to the moment when the mind has consciousness of itself as eternal. The 'feeling' of eternity or the (adequate) affective knowledge of eternity itself referred to in *E*5P23 *could* then very well be the intuition of its own

---

[40] *E*5P23S, G ii, 296; C i, 608 (italics added).

[41] Pierre-François Moreau, *Spinoza. L'expérience et l'éternité* (Paris: Presses Universitaires de France, 1994). We owe to this work an innovative element that is absolutely fundamental to Spinoza studies, namely, the interest it takes in experience, which until then had been unjustly looked down upon. My own work is heir to this new understanding of Spinoza's 'rationalism', although I take this understanding beyond the limits assigned to it by Moreau.

[42] Chantal Jaquet, *Sub specie aeternitatis. Études des concepts de temps, durée et éternité chez Spinoza* (Paris: Kimé, 1997).

essence given to a mind that takes itself as its object, or, quite simply, that conceives any true idea at all.[43]

EXPLANATION OF *E5P26* AND 28 THROUGH
THE NOTION OF AFFECTIVITY

Before examining here some of the problems connected to this view, it would be appropriate to show in what way this identification of the affective phases in the two kinds of adequate knowledge are relevant to explaining the formation of the desire to know at its different levels.

One does indeed find an experience of power, or an affective structure, which allows the mind to desire to know a thing from the standpoint (or under the aspect) of the eternity it involves[44] as soon as that thing is grasped through reason. This is the structure of self-consciousness, or of the certainty of the mind that immediately 'doubles back' every true idea it conceives. This immediate reflexive structure seems to correspond to a logical effect that is simultaneous with what I earlier called the 'first' moment of rational knowledge: the effect is inevitable, and is besides a form of joy, and thus of a strengthening of the mind by its power of thought. This then is the explanation that can be given for the problem raised by *E5P28*; this joy, like every experience of a specific degree of power, has the power to generate the desire for its own strengthening. The first moment of intuition itself just is this experience, in so far as this experience includes knowledge of the principal property of the infinite divine power, namely, its eternity or its necessary self-expression.

---

[43] The most logical course, in my view, is to say that it is an *intuition* that is given in the experience or feeling of eternity—which means that this intuition is given to everyone. I will reply below to the objections that could be raised against such a thesis. One might think that this feeling of eternity corresponds exactly to the mind's becoming self-aware, which 'doubles back' the mind's conception of any true idea; that is, that it corresponds to the moment referred to above as the second moment of rational knowledge. More specifically, the inclusion of the notion of eternity in self-consciousness leads me to think that we are already at the first moment of intuition, then, which almost coincides with the preceding moment, but corresponds, according to the logical divisions I am proposing, to the (also affective) knowledge of eternity as a property of God's attributes. Since the difference between reason and intuition indeed seems negligible here, because the first is transmuted automatically and necessarily into the second, it does not strike me as useful to determine more exactly at what precise 'moment' the feeling of eternity enters into it.

[44] Curley's standard translation of *sub specie aeternitatis* as 'under a species of eternity' seems more confusing than the paraphrases proposed here.

In intuition's two moments, one also has an experience of infinite power (God's attributes in so far as they are eternal) and of finite power (the formal essence of a particular thing). Once one has 'looped the loop', that is, once the mind has returned to the particular object it started from, it feels within itself such a strengthening and such a joy that it can only desire to know more things in this manner. That is why, even if a few true ideas do not a wise man make, our mind has the power of perfecting itself in order to come as close as possible to wisdom, in seeking to know more and more objects in an adequate manner. In doing this, it first relates to God the objects that affect it in the imaginative mode, and it 'has the power' to do so (*E*5P14). In other words, it orders its affections (which still exist) according to an order suitable to the understanding (see *E*5P10 and S), an order that agrees with its essence such as this essence is grasped objectively in God.[45] Following this, the mind which has known certain objects through the properties of the divine attributes, and so through the eternity included in their essence, desires to know more and more objects in the same manner, *sub specie aeternitatis*.

This is what Proposition 26 of Part V of the *Ethics* calls our attention to, a proposition that is itself inexplicable without the joy's power to account for the self-perpetuation of cognitive progress: 'The more the mind is capable of understanding things by the third kind of knowledge, the more it desires to understand them by this kind of knowledge.'[46] For, as if anyone needed reminding, it is this knowledge of the third kind which results in the highest joy or the mind's highest satisfaction,[47] and also the highest form of love,[48] as the mind's intellectual love of God is but a secondary form of this affect of joy.

This is how one can reply to the problem of the interpretation of Proposition 28 of Part V of the *Ethics* with which we began. Before concluding, however, I should examine some of the problems involved in this reading and attempt to resolve them, even though I recognize that the theme of adequate knowledge and its modalities in Spinoza is extremely complex. The explanation I offer here is merely tentative.

---

[45] For a more detailed exposition of this point, see Matheron, 'Vie éternelle', 29.

[46] *E*5P26; G ii, 297; C i, 608.

[47] See *E*5P32D: 'From this [third] kind of knowledge there arises the greatest satisfaction of mind there can be, i.e. joy' (G ii, 300; C i, 611 [altered]).   [48] See *E*5P32C and P36S.

EXAMINATION OF TWO PRINCIPAL OBJECTIONS

Two questions or objections seem to arise quite legitimately from an examination of the reading I have proposed. The first concerns the access to intuition that is supposedly given to everyone, according to my explanation; the second asks to what extent this explanation can account for *everything* that is said about intuition in Spinoza's different works.

If one accepts the division of knowledge into two large kinds (i.e. inadequate and adequate knowledge), instead of into three or four, one is led to regard reason and intuition as two logical steps of the same grasp of the object from the standpoint of eternity. Intuition would be automatically implicated, 'involved', in rational knowledge: whoever has a true idea necessarily also has an intuition. Nonetheless, as the final sentences of the last Scholium of the *Ethics* remind us, the road to wisdom is hard, and those who attain it are rare. From which arises the following question: does not this reading result in diminishing the specificity of the wise man by making everyone wise?

No, simply because having a few true ideas, and even a few intuitive ideas thereby, is not yet to be a wise man. Exactly the same problem arises concerning the feeling of eternity, clearly attributed to everyone by the collective 'we' of *E5P23S*, and which one *can* nevertheless consider characteristic of intuitive knowledge, as I showed earlier. I cannot agree with the notion that the fact that the experience of eternity is shared generally among men proves that it is not included in adequate knowledge, or more particularly, in intuitive knowledge. This disparaging conception of the experience of eternity in relation to intuition persists, rather paradoxically in my view, even at the core of the interpretations that have contributed the most in recent years to the rehabilitation of experience in Spinoza; it takes the form of a difference between 'felt eternity' and 'known eternity.'[49] The main argument in favour of the idea that the experience of eternity is not identical to the conception of the self *sub specie aeternitatis*, and that it is not true knowledge, would seem to rely on the Scholium to Proposition 34 of Part V of the *Ethics*, which states that 'If we attend to the common opinion of men, we shall see that they are indeed conscious of the eternity of their mind, but that

---

[49] See Moreau and Jaquet (for the latter, see esp. pp. 98 f.).

they confuse it with duration, and attribute it to the imagination, *or memory*, which they believe remains after death.'[50] The argument consists in saying that if this feeling of eternity given to everyone were a true idea, it would be impossible for it to be as wrongly interpreted as it obviously is.

But if one argues that, then how is one to account for the fact that *all* men have a true idea of God, as Spinoza explicitly says in *E*2P47, and yet interpret it wrongly? The clarification given by Spinoza in the Scholium of *E*2P47, which says that 'men do not have so clear a knowledge of God as they do of the common notions', in no way diminishes the fact that 'God's infinite essence and his eternity are known *to all*' (my emphasis), as Spinoza reiterates at the beginning of the same Scholium. It is precisely this which grounds the possibility for all men to know by the third kind of knowledge. Exactly the same goes for the experience of eternity. And perhaps even 'exactly' in the strict sense, since the true idea of God that each person has can only be the eternity involved in our objective essence that each person can feel or sense when forming any common notion.

The problem with the argument that differentiates between felt eternity and known eternity (which in a way amounts to once again subordinating experience to the understanding instead of uniting the two) is that it seemingly forgets that one does not become free all at once, with a single true idea, but that it is all a question of proportion. The vocabulary of proportion in the last part of the *Ethics* is striking. I will mention here only the most obvious passages (my emphasis):

This love toward God must engage the mind *most (maxime occupare)*. (*E*5P16)[51]

He who has a body capable of doing *a great many things* . . . has a power of ordering and connecting the affections of his body according to the order of the intellect . . . The result is that it is affected with a love of God, which must occupy, *or* constitute *the greatest part of the mind*. Therefore, he has a mind whose *greatest part* is eternal. (*E*5P39D)[52]

The more the mind knows things by the second and third kind of knowledge, *the greater* the part of it that remains, and consequently, *the greater* the part of it that is not touched by affects which are contrary to our nature, i.e. which are evil.

---

[50] *E*5P34S; G ii, 301–2; C i, 611–12.   [51] G ii, 290; C i, 604.

[52] G ii, 305; C i, 614 [altered].

Therefore, *the more* the mind understands things by the second and third kind of knowledge, *the greater* the part of it that remains unharmed, and hence, *the less* it is acted on by affects, etc. (*E*5P38D)[53]

The proportion of true ideas progressively increases relative to the proportion of false ideas: the true conceptions of the understanding are systematically connected to false causes so long as the mind lacks the strength to demonstrate its judgement, which it acquires when the mind is strengthened, and it is strengthened in knowing more things adequately, and so on. Thus we once again come upon 'the circle of adequate knowledge', a circle which fortunately is not vicious—otherwise ethics would be meaningless and vain. Once adequate ideas occupy a proportionally larger amount of the mind than the ideas of the imagination (which continue to affect it), it is possible to infer that its progress is not 'quasi'-automatic, but automatic; for nothing can stop it from knowing still more and better. *This*, then, is wisdom, or an indefinite progression towards wisdom that nothing can stand in the way of any longer. All men, then, have true ideas, and one can say that their common experience of eternity is a true intuition, but this in no way negates the difficulty of attaining 'wisdom'. In a way there would be a quasi-unconscious degree of intuition itself, which would, at the same time as the mind, become more and more conscious of itself, and more and more powerful and luminous, over the course of ethical development.

On a different level, one might ask how my analysis can account for all the passages in his work where Spinoza explains the different kinds (or modes, or types) of knowledge. I certainly recognize that the example of finding the fourth proportional number, offered repeatedly with slight variations each time, might be difficult to make sense of using this framework for interpreting reason and intuition. For it is true that the conception of reason proposed here appears very different from the calculation performed by mathematicians using the rule of proportion that they take from Euclid's proof (*KV* 2/1n03; *TIE* 24; *E*2P40S2). In the way this arithmetical example is presented in the *Ethics*, Spinoza even seems to limit the possibility of intuition to the intuition of small numbers, leaving us to understand that the laborious route of calculation is

---

[53] G ii, 304; C i, 613 [altered].

absolutely necessary for complex numbers, and that consequently one cannot have an intuition of everything.[54] Obviously, the calculation of a number and the intuition of its proportionality seem very different from the adequate knowledge whose two moments I described earlier. But they are also very different from the definition of intuitive knowledge that Spinoza gives in the *Ethics*, because in these examples one finds nothing of common notions or of the formal essences of particular things that are deduced from knowledge of the formal essence of God's attributes, knowing that this divine essence is the absolute power. This is more a problem of the coherence of Spinoza's texts among themselves than of the present interpretation, and other explanatory frameworks must be adopted to account for these diverging explanations offered by Spinoza.[55]

Finally, Spinoza many times over says that one must surpass rational knowledge in order to reach intuitive knowledge. Indeed, this poses a greater problem to my unifying interpretation of reason and intuition. But we may think that the main reason Spinoza makes this claim is simply an ethical one. For if it is greatly preferable to know by intuition,

---

[54] 'But in the simplest numbers none of this [calculation] is necessary. Given the numbers 1, 2, and 3, no one fails to see that the fourth proportional number is 6—and we see this much more clearly because we infer the fourth number from the ratio which, in one glance, we see the first number to have to the second' (E2P40S2; G ii, 122; C i, 478).

[55] One interpretative hypothesis could perhaps explain this problem of internal coherence. Spinoza's discovery of the theory of common notions as the basis of rational knowledge led him to redefine not only reason in the *Ethics*, but also intuition. From the *Short Treatise* onward, there is a noticeable influence of the ancient Greek model of knowledge, which distinguishes reason from intuition and subordinates the former to the latter. This thesis is put forward by Plato (in the passage on the divided line, *Republic* VI. 509d–511e) as well as Aristotle (see *Analytica Posteriora* II. 19, 100b 7–8; *De Anima* III. 3, 428a 4–5; *Metaphysics* XII. 9, 1074b 35–6; and *Nicomachean Ethics* VI, 3, 1139b 16–17), from whom it derived its legitimacy throughout the Middle Ages. The example of the deduction of the fourth proportional number is completely understandable in the context of this heritage from antiquity, which took mathematics and geometry as models. While modifying his theory in the *Ethics*, Spinoza would not have seen the need to change his example, perhaps because he himself was not aware of the different implications of his theory. However, another interpretation of the example of the fourth proportional number can allow us to account more convincingly for the discrepancy between the description and the illustration of intuitive knowledge in the *Ethics* itself. This interpretation presupposes the persistence of two models of intuition throughout the works of Spinoza. The first one, which may be called the 'empirical' model of intuition, is the one referred to in this essay and corresponds to Spinoza's definition of intuition as a deduction of the individual thing's essence from the attributes of God. Its objects are empirical beings. The 'mathematical' model of intuition, on the other hand, corresponds to the example of the fourth proportional number and can be understood as an intellectual process of *use* stemming from repetition. Its

this is because it is at this stage of knowledge that the mind enjoys the greatest satisfaction of which it is capable. The important thing for Spinoza's ethical objectives, in effect, is not so much the object of knowledge as the form of knowledge, not so much the fact of knowing as what knowing brings us. Without this implying the slightest teleology or utilitarianism with respect to the joy that knowledge brings us, we should bear in mind that it is this joy that constitutes our blessedness or beatitude, even though it is included in the adequate *knowledge* of God. That could justify the superiority claimed for intuition over the other kinds of knowledge, since it is at the two moments of 'intuition' that the experience of joy is given.

In conclusion, the main advantage of this 'circular' reading of adequate knowledge seems to me that it allows us to deal with the problem raised by Proposition 28 of Part V of the *Ethics*, and that it explains why progress in knowledge is indefinite, or why one is not content with just one intuitive idea but is 'automatically' moved to know more adequately, once one has reached a certain stage. As it happens, first, this interpretation accounts for the birth from the second kind of knowledge of the desire to know by the third kind by identifying an affective stage in the second kind of knowledge, that of the mind's self-consciousness or certainty, which *necessarily* leads it to experience the infinite power it bears within itself. This consciousness is equivalent to a knowledge of self and of God. Consciousness of the place occupied by things within this universe of power would be given implicitly in the descent back of the circle of knowledge to the particular object. Second, one can understand why the progress of knowledge can have no end, and is in a position to generate itself in order to give itself the desire to know new objects with the same clarity. For we have seen that the two moments that can be distinguished in intuition correspond to affective experiences, and thus can account for the birth of a desire for intuition's self-perpetuation.

Note that I have left aside the question of the different forms of the mind's love: strictly speaking, there is no 'need' of them to account for

---

objects are numbers, figures, and theoretical truths (for the latter model of intuition, see my 'Habitude, connaissance et vertu chez Spinoza', forthcoming in *Dialogue* 43/1, 2004). This difference in object would resolve the apparent contradiction between the definition and the illustration of intuition.

the transition from one moment to another, since these are all *effects*, forms *derived* from the joy experienced. The primary affect of joy, identified as much in the experience of eternity as in the *acquiescientia sui* (self-contentment) deriving from intuitive knowledge, is enough to account for it. Recognition of the affective origin of the determination to perfect oneself thus provides a plausible explanation, despite the difficulties recognized in the last part of this essay, of the automatic character of adequate knowledge and its basis in an ontology of desire.

Université de Montréal / Princeton University

7

False Enemies: Malebranche, Leibniz, and the Best of All Possible Worlds

EMANUELA SCRIBANO

I. LEIBNIZ AGAINST MALEBRANCHE?

When trying to identify the polemical target of *Discours de métaphysique* § 3, where Leibniz rebuts the thesis of those who 'believe that God could have made things better', editors and commentators are unanimous in identifying Malebranche as the author who would have sustained that God could have done better than He did with the creation of this world.[1] This conviction is not shaken by the doubts which might arise from the variants in the text, which these same editors accurately note and which seem quickly to lead one in a completely different direction. 'Nor can I approve the opinion of *certain moderns*' writes Leibniz in the final version of the *Discours*, correcting an earlier version which reads: 'nor can I approve the opinion of certain *scholastics*'. And again: 'I also believe that a great many passages from Sacred Scripture and the holy fathers will be found favoring my opinion, but scarcely any will be found favoring the opinion of *these moderns*.' This time the 'moderns' substitutes for the 'new scholastics' from the previous version.[2] In the final version of the *Discours*, Leibniz has rendered his critique more general, alluding to all those in recent times who held that God could have created a better world. However, his first thought concerned those 'scholastics' or 'new scholastics'. The earlier version of the *Discours* therefore raises many doubts about the current identification of Leibniz's adversary, since it isn't easy to imagine Malebranche in the guise of a scholastic, even a 'new' one. To this we can also add that Leibniz, in the

---

[1] See, e.g. *Discours de métaphysique*, in A VI. iv 1529–88 at 1533, editor's n. to ll. 12–14 and 1534, editor's n. to l. 11; *Discours de métaphysique*, ed. G. Le Roy (Paris: Vrin, 1970), 211 n. 2.

[2] See the textual notes to A VI. iv 1533, ll. 12 f. and 1534, ll. 7–11.

Theodicée, explicitly indicates that he is in agreement with Malebranche on the question of the choice of the best world.[3]

In the course of the paragraph under discussion, Leibniz alludes to an argument which the 'moderns' use to sustain the thesis that it is always possible for God to create a better world, and makes clear the objective of his adversary's thesis. The 'moderns' at issue here

insist on certain dubious subtleties, for they imagine that nothing is so perfect that there is not something more perfect—this is an error. They also believe that in this way they are able to safeguard God's freedom, as though it were not freedom of the highest sort to act in perfection.

In brief, the 'moderns' hold that there is no world that is the best of all, and, as a consequence, that it isn't possible for God to create it, and that this impossibility is the best assurance for us to be able to attribute to God that freedom of indifference which Leibniz judges imperfect with respect to the 'higher' freedom, the undergirding for the choice necessarily determined for the best. Leibniz's adversary thus uses the thesis that God could always create a better world for the purpose of safeguarding the freedom of indifference in God. Thus we must ask if Malebranche could share in this purpose.

A real point of disagreement between Leibniz and Malebranche, which is certainly not marginal, concerns the relation between the goodness of a world and the simplicity of the means by which the effects are produced. Leibniz inserts the simplicity of the way in which God carries out his project into the perfection of the world. On the other hand, Malebranche considers this simplicity a competitor and antagonist to the maximization of the goodness of a world: a world governed by more complex laws might be better, but less proportionate to divine wisdom, according to Malebranche. In brief, Malebranche reasons by placing goodness and divine wisdom in conflict, and thus puts goodness and the perfection of the world in conflict as well, while Leibniz thinks that they cooperate and can be combined with one another, thus forming the best possible world.[4] It follows that the world most adequate to

---

[3] Cf. *Essais de Théodicée* [*Théodicée*] § 203:'The objection of M. Bayle, which aims to prove that the law of the best imposes a true metaphysical necessity on God, is only an illusion that derives from the abuse of terms. M. Bayle used to have a different view, when he applauded Father Malebranche's view, *which is rather close to mine on this subject*. . . . M. Arnauld . . . had no reason to oppose what this Father had said *approaching what we call the rule of the best*.' Emphasis mine.

[4] Cf. *Théodicée* §§ 206–9 and *DM* 5.

divine wisdom for Malebranche is the best world, and that Leibniz's best world is at the same time the world that is the wisest.[5] It follows that for Malebranche the evil present in the world is a real one, a view that is at odds with what Leibniz thinks. Given this, it is true, for Malebranche, that wisdom prevents God from creating the best world,[6] just as it is true for Leibniz that goodness prevents God from creating the worst world. In both cases, divine judgment on the quality of the world constitutes sufficient reason and is morally determinant for divine choice. This is why the purpose for which the scholastics and the moderns whom Leibniz evokes attribute to God the power to create a better world—the safeguarding of the freedom of indifference in God—militates definitively against including Malebranche in their number. If there is, in fact, a point of agreement between Malebranche and Leibniz, it is in the thesis that while divine power extends to other possible worlds, the divine choice is limited to the actual world, that is, that it would be impossible for God to create any world whatsoever different from the one that He actually created.[7] The refutation of the freedom of indifference in

---

[5]   That this is the true point of disagreement between Leibniz and Malebranche is expressed explicitly in their epistolary exchange. Cf. Malebranche to Leibniz, 14 Dec. 1711, in GP i. 358–9: 'I am persuaded, as you are, Sir, that God has made His creatures as well as He could, acting, nevertheless, as He should act, that is, acting in accordance with His law, which can only be the immutable order of His divine perfections. And thus His work is the most perfect that it could be, not absolutely, but with respect to the means by which it was carried out. For God doesn't honor Himself only through the excellence of His work, but also by the simplicity and the fruitfulness of His means. Of all the possible combinations of the excellence of His works and the wisdom of His means, that which carries the most the character of the divine attributes is the one that He has chosen.' Leibniz to Malebranche, Jan. 1712, GP i. 360: In fact, when I consider the work of God, I consider his means as a part of the work, and the simplicity joined to the fruitfulness of the means makes up a part of the excellence of the work: for in the whole the means make up a part of the end.' The same Leibniz, in the *Théodicée*, presents this point of disagreement as easily reconciled. Cf. *Théodicée* § 208–9: 'One could also reduce these two conditions, simplicity and fruitfulness, to a single benefit, which is to produce the most perfection possible; and, by this means, *Father Malebranche's system reduces to mine on this point . . . Now, since everything comes back to the greatest perfection, we come back to the law of the best.'* My emphasis.

[6]   Cf. *Traité de la nature et de la grace* [*TNG*] I. xiv, in Malebranche, *OC* v 29: 'God could doubtless make a world more perfect than the one that we inhabit. . . . But to make this more perfect world, He would have had to change the simplicity of his means . . . and then between the action of God and His Work, there would no longer be the proportion *which is necessary for determining an infinitely wise Being to act'* (my emphasis).

[7]   Cf. Malebranche *TNG* I. xiii, in *OC* v. 28: 'God, discovering in the infinite treasures of His wisdom an infinity of possible worlds . . . has determined Himself to create the one which He would have had to produce and to conserve it through the simplest law's; and *TNG* I. xxxviii, in *OC* v. 47: 'His wisdom renders Him impotent, so to speak. For since it *requires* Him to act for

God in favor of 'the highest freedom', that which consists in self-determination 'following sovereign reason', is clear both in Malebranche and in Leibniz.

The editors of the recent critical edition of the *Discours* in the Akademie Edition of Leibniz's works refer to two passages in Malebranche to justify their identification of this author as Leibniz's adversary. But in both of these passages, Malebranche, while indeed affirming that God *could have* created a better world, doesn't hold that God could have *willed* to create it, that is, he doesn't hold that God's volition is indifferent with respect to the choice of a world. In the *Traité de la nature et de la grâce*, Malebranche affirms that 'God could doubtless have made a world more perfect than that in which we live',[8] since there surely exist worlds better than this one; but an analogous possibility for His volition to determine itself does not correspond to the capacity of His power, since a world better than this one would not present 'this proportion which is necessary to determine an infinitely wise Being to act'.[9] That is, God would not have been able to choose such a better world which, indeed, He had the power to create. For Malebranche as well, the choice is either necessarily determined by the quality of its object, or it doesn't come to pass.

At first glance, the second passage cited by the editors of the Akademie Edition seems more promising. At issue is *Eclaircissement* XVII, § 40 from the *Recherche de la vérité*:

For God wills to honor Himself not only through the excellence of His work, but also through the wisdom of His ways. If He had in view only the excellence of the work, to which work would He determine Himself in order to honor Himself perfectly, *He who can produce an infinity of works one more perfect than the next*? But He acts as wisely as possible, or in the way worthiest of His attributes, in the order of which He found His law and all His motives, attributes He cannot contradict or ignore; for He loves them invincibly since His volition is but the love He bears for them—He acts, I say, in the best way possible when from all possible works He determines Himself to produce, not the one most perfect in all its parts, but the one that together with the ways by which it was produced most perfectly expresses His attributes.[10]

the most simple means' Leibniz, *Théodicée* § 234: 'God has chosen between different courses of action, all of which are possible; thus, metaphysically speaking, He could choose to do that which is not at all the best; but *He cannot do it* morally speaking.' My emphasis.

[8] Malebranche, *TNG* I.xiv, in *OC* v. 29.   [9] *TNG* I.xiv, in *OC* v 29.

[10] *OC* iii. 341, in N. Malebranche, *The Search after Truth* and *Elucidations of the Search after Truth*, trans. T. M. Lennon and P. J. Olscamp (Columbus: Ohio State University Press, 1980), 743.

This passage presents an unquestionable advantage for those who intend to identify Malebranche as Leibniz's adversary: it in fact contains the explicit declaration that God could have made *an infinity* of worlds more perfect than this one, or rather, that there doesn't exist a world that is most perfect in absolute terms. As we know, at question is the thesis in which Leibniz's adversary holds the impossibility of creating the best world. However, this partial agreement with the author Leibniz criticizes shouldn't make us forget the disagreement: Malebranche, in fact, holds that if God chose the world using the criterion of the best, he would never succeed in choosing because worlds are perfectible to infinity. Far from using the argument of infinite perfectibility to defend the freedom of indifference in God, Malebranche uses it to sustain that there cannot be a criterion of the best which God follows, otherwise God would never be determined to decide. In brief, in this passage, Malebranche disagrees with Leibniz over the fact that there is a best of all possible worlds. But he agrees with Leibniz on the fact that, in the absence of a preponderance of reason, choice is impossible, while, as we know, Leibniz's adversary proposes to use his argument to defend the indifferent choice of God—the only thing possible in the absence of a best world. Because of this, that is, because he is convinced that in the absence of a preponderant reason, choice is not possible, Malebranche in the passage just cited from *Eclaircissement* XVII proposes to join to the criterion of the best the criterion of the wisest means, since these criteria succeed in obtaining the maximal level of perfection which alone allows God to determine himself. Therefore, not even this passage lends itself to identifying Malebranche as the author who would deny the existence of the best of all possible worlds in order to *safeguard* the freedom of indifference in God, since Malebranche seeks an aid to *neutralizing* the freedom of indifference and the impossibility of a choice which, from his way of understanding the matter, would imply the search for the best of all possible worlds.

The obstacles to the identification of Malebranche as the adversary of Leibniz are, if possible, accentuated by §§ 193–5 of the *Essais de théodicée*, dedicated to an analogous theme. There Leibniz repeats the critique of the *Discours*, but with significant adjustments. § 193 is dedicated to stigmatizing the authors 'who hold that God could do better'. § 194 repeats the criticism of the *Discours*: those who reason in this way make God act badly, since 'the lesser good has the nature of evil'.[11] § 195 is dedicated to

---

[11] Cf. *DM* 3.

refuting the 'weak' opinion already examined in the *Discours* in accordance with which one seeks to sustain the thesis that God could have created a better world: 'Someone will say that it is impossible to produce the best, because there is not a perfect creature and it is always possible to produce one still better.' At issue here is the same opinion refuted in § 3 *Discours*: 'Furthermore, these moderns insist on certain insubstantial subtleties, since they imagine that nothing is so perfect that there isn't something even more perfect, which is an error.' Why this is an error isn't at all clear in the *Théodicée*, just as it wasn't in the final version of the *Discours*. In the preceding version of the *Discours* Leibniz motivated his refutation of the impossibility of the best world with the consideration of a thesis which will return in later texts: it isn't true that there isn't a most perfect creature; the right triangle, for example, is the most perfect of triangles, the circle the most perfect of figures, etc.[12] The discussion of this claim is eliminated in the final version of the *Discours*, but the reason why the thesis that there isn't a best world is erroneous remains, simply, unarticulated, just as it remains unmotivated why the contrary opinion is true. In place of the reasoning that would refute his adversary, in the *Théodicée* Leibniz limits himself to showing that the reasoning about creatures—that is, that there is always a creature more perfect than any given creature—cannot extend to the universe, for the good reason that the universe and individual substances are ontologically dissimilar:

> I respond that what one can say about a creature or about a particular substance, which can always be surpassed by another, ought not to be applied to the universe, which, since it must extend through all future eternity, is infinite. Furthermore, there is an infinity of creatures in the least parcel of matter because of the actual division of the continuum to infinity. And the infinite, that is, the collection of an infinite number of substances, properly speaking isn't a whole, no more than is the infinite number itself, of which one cannot say if it is even or odd.[13]

In this way, the text of the *Théodicée* adds a further characteristic to the identity of Leibniz's adversary: the adversary appears to have reasoned

---

[12] In a passage later suppressed, Leibniz wrote: 'for example, there are an infinity of regular figures, but one is the most perfect, namely the circle; if he were required to make a triangle, and there was no specification of the kind of triangle, God would certainly make an equilateral triangle since, absolutely speaking, it is the most perfect.' See A VI.iv 1534, note to l. 12. See also *De rerum originatione radicali* (1697), in GP vii. 302–8 at 304; and *Tentamen anagogicum* (1697), GP vii. 270–9 at 278.   [13] *Théodicée* § 205.

about individual creatures and denied that there is a most perfect creature, thinking, perhaps, that the reasoning constructed for the creature can be transferred to the entire universe. But, once again, this author cannot be Malebranche who, like Leibniz, always reasons in terms of a more perfect world, and not in terms of a more perfect creature.[14]

If too many reasons militate against the commonly held polemical target of *Discours de métaphysique* § 3, let us then try to follow Leibniz's indications literally, and let us look among the 'new scholastics'. The search among them leads quickly to a favorable result. The *Disputationes metaphysicae* of Suárez, in fact, contains the passage to which Leibniz is certainly referring. At issue here is section XVII of *Disputatio XXX*, which Suárez dedicates to the power of God, considered within the limits by which it is knowable through natural reason. In this section, Suárez combats two opposing theses: that in accordance with which God could produce an infinite effect, and that in accordance with which God cannot produce a world different from the actual one. This last thesis is defended by those theoreticians who hold that there is one species better than all other possible species, and thus that the power of God exercises itself necessarily in producing this species:

> We should avoid the other extreme, that of those theologians who say that divine power cannot always make more or better species of things, but that God himself can know a certain species, capable of being created, that is so perfect that God cannot create one more perfect.

This 'error', which is exactly the same as the position Leibniz will hold, as we have seen, is attributed by Suárez to Durandus, Aureolus, Capreolus, and Scotus. The only foundation of this thesis, continues Suárez, is the conviction that there must be a most perfect species of all because it isn't possible 'to have a progression to infinity in specific perfections'.[15] But this foundation

> is very weak: for there is no contradiction in the fact that possible species go to infinity. For it is established that in the species of numbers, one can go to infinity, and it is the same with respect to the division of the continuum. It is also the case with respect to the size of a possible body. . . . Therefore in the whole collection of possible species, which God has present to Him in the strongest sense, He is acquainted with no species that is more perfect than all others. Nor is this

---

[14] Cf. TNG i.xiv, in Malebranche, OC v 29, quoted in n. 6 above.
[15] F. Suárez, *Disputationes metaphysicae* [*Disp. met.*], Disp. XXX, sect. xvii, xix.

an unwelcome conclusion, since there is no such thing, just as God is not acquainted with the greatest [*sic*] part in the continuum, since there is no such thing. And so that progression of possible species has no intrinsic terminus . . . but only an extrinsic one, namely God himself, who knows himself, or rather, knows that He cannot create something equal to himself, but, however, that He can create anything He likes that is less perfect, which is not something of determinate perfection, but is a certain syncategorematically infinite collection . . . in which there is no greatest term.[16]

As with Leibniz's adversary, Suárez sustains here the impossibility that there is a species that is most perfect: 'Therefore in the whole collection of possible species . . . He is acquainted with no species that is more perfect than all others . . . since there is no such thing.' Suárez puts forward this argument to defend the possibility that God could create a species better than any other species that currently exists, that is, to defend the freedom of indifference, which both Leibniz and Malebranche deplore. This is the subject to which Suárez had dedicated the preceding section, 'What can be demonstrated about the divine volition by natural reason'[17] In that section, Suárez had confronted those who affirm that although the power of God is not necessitated in its operation— otherwise it would be obligated to produce everything that can be produced—His volition is, nevertheless, linked to a particular end in such a way that the particular characteristics of the determinate end render a different choice impossible (again the position that Leibniz will take: God can do differently, but cannot will differently):

it can be understood that God acts, or wills from the necessity of His nature, not absolutely simply, with respect to His power, that is, not by willing necessarily to do as much as possible, nor by applying infinitely His infinite power (*virtus*) to acting, but that He acts at very least from necessity with respect to the end that He has taken up.

Against these adversaries, Suárez defended the freedom of indifference in the divine volition, maintaining that it is always possible for God to create a universe that is different and better:

But, on the contrary, concerning this I look for the end for which divine volition is determined to willing this universe with necessity, and its good, since

---

[16] F. Suárez, *Disputationes metaphysicae* [*Disp. met.*], Disp. XXX, sect. xvii, xx.

[17] Ibid., Disp. XXX, sect. xvi.

God's power is not limited to this, but can bring about another universe, either similar, or more perfect.[18]

The successive sections, dedicated to divine power, are charged with explaining why it is always possible to create a species better than those which exist. Like Leibniz's adversary in the *Théodicée*, Suárez therefore maintains that there is no best world, using this thesis to ground the freedom of indifference in God and, in the end, links the case of the most perfect universe (discussed in the section dedicated to God's freedom) with that of the most perfect creature (discussed in the section dedicated to the power of God, in support of the thesis of the freedom of indifference). Suárez, in brief, satisfies all of the conditions for being identified as Leibniz's adversary.

Finally, for the final confirmation of the identification of Suárez as Leibniz's adversary, it should be noted that the text of the *Théodicée* presents almost a literal quotation of Suárez's text. 'Someone will say that it is impossible to produce the best, *because there is not a perfect creature* and it is always possible to produce one still better', Leibniz maintains in *Théodicée* § 194, echoing Suárez: 'He is acquainted with no species that is more perfect than all others. Nor is this an unwelcome conclusion, *since there is no such thing.*'[19]

2. IS THE BEST OF ALL POSSIBLE WORLDS POSSIBLE?

The discovery of the Suárezian source of the argument given in Leibniz helps us also to dispel, at least in part, the annoying embarrassment that the reading of *Théodicée* § 195 provokes in the reader. Immediately after reporting Suárez's opinion in accordance with which the creation of the

---

[18] Ibid., Disp. XXX, sect. xvi, xix.

[19] A later indication of the fact that Leibniz was thinking of Suárez can be found in a passage of the letter to Des Bosses of 11 July 1706, put in parentheses by Leibniz himself and thus reproduced in a note in Gerhard's edition. Leibniz writes: 'For even if a *certain one of your group* (*quidam vestrorum*) might doubt it, I think that it should be held as certain that God has made what was the best to be made' (GP ii. 311 n.). Since this letter was sent to a Jesuit, it is obvious that Leibniz had in mind here a Jesuit theologian and not Malebranche. Also in his Leibniz to Des Bosses on 4 Oct. 1706, Suárez is named as 'Suaresium vestrum', 'your Suárez' (GP ii 320). I would like to thank Matteo Favaretti for having called these passages to my attention. On Leibniz and Suárez, see A. Robinet, 'Suárez im Werk von Leibniz', *Studia Leibnitiana* 13 (1981), 76–96.

most perfect creature is impossible because there is no such thing,
Leibniz replies in this way:

> I respond that what one can say about a creature or about a particular substance,
> which can always be surpassed by another, ought not to be applied to the
> universe, which, since it must extend through all future eternity, is infinite.
> Furthermore, there is an infinity of creatures in the least parcel of matter
> because of the actual division of the continuum to infinity. And the infinite, that
> is, the collection of an infinite number of substances, properly speaking isn't a
> whole, no more than the infinite number itself, of which one cannot say if it is
> even or odd.

It appears that here Leibniz is disposed to concede that a most perfect
creature isn't possible, but he denies that this could hold for the universe
for the good reason that the universe is infinite, and the infinite, in contrast with the individual creature, isn't a whole, but an aggregate, infinite,
indeed, made up of individual substances. Furthermore, if we want to be
rigorous, creatures are also aggregates, since every creature is divisible to
infinity: 'there is an infinity of creatures in the least parcel of matter
because of the actual division of the continuum to infinity.' Thus the
universe is not an individual but an aggregate, as is an infinite number 'of
which one cannot say if it is even or odd', and what holds for individuals doesn't hold in its case. Therefore Leibniz seems to imply that in
infinite aggregates, exactly because they are infinite, one can attain a
maximal perfection which, on the contrary, one cannot attain in finite
creatures. But this reading seems difficult to sustain within Leibniz's
thought, as the example of the infinite number that Leibniz advances to
reinforce his reasoning demonstrates—*no more than the infinite number
itself, of which one cannot say if it is even or odd.* The case of the number, in
fact, is the classic Leibnizian example, along with that of motion and of
the size of a figure, which cannot be a perfection since it isn't susceptible to a greatest, as one finds reaffirmed in *Discours* § 1: 'forms or natures
which are not susceptible to a highest degree are not perfections, as for
example the nature of number or of figure. Since the greatest number of
all . . ., as well as the largest of all figures, implies a contradiction.' How,
then, can the example of the number be brought forward to refute the
opposite thesis, that is, that the infinite is susceptible to a greatest?
Perhaps Leibniz here remains sufficiently limited to the refutation of the
legitimacy of the passage from the impossibility of a most perfect creature (which he seems to concede) to the impossibility of a greatest

aggregate (which he doesn't concede), or rather, perhaps Leibniz limits himself to contesting the transference of the reasoning which Suárez had constructed for the creature to the universe. In such a case, the only thesis that the character of the world as an infinite aggregate could refute would the thesis explained immediately after, that is, the thesis of the divinity of the world and the thesis that God is the soul of the world, since the world cannot be conceived as an individual substance: 'The very same thing serves to refute those who make a god of the world, or who conceive of God as a soul of the world; the world or the universe cannot be considered as an animal or as a substance.' In the confrontations with Suárez, Leibniz, on the other hand, would limit himself to the passage from what is demonstrated for a creature to what holds for the universe, without entering into the merit of the thesis that remains valid for the creature, and, as a consequence, for the universe.

This 'minimalist' reading of Leibniz's argument, the only one *prima facie* compatible with his philosophy, finds legitimization in the hypothesis that Leibniz's polemical target is Suárez: as we know, it is Suárez who presented the demonstration that God can create things differently derived from the non-existence of a species that is best of all. Suárez thus would be refuted solely by the irreducibility of the case of the most perfect universe to the case of the most perfect species.

However, if the oddity of Leibniz's reasoning might receive a certain justification from his confrontation with the text from Suárez, we do not fail to notice the particular awkwardness of the argument, which, if completed by a reader knowledgeable in Leibniz's thought, risks being turned against itself. Why shouldn't the example of the continuum, of number, of figure, even militate in favor of the thesis sustained by Suárez, since on this point, Leibniz, who thinks like Suárez himself, as will be remembered, cited the example of the infinite division of the continuum and of the size of a figure as an argument in favor of the impossibility of attaining a greatest in the infinite:

For it is established that in the species of numbers, one can go to infinity, and it is the same with respect to the division of the continuum. It is also the case with respect to the size of a possible body.[20]

Why should the fact that the universe is infinite be an advantage for Leibniz? Indeed the infinity of the world would seem to place it among

---

[20] Suárez, *Disp. met.*, Disp. XXX, sect. xvii.

those things that are not subject to a greatest, such as number, the division of the continuum, etc. The impression is that in every case, the argument chosen to refute Suárez is a *faux pas* on Leibniz's part, since it drives Leibniz to compare the world to all those things which he himself had always declared to not to be subject to a greatest.

But, looking more carefully, Leibniz has gradually made a significant decision between the first drafting of the *Discours* and the text of the *Théodicée*, a choice that shows well how, over all these years, Suárez's challenge had worked away at Leibniz beneath the surface. In the *Discours*, Leibniz limited himself to claiming that the opinion of those who sustain that the best world is impossible is surely erroneous, setting aside in any way the motivation for his conviction: 'they imagine that nothing is so perfect that there isn't something even more perfect, which is an error.' Later, in the *Théodicée*, Leibniz is willing to concede that this proposition of his adversaries is not entirely in error. Suárez had affirmed that God cannot create a being as perfect as He himself is; He must therefore create choosing among those beings which have finite perfection. But in this order, God finds himself facing two other impossibilities: that of the most perfect creature, because such a creature doesn't exist, and that of creating all together or through a successive progression the entire scale of creatures, since the series is potentially but not actually infinite and thus cannot be exhausted:

He can create anything He likes that is less perfect, which is not something of determinate perfection, but is a certain syncategorematically infinite collection . . . in which there is no highest term. And thereby it also happens that . . . the whole collection cannot be produced at the same time, nor can it be exhausted successively.[21]

The world of creatures is a collection that can be augmented infinitely, and thus can never be created all at once, nor can the entire series be exhausted by creating things successively. In this very affirmation, Leibniz should have seen a way out of the difficulty for the creation of the most perfect world that comes from the infinite regress in the scale of perfections. In the *Théodicée*, Leibniz, in fact, decides to insert the hypothesis that among the characteristics that might be able to belong to the most perfect world there might be an indefinite progression of

---

[21] Suárez, Disp. met., xx.

perfections, in the situation in which the creation of the most perfect all together and at one time as impeded by the very nature of things, as Suárez thought: 'Thus it might be the case that the universe always becomes better and better, if it were in the nature of things that it is never able to attain the best all at once.'[22]

Surprisingly, Leibniz accepts here the admission that the nature of things might prevent a universe better than all others from being realized all at once and thus seeks to insert the progression to infinity among the perfections of which an infinite aggregate is susceptible within the best world. This decision can explain Leibniz's apparently counterproductive move to lay out the attack on Suárez only on the illegitimacy of transferring that which holds for one creature to that which holds for the world, and to meet head-on the difficulty posed by the progression to infinity, comparing, as we know, the world to number. Leibniz no longer fears arguments in response that are drawn from the example of number or the continuum, since he decided to insert the indefinitely increasing perfection of the world within the hypothesis of the best world. In this way, to the illegitimacy of the passage from the reasoning concerning the creature to the reasoning concerning the infinite universe, Leibniz adds the thesis of the compatibility between the infinite increase in perfection and the existence of a world better than every other world, a thesis that neutralizes the objection against the existence of the best possible world that Suárez derived from the progression to infinity.

At the root of all, is, however, a choice already announced at the time of the *Discours*, that is, the renunciation of any argument in favor of the possibility of the best world which is not an obsessive appeal to the validity of the principle of sufficient reason. As we know, in the *Discours* Leibniz had renounced the argument according to which within any sort, we can always find creatures more perfect. At the end of this text, Leibniz began to put into action the strategy that will remain the only one used in the *Théodicée*: since only the choice of the best makes the determination of the divine volition possible, that which exists must be the best world: 'to believe that God acts in some matter without having any reason for His volition, *outside of the fact that it appears that this could not be*, is a view that scarcely conforms to his glory.'[23] In effect, the difficulty of maintaining that the best universe is at least possible, prefaced by

[22] *Théodicée* § 202.   [23] *DM* 3.

maintaining, against Suárez, that God should have chosen it, would seem to be difficult even for Leibniz if, in the *Théodicée*, for the first time explicitly, he declares it impossible to know *how* the best world is possible: 'Thus it might be the case that the universe always becomes better and better, if it were in the nature of things that it is never able to attain the best all at once. *But these are problems which are difficult to judge.*'[24] Leibniz makes explicit here the renunciation of all demonstrations of the possibility of the best world, and limits himself to asserting in virtue of the principle of sufficient reason that the best world *must* exist, simply because *a* world exists. The entire burden of the proof that the best world is possible rests on the shoulders of § 196:

It is not a creature that is at issue here, but the universe, and my adversary would be obliged to hold that a possible universe could be better than another, to infinity. But it is in this that he is mistaken, and it is this that he will not be able to prove. *If this opinion were true, it would follow that God would not have been able to produce any world; for He is unable to act without reason, and this would, indeed, be to act against reason.*

The entire proof that this is the best of all possible worlds reduces thus to the establishment of its existence and to the validity of the principle of sufficient reason. If this world exists, it must be the best, otherwise God would not have been determined to action and nothing would exist, and if this best world exists, it is possible: *Ab esse ad posse* ('from what is to what can be)', a reasoning familiar to Leibniz in the face of the dilemmas of the infinite.[25] And it is on the principle of sufficient reason, then, that we will test the supposed opposition between Leibniz and Malebranche.

3. MALEBRANCHE AND LEIBNIZ

According to the Leibniz of the *Discours*, it is 'the moderns' who sustain the thesis of the impossibility of the best world. There is much malice in

---

[24]   *Théodicée* § 202.

[25]   He made use of this kind of reasoning in relation to the possibility of a necessary being in a letter to the editor of the *Journal de Trévoux* of 1701, in GP iv. 405–6 at 406. In *Théodicée* § 416, the principle of sufficient reason is the only ground for claiming that in the hierarchy of perfections there has to be a maximally perfect world, but not a least perfect one: 'among infinitely many possible worlds, there is the best of all, otherwise God wouldn't have chosen to create any; but there is no world such that there is no other less perfect than it' Cf. also *DM* 3.

the decision to speak only of the 'moderns' as opposed to the 'scholastics', be they 'new' scholastics, as they were called in the preceding version. In this way Leibniz seeks to present the thesis that he aims to refute as if it were an eccentricity of modern times, and to eliminate the impression that it is he, rather, who is the true 'modern'; in brief, Leibniz seeks to induce in the reader the conviction that the opinion according to which God necessarily chooses the best world is a thesis close to the tradition, in contrast with the thesis which attributes to God a freedom of indifference, a thesis whose antiquity and authoritativeness Leibniz wants to hide. But it is easy to show that this attempt is unfounded. Leibniz's enemy, Suárez, in fact, is only reusing an argument that in its mature formulation goes back to St Thomas Aquinas.

As I have tried to show elsewhere,[26] the relation between God and the world that Malebranche and Leibniz theorized is opposed to the relation between God and the world outlined by Thomas, because, in contrast with Thomas, Malebranche and Leibniz think that there can be a common measure between the quality of a world and God's reason, a common measure such that the quality of a world can constitute an absolute motivation for the divine choice. The reason why it is always possible to create a better world, according to Thomas, is because there is no quantifiable relation between the infinite perfection of God and the perfection of creatures:

Divine goodness is an end that exceeds created things in all proportions. Whence divine wisdom is not determined to any certain order of things, in such a way that another course of things could not flow out of it.[27]

Finite perfections are always real, since they participate in the divine perfections, but yet, even if one is greater than another, they are all infinitely distant from divine perfection:

the order placed in things by divine wisdom, in which consists the very notion of his justice . . . is not so comparable to divine justice so as to limit divine wisdom to this order.[28]

---

[26] E. Scribano, 'Fénelon contro Malebranche sulla contingenza del mondo', in L. Simonutti (ed.), *Dal necessario al possibile* (Milan: F. Angeli, 2001), 245–63.

[27] *Summa th.* Iq25a5c. Cf. also *De potentia* q1a5c: 'Creatures are not commensurable with divine goodness and justice as though without them, divine goodness could not be manifested . . . . And so it can be manifested through other creatures ordered in another way: and therefore the divine volition can extend itself to other things than those that it created without prejudice to His goodness, justice, and wisdom.'   [28] *Summa th.* Iq25a5c.

Hence no finite perfection is related to the perfection of God in such a way that it can constitute a sufficient reason for the choice. The disproportion between any perfection at all in the world and the divine perfection is the safeguard of the freedom of indifference in God, for whose volition we can never find a determinate reason for choice in the finite. This is why God can always do something better than what he did.[29]

Suárez, with his argument directed against those who think that God is morally obligated to create the best world, presented a variant of the Thomistic theory. No world could be as perfect as God, hence the choice is always made with indifference, nor is the divine choice carried out in contempt of the consciousness of which is the best world, since the best world doesn't exist. Freedom of choice thus doesn't include the power to choose the lesser good, as Leibniz thought, since, even though the best of all worlds doesn't exist, any choice has a good as its object. And in fact Suárez explicitly imitates Thomas' argument to justify the impossibility that there is a best possible creature:

The preceding opinion [that of those who affirm that it is possible for there to be one creature more perfect than all] greatly decreases the omnipotence of God, since if God could not make something better than some designated created substance however perfect, it would not be due to an inconsistency. For, *since it is finite and imperfectly participates in the divine, there is no inconsistency deriving from the thing itself that prevents there from being some other more perfect substance that can be created, which would have a greater participation in the divine.* Therefore, if that could not be, it could only come from a defect in the divine power.

Do we dare to say, perhaps, Suárez continues, that God couldn't create an angel better than any existent angel?

However, it is confirmed and declared, that since all intellectual substance is in the image of God, and *there is no perfect image of him, but all are infinitely distant,* therefore whatever is done, however much it appears in itself perfectly, another can be made more similar to God, an understanding more pure and simple. And the same argument can be made with respect to the species of other degrees, to the extent to which they participate in the divine being and are His signs.[30]

The defense of God's freedom of indifference is thus a consequence of a deeper thesis, that of the incommensurability between the finite and the infinite. And for the contrary view, that of Leibniz and Malebranche,

---

[29] 'quamlibet re a se facta potest Deus facere aliam meliorem' (Thomas, *Summa th.* Iq26a6c).

[30] *Disp. met.*, Disp. XXX, sect. xvii, xix. Emphasis mine.

moral necessity in God hides a deeper commitment, that of the commensurability of the valuation of the world and the reasons for divine choice.[31]

In the passage presented by other commentators as a proof of Malebranche as the polemical target of Leibniz, Malebranche represents an advanced stage of the abandonment of the Thomistic way, but nevertheless he is still an intermediate between Thomas and Leibniz. Malebranche, in fact, accepts that in the world we can never find a determinant reason for the choice of one universe rather than another. Worlds are perfectible to infinity, and no one can construct a determinant reason for divine choice. Also for Malebranche, therefore, we must accept the principle according to which the finite and the infinite are not proportional. Nevertheless, Malebranche is convinced that one such proportion should be constructed to render divine choice possible. There must be a proportion between finite and infinite, since God is determined to create, and it is God who institutes such a proportion by inserting an element of the infinite, of the divine into the finite, the laws of nature which, to the extent to which they are direct manifestations of the attribute of wisdom in God, create in the finite that determining reason which is lacking in the finite, taken in itself.[32] In brief, Malebranche shares with Leibniz's adversary the thesis that there is no best of all possible worlds, but is in agreement with Leibniz that in this condition, no choice would be possible. Malebranche thus shares the heart of the Leibnizian theodicy, the validity of the principle of sufficient reason, and thus the necessity for instituting a proportion between the finite and the infinite which can determine God to choice.

The conceptual leap accomplished by Leibniz after Malebranche— the finite is in itself a sufficient reason for divine choice—should not be underestimated. But we shouldn't value any less the affinities that Leibniz has with Malebranche, affinities that distance both of them from the Thomist conceptual world which, at least on this point, Suárez still

---

[31] In general, on the search for univocity between God and finite things, it is always worth consulting A. Funkenstein, *Theology and the Scientific Imagination from the Middle Ages to the Seventeenth Century* (Princeton: Princeton University Press, 1986).

[32] That the divine choice is determined by the presence of a reflection of God's attributes in the laws of nature is, however, Malebranche's constant position. See *TNG* I.xii, additions, in OC v. 27–8: 'From this infinite number of ways through which God could have executed his plan, we see that which He should prefer above all others. *It is doubtless that which most bears the character of the divine attributes.*' Emphasis mine.

represents with fidelity: for both Leibniz and Malebranche the world should be able to attain a proportion with the infinite that can be a motive for the divine choice, and the distance between the world and God should be measurable; in the finite God should find a sufficient reason for choice. If the world were not ruled by the most simple laws, Malebranche affirmed, 'there would no longer be *the proportion* between the action of God and His world, which is necessary for determining an infinitely wise Being to act.'[33] Malebranche, like Leibniz, therefore exemplified the theological errors against which Thomas and then Suárez set out their position: 'In this those who err were deceived: for they judged that the order of creatures is as it were *commensurable* with divine goodness, and that He could not exist without it;'[34] 'divine goodness is an end that exceeds created things *in all proportions*';[35] 'no [substance] is His perfect image, but is *infinitely distant*.'[36]

To identify Malebranche as Leibniz's adversary thus is not only a 'learned' error. It risks, in fact, obscuring the true theological revolution that unites Malebranche and Leibniz. Both in fact travel the road of the commensurability of the finite world with God, in opposition to the Thomist theology. The sharing of the principle of sufficient reason and the common conviction that it can be applied to God are the more evident symptom of the break by these two representatives of modern rationalism in the confrontation with an intellectual world whose theoretical tools had the end of safeguarding the disproportion between God and the world.

Università di Siena
[Translated by Daniel Garber]

---

[33] Cf. *TNG* I. xiv, in Malebranche, OC v. 29, quoted in n. 6 above.
[34] Thomas, *De potentia* q1a5c.   [35] Thomas, *Summa th.* Iq25a5c.
[36] F. Suárez, *Disp. met.*, Disp. XXX, sect. xvii, xix.

8

The Enigma of Leibniz's Atomism

RICHARD ARTHUR

I. THE ENIGMA

Reminiscing about his early views on the continuum problem in a dialogue penned in 1689,[1] Leibniz recalled the period in his youth when he had enthusiastically subscribed to the 'New Philosophy', embracing the composition of the continuum out of points and the doctrine that 'a slower motion is one interrupted by small intervals of rest.'[2] Speaking of himself through the character Lubinianus, he continues:

And I indulged other dogmas of this kind, to which people are prone when they are willing to entertain every imagination, and do not notice the infinity lurking everywhere in things. But although when I became a geometer I relinquished these opinions, atoms and the vacuum held out for a long time, like certain relics in my mind rebelling against the idea of infinity; for even though

For their comments on oral presentations of this essay I am grateful to members of my audiences at the Midwest Seminar in Chicago (December 1996), University of Toronto (February 1995), Middlebury College (March 1996), McGill University (March 1997), and the Dipartimento di Filosofia, Università di Bologna (March 1998). I am also much indebted to Justin Smith for his close reading of a long and unwieldy earlier written version, and to Catherine Wilson, Daniel Garber, Philip Beeley, and an indefatigable anonymous referee for helpful advice on how to improve it.

[1] From the second dialogue of his *Phoranomus: Ôr, on Power and the Laws of Nature* [*Phoranomus*] (July 1689); these dialogues have been transcribed and annotated in a critical edition by A. Robinet, in *Physis* 28 3 (1991), 429–541, and 28 23 (1991), 797–885. The extracts to follow are from 803. They are my translations, as are all English renderings of Latin or French passages in this paper; here, as elsewhere, I have used 'ôr' with a circumflexed 'o' to denote the 'or of equivalence', translating *seu* or *sive*. Many of the translated passages from Leibniz are quoted from G. W. *Leibniz: The Labyrinth of the Continuum Writings from 1672 to 1686* [*Labyrinth*], ed. and trans. R. T. W. Arthur (New Haven: Yale University Press, 2001).

[2] This position, proposed by the 'Zenonist' faction of Jesuit philosophers, was endorsed by Rodrigo Arriaga in his *Cursus Philosophicus* (Antwerp, 1632), 490 ff., and by Pierre Gassendi in

I conceded that every continuum could be divided to infinity in thought, I still did not grasp that in reality there were parts in things exceeding every number, as a consequence of motion in a plenum.

That 'atoms and the vacuum held out for a long time' among Leibniz's cherished views is readily confirmed by an examination of his manuscripts. One may find papers containing some measure of commitment to atomism intermittently throughout the period from 1666 to 1676; moreover, if his later memory is to be trusted, he first 'gave himself over to' atomism as early as 1661.[3] As for his reasons for rejecting atoms, Leibniz's mature objections based on the actually infinite division of matter are well known. This passage from the correspondence with Clarke is representative:

> The least corpuscle is actually divided *ad infinitum* and contains a world of new created things, which the universe would lack if this corpuscle were an atom, that is, a body all of a piece and not subdivided . . . What reason can be assigned for limiting nature in the process of subdivision?[4]

According to this scenario, then, one would expect to find some definitive text or texts from the 1670s in which Leibniz discovers his mature objection to atoms, and presents it accordingly. This is the line taken by the French scholar André Robinet, for example, who locates the crucial change in Leibniz's thinking as his rejection of indivisibles in

---

his *Animadversiones in decimum librum Diogenis Laertii* [*Animadversiones*] (Lyons, 1649; reprint edn. New York and London: Garland), 455–6. Leibniz might have learnt of it from reading Libert Froidmont's refutation in his *Labyrinthus sive de compositione continui* (1631), 62 ff. See also Philip Beeley's discussion of this doctrine in his *Mechanismus und Kontinuität* [*Kontinuität*] (Stuttgart: Franz Steiner, 1996), 298–300.

[3] In a letter to Rémond in July 1714, Leibniz recalls: 'As for Gassendi, . . . I am not as content with his meditations at present as I was when I was starting to abandon the opinions of the school, while still myself a schoolboy. Since the doctrine of atoms is satisfying to the imagination, I gave myself over to it completely, and the void of Democritus or Epicurus, together with the impregnable corpuscles of these authors, appeared to me to relieve all difficulties.' (GP III 620). In a letter the previous January, he described himself as having begun to deliberate whether to opt for the moderns over the scholastics 'at the age of 15' (GP III 606). Willy Kabitz argues that Aristotelian principles in his early writings at university show that Leibniz must have misremembered, and that he could not have gone over to the moderns until 1664 at the earliest (Willy Kabitz, *Die Philosophie des jungen Leibniz* (Hildesheim and New York: Georg Olms, 1974), 49–50.

[4] Postscript to Leibniz's fourth paper, *Leibniz: Philosophical Writings*, trans. Mary Morris and G. H. R. Parkinson (Rutland,VT: J. M. Dent/Charles E. Tuttle, 1995), 220, 221.

the fragment *De minimo et maximo* (Nov. 1672–mid-Jan. 1673).[5] He then identifies the text in which Leibniz gives a definitive statement of the resulting position as the dialogue *Pacidius Philalethi*,[6] a detailed investigation of the problems of the continuum which Leibniz wrote in November 1676[7] on board a ship from England to Holland (where he would visit Spinoza and other leading Dutch scholars on his way back to Hanover). For in that dialogue Leibniz's spokesman Pacidius eloquently presents the position that has become familiar to us in his mature works:

I myself admit neither Gassendi's atoms, ôr a body that is perfectly solid, nor Descartes's subtle matter, ôr a body that is perfectly fluid . . . (A VI.iii 554; *Labyrinth*, 185)

But there is no reason why these miraculous leaps should be ascribed to this rather than that grade of corpuscles—unless, of course, we admit atoms, ôr bodies so firm that they do not suffer any subdivision or bending . . . But I do not think that there are such bodies in the nature of things . . . since there is no reason why God should have put a stop to his handiwork at this point and left only these creatures without a variety of other creatures inside them, as if they were paralyzed or dead . . . (A VI. iii 561; *Labyrinth*, 199)

Accordingly I am of the following opinion: there is no portion of matter which is not actually divided into further parts, so that there is no body so small that there is not a world of infinitary creatures in it. (A VI. iii 565; *Labyrinth*, 209)[8]

---

[5] André Robinet, *Architectonique disjonctive automates systemiques et idealité transcendentale dans l'œuvre de G. W. Leibniz* [*Architectonique*] (Paris: J. Vrin, 1986), 186–7. This fragment is edited by the Akademie as '*De minimo et maximo. De corporibus et mentibus*', A VI.iii 97–101, and translated as 'On Minimum and Maximum; on Bodies and Minds' in *Labyrinth*, 9–19. Robinet cites it by its *incipit* (opening words) *Nullum datur Minimum . . .*, rather than by the Akademie title.

[6] Robinet, *Architectonique*, 187–9, esp. 188: '[Dans le *Pacidius Philalethi*] les points ne sont pas des indivisibles, les points sont des extrémités, des limites . . . Il s'ensuit que la conception de la matière ne peut plus reposer sur l'indivisible-point puisqu'elle est infiniment divisible en acte, passant sous le modèle de la poursuite de la division vers l'infiniment petit . . . Et remarquons ensuite que l'éviction du vide et de l'atome s'ensuit.'

[7] Leibniz wrote the *Pacidius* during the last ten days of October (Old Style) on board a ship bound for Holland, whilst waiting in the Thames estuary for cargo and optimal sailing conditions. I give all dates here New Style, which makes its composition the first ten days or so of November.

[8] He has the interlocutor Gallutius respond: 'This is an admirable idea of reality you are presenting us with, since so much would have to be missing in order for there to be atoms; whereas the idea that there should rather be a kind of world of infinitary things in any

Awkwardly for this interpretation, though, Leibniz does not give up atoms as soon as he gives up indivisibles. In fact, over three years after *De minimo et maximo* and only a few months before he wrote the *Pacidius*, Leibniz was writing in his unpublished papers of being more and more persuaded of the very same 'perfectly solid' atoms he rejects in the latter.[9] Still, one might put this down to the fact that Leibniz took a long time to convince himself that the infinite division of the continuum was not merely theoretical, and that 'there really were parts in things exceeding every number.' The real enigma, I propose, is that this thesis, that the continuum is not just potentially but actually divided into an infinity of parts, is one he seems to have held from as early as 1666, and consistently from then on, even while proposing atoms. Here is the evidence.

In his *Dissertatio de arte combinatoria* of March 1666, Leibniz advocates a combinatoric of atoms as 'the only way of penetrating into the secrets of nature—if it is indeed true that large things are composed of small ones, whether you call these atoms or molecules' (A.VI.i 187), citing Kepler's *Harmonice* as well as Gassendi's *Animadversiones* (1649), Magnen's *Democritus reviviscens* (1648), and the classical atomists (A VI.i 216). Yet in the fourth axiom of the demonstration of God's existence preceding the dissertation he had proposed that 'Each body has infinite parts, ôr, as is commonly said, the Continuum is divisible to infinity' (A VI.i 169). Granted, at first sight this seems to fit the description Leibniz gave in the *Phoranomus* of his early views. Atoms still have a certain claim on his thought, but he has only conceded that the continuum is infinitely *divisible*. The mention of infinite parts in the first clause of axiom 4 seems dubious as evidence for his subscribing to an infinity of parts in things in reality, an *actually* infinite division. For on the standard Aristotelian interpretation, a body has infinite parts only *potentially*, i.e. in the sense that any parts into which it is actually divided are susceptible of further division. However, as Philip Beeley has argued, Leibniz uses this axiom to prove that the force of motion of a body must be

corpuscle you please is something which, as far as I know, has not been adequately considered before now' (A VI.iii 566; *Labyrinth*, 211).

[9] Indeed, he still advocates them *after* writing the *Pacidius*, if the dating of the *Catena Mirabilium Demonstrationum de Summa Rerum* as December 12, 1676 is correct. He writes: 'Supposing plenitude, *atoms* are demonstrated; indeed, even without plenitude, from the mere consideration that every flexible body is divided into points. It seems very much in accord with reason that primitive *bodies* should all be spherical.' I am inclined to doubt that Leibniz could have written this piece then, however, although I will not argue that here.

infinite, on the grounds that the motion of the body as a whole presupposes the coming-into-motion of every single part, and thus a moving principle in each one. But the infinitude of the force follows from this only if a body has infinite parts that are actual, and not merely potential. Therefore a body must have an actual infinity of parts.[10]

Five years later Leibniz is unequivocally committed to actually infinite division, but now sees it as refuting atomism, just as in his mature work. In the fragment 'On Primary Matter' of 1671, he writes (his stress): '*Matter is actually divided into infinite parts. There is in any body whatever an infinity of creatures. All bodies cohere with one another. Yet every body separates from every other, although not without resistance. There are no atoms*, ôr bodies whose parts never separate.' Yet later in 1671, in the *Hypothesis de systemate mundi*, he describes the world as 'a space full of globes, touching each other only at points', with voids in the gaps between them. All bodies are either 'naturally dissoluble, or they are indissoluble, i.e. atoms'. Although atoms are 'the only integral bodies', 'it suffices for a body to be integral only at its surface', and to be 'again composed of infinite globes inside' (A VI.ii 294). Similarly in his Paris manuscripts of 1676 one may find Leibniz explicitly upholding both the reality of atoms and the actually infinite division of the continuum, sometimes even in the same passage, as we shall see.

Thus the enigma of Leibniz's atomism is this: if we take atoms in the orthodox sense of finite parts of matter that are not further divided, then Leibniz's thesis that matter is actually infinitely divided *directly precludes them*, as he himself urges in his mature writings. Yet this thesis of the actually infinite division of matter is one he had maintained throughout the period in which he had intermittently advanced atoms.

2. LEIBNIZ'S ATOMS: SOME INTERPRETATIONS

At first blush this difficulty seems intractable. For if atoms are physically indivisible finite parts of matter beyond which it cannot be further divided, this is in blatant contradiction with the thesis that matter is

---

[10] See Philip Beeley, *Kontinuität*, 57. The suggestion that this axiom does concern actual parts had been made previously by Daniel Garber in his 'Motion and Metaphysics in the Young Leibniz', in Michael Hooker (ed.), *Leibniz: Critical and Interpretive Essays* (Minneapolis: University of Minnesota Press, 1982), 160–84, at 168.

infinitely divided. Although the difficulty has perhaps not been pointed out before in quite so stark a fashion, several commentators have shown some awareness of the problematic nature of Leibniz's dalliance with atoms in his youth, and in this section I wish to consider some of the different approaches that have been taken. This will introduce us economically to many of the central features of Leibniz's early atomism, as well as motivate my own resolution of the enigma in the following sections. One such approach is that of Robinet already mentioned above, who identifies Leibniz's atoms, not with finite parts of matter, but with the infinitely small parts or indivisibles he espoused in the early 1670s. Another, that of Philip Beeley, is to deny that Leibniz was ever 'committed' to atoms after he went to university, and to interpret his appeals to atoms or physical indivisibles as simply the trying out of hypotheses. A third, that pursued by Christia Mercer, is to interpret his atoms as atoms of substance of the type he advocated in the 1680s and 1690s: these would have bodies that are physically divisible, even though the substantial atoms themselves would be metaphysically indivisible. Although each of these proposals has merit, I shall argue that none can be regarded as providing a wholly satisfactory resolution to the enigma.

According to Robinet, Leibniz's atoms are identical to the *indivisibles* he had posited in his *Theoria motus abstracti* (*TMA*), composed together with his *Hypothesis physica nova* (*HPN*) in 1670, and sent to the Royal Society and Académie des sciences in 1671. On the one hand, the indivisibles are inferred from the fact that continuous matter is actually infinitely divided, not just indefinitely divided, as Descartes had proposed. On the other hand, indivisibles of a line (identified with the indivisibles of Cavalieri's geometry) are justified in terms of motion: an indivisible line is the space traversed by a body with a definite endeavour (*conatus*) at an instant: the greater the endeavour, the greater the indivisible space traversed. One of the main results that Leibniz derives from this theory is that 'bodies are momentaneous minds' (A VI.ii 266). Robinet interprets this to mean that the body itself is the point that is proportional to endeavour: 'the "conatus-body" which is a point and not a line, does not endure longer than a moment'.[11] But at the same time this 'conatus-body' is a 'conatus-mind', a mind lasting no longer

---

[11] 'Ainsi le "conatus-corps" qui est point et non pas ligne, ne dure pas plus d'un moment: il reste "intra-punctum" ' (*Architectonique*, 162).

than a moment.[12] According to Robinet, this strong connection of Cavalierian indivisibles with minds undergirds Leibniz's early theory: 'under the atomistic model of Cavalieri's indivisible point, the science of mind had to be compatible with the mechanical treatment of the physics of body: the concept of "conatus" and its double acceptation furnished the argument'.[13]

As Robinet observes, however, within two years of devising this novel theory of indivisibles, Leibniz has rejected them.[14] In his *De minimo et maximo* written in the Winter of 1672–3, Leibniz now identifies indivisibles with the minima he had hitherto eschewed, and rejects both. He still upholds the existence of 'infinitely small things in the continuum, that is, things smaller than any given sensible thing'. But these infinitely small things cannot be indivisibles, he now recognizes, on pain of the same contradictions as arise from trying to compose a line from points.[15] This is the decisive change of position that Robinet is alluding to when he says 'l'éviction de l'indivisible ruine le concept de l'atome physique (the eschewing of the indivisible lays the concept of the physical atom to ruin)'.[16] So we get a neat explanation of Leibniz's adoption and subsequent rejection of atomism. As long as he upholds his early theory of the continuum, he supports atoms as the indivisible constituents of the material continuum, the indivisible parts into which it is infinitely divided.[17] Once he abandons indivisibles, he is bound to reject atoms too.

---

[12] 'les structures de la *TMA* et de son environnement métaphysique postulent . . . un concept du "conatus-corps" qui est un esprit momentané, un concept du "conatus-esprit" qui practique l'auto-conservation' (ibid. 162).

[13] 'Jusque-là sous le modèle atomistique du point indivisible de Cavalieri, la science de l'esprit devait être compatible avec le traitement mécaniste de la physique du corps: le concept "conatus" et sa double accentuation en fournissaient l'argument' (ibid. 185).

[14] Actually, as Philip Beeley has observed, Leibniz seems to have decided to reject the identification of points with indivisibles a year earlier than Robinet had supposed, having already written in a letter to Arnauld dated November 1671: 'there are no indivisibles, but there are unextended things' (A II.i 172). See Beeley's discussion in his *Kontinuität*, esp. 258–9. See also A VI.ii 165.

[15] Since 'every indivisible point can be understood as the boundary of a line' (A VI.iii 97), one can show that the number of such indivisibles in the diagonal of a square is both equal to and greater than the number in the side, thus yielding a contradiction.

[16] 'S'il n'est pas question de remettre en selle l'atomisme physique, cependant les arguments plaident en sa faveur sur le plan métaphysique: mais *l'éviction de l'indivisible ruine le concept de l'atome physique*. Par contre il se pourrait qu'il y eût des atomes métaphysiques qui seraient indivisibles, mais dont la nature serait mentale' (*Architectonique*, 189).

[17] 'Le corps et l'âme sont ponctualisés, rendus indivisibles par l'essence même du modèle de Cavalieri' (ibid. 160).

There is of course the embarrassment of the nearly four-year gap
between this paper of 1672–3 and his rejection of atoms in the *Pacidius*
in late 1676, during which time Leibniz entertains atoms on various
occasions. But Robinet explains these references to atoms away as the
'ephemeral hypotheses' of the experimental style of his philosophy in
this period.[18]

This identification of Leibniz's atoms with his indivisibles has some
obvious attractions. First, since atoms traditionally *are* the indivisibles
that are inferred from the division of matter, it would seem redundant to
have two kinds of physical indivisibles. Second, even if classically the
physical continuum is composed of only a finite number of atoms,[19]
there was ample precedent for claiming that it was composed of an actual
infinity of them: in his *Two New Sciences* Galileo Galilei had resolved the
continuum into infinitely many atoms separated by indivisible voids.
Third, even though Leibniz cites Cavalieri as considering *indivisibles* as the
rudiments or beginnings of lines and figures, there was a precedent for
identifying *atoms* as the rudiments of lines, not only in the Platonic tradition, but in Magnen's more recent revival of Democritean atomism.[20]

Still, despite these points in its favour, I believe there are several reasons
why this tidy hypothesis of Robinet's will not work. First and foremost,
Leibniz's indivisibles are *points*. Although they compose the physical continuum and some are smaller than others, they are not themselves bodies.[21]
Instead, they are described as the unextended boundaries or 'beginnings'
of bodies.[22] Second, in the *Theoria motus concreti* (*TMC*), the concrete part

---

[18] 'Car le concept de l'atome subit de violentes torsions pendant ce travail fragmentaire de
1676 . . . Ce reclassement des structures [leading to metaphysical atoms] est obtenu à la suite
d'hypothèses éphémères, toutes ces pièces restant sur le style du "videndum est"'
(Architectonique, 189).

[19] Cf. Magnen, *Democritus reviviscens sive De atomis* [*Democritus*] (Lyons, 1648), Prop. XIX,
174: '*Continuum componitur ex atomis, sive corpusculis finitis numero* (The continuum is composed
of atoms, ôr corpuscles finite in number)'.

[20] Cf. Magnen, *Democritus*, 160: '*Atomi simplices, sunt elementorum indivisibiles particulæ, &
linearum physicarum radices.* (Simple atoms are the indivisible particles of the elements, and the
roots of physical lines.)' The Platonic origin of this doctrine is reported by Aristotle: '[Plato]
called indivisible (ἄτομοL) lines the origin of the line, and this he often postulated'
(*Metaphysics* I 9, 992ᵃ19–22).

[21] Thus Leibniz writes to Oldenburg: 'for indivisibles are boundaries of things . . . therefore the
two points or extremities of body, that of the one pushing and that of the one pushed, penetrate
one another (for there is such a thing as a penetration of points, although not of bodies)' (A II.i 64).

[22] In Robinet's defence, Leibniz is not very clear on this issue in 1671. Certainly he describes
bodies as momentary minds, but he also sometimes describes minds as consisting in a point,

of the *HPN* that Leibniz sent to the Royal Society in England, he explicitly criticizes standard atomism and corpuscularianism, writing:

> I have always believed that whatever may be said about atoms with various figures, about vortices, shavings and branches, about hooks, claws, globules and so much other apparatus proper to the game of the learned, is too remote from the simplicity of nature and from any experiments, and too naïve to be connected in any obvious way with the phenomena.   (A VI.ii 248)

He proposes instead a theory of the constitution of matter from *bullae*, tiny hollow bubbles formed like glass beads in a glassworks by the action of the sun on the earth's aether.[23] The great advantage of his theory, he claims, is that with it he can explain the cohesion of these ultimate constituents in terms of the overlapping of indivisibles, whereas the atomists and corpuscularians alike have to take the cohesion of their basic particles as an ἄρρητον or unexplained given.[24]

Leibniz's theory of cohesion is of great interest in its own right, although rather too complex to explain in detail here. The basic idea is that the indivisibles of a body are not minima, or partless points, but have an infinitely small quantity that is proportional to the body's endeavour to move at a given instant. The endpoint of a body in motion therefore occupies a greater (yet still infinitely small) space than one at rest. Consequently, when one body impels another, or endeavours to move it, it has already begun to penetrate it. This is because at the moment of contact, the extreme point of the impinging body occupies a space that is greater than the extreme point of the body at rest, so that they overlap.

which would seem to entail that bodies are momentary points. But in the *TMA* he describes a point as corresponding to a single endeavour, i.e. a thought, not a mind. In order to constitute a 'harmony' or 'storehouse of endeavours', it seems that a mind needs a structure in which more than one endeavour can be conserved, and thus a plurality of such points.

[23] 'For whenever subtle things endeavour to break through dense ones, and there is some obstruction, the dense things are formed into certain hollow bubbles, and an internal motion of parts, and thus a consistency or cohesion, is produced . . . . The same thing is established in the workshops of glassmakers, where, by a circular motion of fire and a straight one of spirit, glasses, the simplest artificial kind, are produced; similarly, by a circular motion of the earth and a straight one of light, bubbles are produced' (*TMC*: A VI. ii 226).

[24] In a letter to Oldenburg in September 1670, Leibniz writes 'Hobbes himself assumes a consistency ôr cohesion in things as a kind of ἄρρητον' (A II.i 63–4). As Beeley reminds us (*Kontinuität*, 71), this objection, that explanations of cohesion in terms of particles already assumed to be cohering would lead to an infinite regress, had been made by many opponents of atomism such as Froidmont, White, Glanvill, and Hobbes himself.

Therefore 'whatever things move in such a way that one endeavours to enter the other's place, cohere together while the endeavour lasts'.[25] As he writes to Pierre de Carcavy in June 1671, it is by means of 'my theory of abstract motion that I explain the original cohesion by means of which certain insensible bodies, as if fornicating, obtain their *primary hardness* (which cause suffices for those of us of intelligence to suppose, for otherwise nothing will prohibit there from being a progression to infinity . . .)' (A II.1 126–7). This done, he can explain the *secondary hardness* of his *bullae*, 'how they are made firm by a motion returning on itself around their own centers', so that, with the infinite regress thus broken, he has 'explained the elements of sensible things by the origin of *bullae*' (127). These spinning hollow *bullae*, together with the solid globules which he also assumes in the early 1670s, are then Leibniz's 'atoms' of this period, although he prefers the collective term *terrellae* (literally, 'earthlets').[26]

Of course, even if Leibniz's atoms are not the indivisibles themselves, but the *bullae* composed from them, Robinet could still be correct in his claim that Leibniz's rejection of atoms is a consequence of his 'éviction de l'indivisible' in 1672. But we are now in a position to see that this does not follow. For nothing in Leibniz's theory of cohesion depends on the points being indivisible, but only on their proportionality to the infinitely small elements of motion, ôr endeavours. As can be confirmed by an examination of Leibniz's manuscripts and letters from this period, this construal of points in terms of endeavours is strengthened rather than weakened by the rejection of indivisibles; and Leibniz continued to promote his endeavour theory of cohesion for some years afterwards.

To summarize: Robinet's identification of atoms with indivisibles fails because in the *TMA* indivisibles are *points*, not bodies,[27] and

[25] Leibniz to Oldenburg, 28 Sept. 1670 (A II.i 64). He gives a similar account in late 1672: 'Hence it follows that whatever endeavours to move into another's place already at its boundary begins to exist in the other's place, i.e. their boundaries are one, i.e. penetrate each other; and consequently one cannot be impelled without the other. And consequently these bodies are continuous' (A VI.iii 96; *Labyrinth*, 21–3).

[26] I give more extensive accounts of Leibniz's views on cohesion in Richard Arthur, 'Cohesion, Division and Harmony: Physical Aspects of Leibniz's Continuum Problem (1671–1686)', *Perspectives on Science*, **6**, 1–2 (1999), 110–35; and in *Labyrinth*, Introduction, pp. xxxvii–xliii.

[27] This criticism must be softened by the qualification that on two other occasions Leibniz did refer to bodies as points: in his letter to Duke Johann Friedrich of May 1671 Leibniz refers to 'physical points' as atoms (A II.i 115), and in February 1676 he refers to 'points, i.e. bodies smaller than any that can be assigned' (A VI.iii 473–4; *Labyrinth*, 47).

because Leibniz offers his theory of *bullae* in the *HPN* as a preferable alternative to atomism in that, unlike the latter, it gives an explanation of the cohesion of its elementary particles. Thus he does not begin by supposing bodies that are physically indivisible, but explains their firmness in terms of his endeavour theory of mutually cohering, unextended points. Moreover, since his rejection of indivisibles in 1671–2 is only a reinterpretation of his theory of points in terms of endeavours, it is not in itself inimical to his endeavour theory of cohesion, or to the *bullae* or globules whose cohesion is explained in terms of this theory. It is therefore insufficient to explain any change of attitude towards atoms between 1671 and 1676, or why, by his own testimony in the *Phoranomus*, 'atoms and the vacuum held out for a long time' after he had 'become a geometer' and abandoned his earlier views on the continuum.

A different tack is taken by Philip Beeley, who objects to the idea that Leibniz can be seen as 'committed to atomism' at all during the Paris period. Granting that Leibniz 'does at this time in numerous philosophical drafts refer to atoms', he argues that the mere mention of atoms or physical indivisibles is not enough to warrant a claim that Leibniz is committed to atomism. The idea that for a time in Paris he embraced atomism is 'a mistake' resulting in part 'from overinterpretation of workshop drafts'. The various manuscripts involving atoms should properly be regarded, he claims, as further experiments in 'Leibniz's workshop of ideas', hypotheses studied for the sake of theoretical exploration.[28] These are what Catherine Wilson has called 'momentarily adopted trial positions',[29] and what Robinet has likewise aptly referred to as 'a series of ephemeral hypotheses . . . in the style of *"videndum est"* [i.e. "It must be seen whether . . . "].[30] In a similar vein, Beeley has observed more recently that Leibniz was surprisingly open to exploring hypotheses with which he did not entirely agree for the sake of a cooperative pursuit of knowledge.[31] Although in his interchanges with other scholars he

---

[28] All of these quotations are from Beeley's comments in 'Response to Arthur, Mercer, Smith and Wilson' ["Response"] (a discussion forum on his *Kontinuität und Mechanismus* (1996), 65–82 in *Leibniz Society Review*, **7**, (Dec. 1997), esp. 74, 82.

[29] Catherine Wilson, Review of Beeley's *Kontinuität und Mechanismus, Leibniz Society Review* **7** (Dec. 1997), 61.

[30] 'Ce reclassement des structures est obtenu à suite d'hypothèses éphémères, toutes ces pièces restant sur le style du "videndum est" ' (Robinet, *Architectonique*, 189).

[31] Philip Beeley, 'Pragmatism and Perspectivism in Leibniz' ['Pragmatism'], in Hans Poser (ed.), *Nihil Sine Ratione* (Berlin: Gottfried-Willhelm-Leibniz-Gesellschaft, 2001), 86–92.

holds fast to certain ideas deeply entrenched in his metaphysics (what we might call, following Lakatos, the 'hard core of his research programme'), such as in this case the actual division of matter to infinity and the consequent rejection of atoms, Leibniz nevertheless 'finds it perfectly acceptable that the physicist set a certain limit to the analysis of matter' in his scientific practice.[32]

Beeley's point here about Leibniz's lack of dogmatism must, I believe, be granted without reservation, especially with regard to the heady and inspired manuscripts penned in Mainz and Paris. In these Leibniz seems prepared to let the logical current of his reasoning carry him into uncharted waters, and even to relish this, despite the heretical shores he sometimes reaches in his conclusions. An explanation in terms of his lack of dogmatism, then, might well explain Leibniz's apparent commitment to atomism in certain cases. Perhaps it explains the atomism of the draft *Hypothesis de systemate mundi*, which is explicitly based on hypotheses (such as the non-existence of the plenum) which contradict those of the *Hypothesis physica nova*, in which it is mentioned as a separate project lying outside the scope of that work.[33] It is also consistent with the way Leibniz broaches the issue of atomism in 'On the Secrets of the Sublime' in Paris in February 1676: 'Does it seem in accord with reason for there to be atoms?' On the other hand, though, the answer given to the question in the sequel is unambiguously affirmative: 'If an atom once exists it will always exist. For the liquid matter of the surrounding plenum will immediately endeavour to dissipate it, since it disturbs its motion, as can easily be shown. If some large body that to some extent resists dissipation moves in a liquid, it will at once form a kind of *terrella*, and a vortex' (A VI.iii 473; *Labyrinth*, 47). And in manuscripts written in the succeeding months, Leibniz's tone grows progressively more assertive:

Since, therefore, I have established on other grounds that there is some portion of matter that is solid and unbreakable—for no adhesive can be allowed in the primary origins of things, as I judge to be easily demonstrable—and since, moreover, connection cannot be explained in terms of matter and motion

---

[32] Beeley quotes Leibniz's letter to Des Billettes of March 1697, which I translate: 'thus there are no atoms, nor perfectly fluid matter, nor perfect globes, and I believe I have a demonstration of that. But just as architects only need to push the analysis of materials down to a certain point, I believe that physicists likewise can arrive at a certain analysis of sensible bodies which serves their practical needs' (A I.xiii 656; Beeley, 'Pragmatism', 87).

[33] See A VI.ii 225, II.20–2.

alone, as I believe I have shown satisfactorily elsewhere, it follows that thought enters into the formation of this portion, and that, whatever its size, it becomes a body that is single and indissectible, i.e. an atom, whenever it has a single mind. (A VI.iii 393; *Labyrinth*, 57)

I am more and more persuaded about indissectible bodies; and since these did not originate through motion, they must be the simplest, and therefore spherical, for all other shapes are subject to variety. So it seems indubitable that there are infinitely many spherical atoms. (A VI.iii 524; *Labyrinth*, 61)

Although Leibniz certainly changes his mind about whether he has indeed 'satisfactorily shown' that connection cannot be explained in terms of matter and motion, the talk of 'indubitability' and 'demonstration' shows him writing in a decidedly affirmatory mode; that is, even if the existence of atoms is a hypothesis, it is one that at this time he regards himself as having demonstrated.

Beeley also buttresses his case for a consistent anti-atomism on Leibniz's part by a subtle reinterpretation of the doctrine of indivisibles in the *TMA*. On his reading, Leibniz, like Ockham, understands points in terms of lines, though not as their endpoints: they are not minima, or smallest assignable parts, but lines smaller than any that can be assigned.[34] According to Beeley, this means there is an 'ontological relativization of the concept of a point' (*Kontinuität*, 243). Points, as lines smaller than any assignable, are indivisible relative to the division of the original continuum, for there are none smaller in relation to the line; but they themselves may be infinite in comparison with other points, and so on down. As for Leibniz's rejection of indivisibles in 1671–2, Beeley claims that his abandoning of this feature is not a major change of position, but merely a making explicit of something already implicit in the nature of point, the fact that it is not partless. This is therefore not so much a change of doctrine as Leibniz's finally recognizing the inconsistency of construing points both as indivisible and as infinitely small lines. Points, therefore, were never really indivisible for Leibniz; and after 1671–2 indivisibles are only endpoints of lines, absolute minima, distinct from the actually infinitely small actuals. Thus, in keeping with his

---

[34] Such a point may therefore be understood as containing parts, as Leibniz explains to Oldenburg in 1671: 'especially admirable is the nature of points: for although a point is not divisible into parts supposed *extra partes*, it is still divisible into parts . . . previously penetrating one another' (A II.i 64).

anti-atomism, Leibniz was never committed to physical indivisibles in any absolute sense.

The problem is that in de-emphasizing the importance of this change, Beeley makes it harder to see how Leibniz could ever have invested his talk of 'indivisibles' in the *TMA* with any philosophical significance.[35] Yet he certainly did, going so far as to explain the indestructibility of minds as due to the indivisibility of the points in which they inhere. In his 'On the Use and Necessity of Demonstrations of the Immortality of the Soul', sent to Duke Johann Friedrich in May 1671, Leibniz wrote:

> For I shall demonstrate that mind consists in a point . . . Whence it will follow that mind can no more be destroyed than a point. For a point is indivisible, and therefore cannot be destroyed. Therefore body is obliterated, and dispersed to all corners of the earth. Mind endures forever, safe and sound in its point. For who can obliterate a point? (A II.i 113)

Now with his rejection of the indivisibility of points, this warrant for the non-dissolution of minds is lost. On Beeley's interpretation, however, it was only ever an illusion, which Leibniz recognized as such in late 1671, after which he consistently distinguished actually infinitely small actuals from indivisible elements in matter, which latter he rejected from then on. But this will not explain why in 1676 he should have begun to experiment in earnest with atoms that are strictly indissectible and perfectly solid, whose 'solidity ôr unity . . . is due to mind' (A VI.iii 509; *Labyrinth*, 117), arguing that 'If there were no atoms, everything would be dissolved, given the plenum' (A VI.iii 525; *Labyrinth*, 61). Beeley claims that in these drafts Leibniz was not embracing atomism; rather, in his opinion, 'what he was really trying to do was to solve the fundamental problem with which the *Theoria motus abstracti* and *Hypothesis physica nova* had left him: how to integrate minds into the system.' But granting that in 1676 his atoms perform this function, they would seem to be something more substantial than an arbitrary limitation of the physicist's

---

[35] Since writing this I have discovered that substantially the same criticism of Beeley's interpretation has already been made by O. Bradley Bassler in his 'The Leibnizian Continuum in 1671', *Studia Leibnitiana* 301 (1998), 1–23. Bassler writes: 'Since Beeley takes the identification of the point with an infinitely small (divisible?) line in the *TMA* as an indication that points are homogeneous with lines, Beeley's reaction is understandably to see this [rejection of indivisibles] as "Bedeutungswandel ohne inhaltiche Konsequenz" (*Kontinuität*, 258)' (19). Bassler charges that Beeley 'fail[s] to take Leibniz's declared position—in particular the indivisibility of points—seriously from the outset' (21).

analysis of the division of matter; and granting that this function was previously performed by indivisible points, it would seem that the idea of physical indivisibles of some kind is more than a 'momentarily adopted trial position'. Nor is it clear how the fact that atoms contain minds is supposed to detract from Leibniz's being committed to them.

This last feature of Leibniz's thought on atoms, their connection with minds and metaphysical unity, prompts consideration of a third interpretation of Leibniz's thought on atoms, that offered by Christia Mercer, first in concert with Robert Sleigh and subsequently in her new book, *Leibniz's Metaphysics*.[36] In this connection we may note that in Leibniz's early metaphysics it is the union of matter with a concurrent mind that constitutes *corporeal substance*; in the *TMA* and associated manuscripts 'the door is opened for pursuing the true distinction between bodies and minds' by means of the Hobbesian identification of thoughts as endeavours (*conatus*), with Hobbes's materialist intent inverted so that minds are more basic; in the Paris writings thought is described as 'entering into the formation' of a portion of matter, so that 'whatever its size, it becomes a body that is single and indissectible, ôr an atom, whenever it has a single mind'[37]; and finally, in the 1680s, corporeal substances, explicitly identified as *substantial atoms*, are described as containing indestructible minds, souls, or substantial forms, making it 'probable that they have always existed from the beginning of things'.[38]

Such considerations have led Mercer to propose a continuity thesis that is in a way the obverse of Beeley's: Leibniz *always* upheld atoms, from 1668 onwards, although these are to be conceived of as *atoms of substance* or corporeal substances, *not* the purely material atoms of Democritus and Epicurus, which Leibniz rejects (on the latter point, Beeley and Mercer agree). The origins of this position, according to Mercer, are to be found in Leibniz's theological project of 1668 where he gives his first theory of substance, with mind functioning as an active, organizing principle for body, playing the role of an Aristotelian substantial form. 'A mind makes the body substantial by constituting its

---

[36] Christia Mercer and R. C. Sleigh, Jr., 'Metaphysics: The Early Period to the *Discourse on Metaphysics*' ['Early'], in Nicholas Jolley (ed.), *The Cambridge Companion to Leibniz*, (Cambridge: Cambridge University Press, 1995), 67–123; Christia Mercer: *Leibniz's Metaphysics: Its Origins and Development* [*Leibniz's Metaphysics*] (Cambridge and New York: Cambridge University Press, 2001).

[37] 'Notes on Science and Metaphysics', 18 Mar. 1676; A. VI. iii 393; *Labyrinth*, 57.

[38] 'Wonders concerning the Nature of Corporeal Substance', A VI.iv 1466; *Labyrinth*, 265.

principle of activity', says Mercer (75), quoting Leibniz's 'the substance
of the body is union with a sustaining mind' (A VI.i 508–9).[39] In the first
version of this theory, the substance of each human body is provided by
union with its human mind, whereas non-human bodies are made substantial by union with the 'universal mind' or God. Moreover, this union
is not merely metaphysical but physical. In the *Confession of Nature
against the Atheists* of 1668 Leibniz offers the necessity of a divine origin
for the firmness or cohesion of atoms as an opportunity for proving the
existence of God:

> Thus in providing a reason for atoms, it is right that we should have recourse to
> God, who is responsible for the firmness in these ultimate foundations of things.
> And I'm surprised that neither *Gassendi* nor anyone else among the very acute
> philosophers of our age has noticed this splendid occasion for demonstrating
> Divine Existence.   (A VI.i 492)

But by 1671 a different conception has emerged, in which every body
contains its own principle of activity (84). In a letter to Duke Johann
Friedrich of May 1671, Leibniz asserts that every substance has a 'kernel
of substance' that can either 'spread throughout the body' or 'draw itself
back into an invisible center'. Mercer identifies this 'kernel' with the
mind or principle of activity, writing: 'the mind or kernel of every
corporeal substance causes and maintains its organization, . . . an
organization of matter that can be more or less "spread out" ' (82). This
combination of variable matter with constant substantial form, claims
Mercer, is what Leibniz means by his references in 1676 to 'indissectible
bodies':

> Mind takes some portion of matter, acts as the 'cement' of the parts of matter, and
> thereby produces a 'naturally indestructible' atom [A VI.iii 474 ff.]. Nor should
> the term *atom* mislead us: for Leibniz an atom is indestructible, but it is not invari-
> able; it is the fundamental unit of the physical world, but it is constituted of mind
> and matter. Mind functions as the metaphysical glue or 'cement' of an atom or

---

[39] Here I shall follow the account Mercer gives in her part of the article with Sleigh
('Early'), which is more explicit than her recent book about her views on Leibniz's atoms. Her
position in the latter, however, seems essentially the same: Leibniz was committed to substantial atoms from 1669 onwards, despite his fluctuating views on cohesion, continuity, and
motion. See e.g. Mercer, *Leibniz's Metaphysics*, 282, 293. (Page number references in the text are
to the article, unless otherwise stated.)

corporeal substance by persistently producing an organization with some chunk of matter; exactly which chunk it organizes is unimportant. (88)

Thus for Mercer there is a perfect continuity from Leibniz's speculations of 1671 concerning the 'kernel of substance' to his mature theory of corporeal substance. The natural indivisibility of atoms or corporeal substances, i.e. 'the indestructibility of the union formed between mind and matter', is a consequence of the fact that 'whatever acts cannot be destroyed' (A VI.iii 521; *Labyrinth*, 121), and that mind 'will organize some matter as long as it acts' (88).[40] Moreover, in addition to acting as the 'metaphysical cement' or organizational principle, 'mind constitutes both the identity of the substance whose cement it is and the source of its individuation' (88). Although there is an important modification in 1678 or shortly thereafter, when Leibniz rehabilitates the notion of a substantial form, and distinguishes minds as a privileged subclass of such forms or souls, the basic idea is the same. It is the mind's (or mind-like substantial form's) ability to retain memories of its past actions that distinguishes it from a merely material body, which would by itself be incapable of action and passion.

Again, this interpretation has much to recommend it. Most obviously, it explains how Leibniz could simultaneously countenance both 'atoms' and the actually infinite division of matter: the atoms are indestructible by virtue of the mind they contain, even while their matter varies and is divided infinitely within. Moreover, the commonality Mercer identifies between many of the themes and ideas from Leibniz's first writings about substance and those of his mature metaphysics seems undeniable. There can be little doubt that the same concern with the inadequacy of a purely materialist account of body that informed his earliest writings also informs his later ones: throughout he saw it as necessary for body, or at least certain bodies, to be united and organized by an immaterial principle of unity. Unless somewhere in matter there are such perduring substantial unities, he never tired of arguing, there would be nothing substantial at all in matter, which would long ago have dissolved into a powder of points. As Leibniz mentions on numerous

---

[40] In her new book, Christia Mercer separates out the problem of cohesion from the problem of metaphysical unity, arguing that in the *TMA* and letters to Hobbes and Oldenburg of 1670, a body consists in 'an infinity of substantial atoms which have momentary minds, and whose momentary endeavors constitute the cohesion among the atoms' (*Leibniz's Metaphysics*, 282). This seems to equate Leibniz's substantial atoms with his indivisible points, in agreement with Robinet.

occasions, this is the very argument that Cordemoy had used to promote his own version of atomism.[41]

Undeniable also is the theological connection to which Mercer draws our attention. As she points out, it was certainly part of the context of Leibniz's early atomism that he was trying to solve traditional problems such as the resurrection of the body, the topic of the essay he appended to his letter to Duke Johann Friedrich in 1671. 'Because substantial identity depends wholly on the mind, as long as the mind remains the same so will the body or corporeal substance' ('Early', 89). Thus despite the dramatic change in death, where the volume of matter organized by the soul shrinks to some minute portion, at resurrection the kernel of substance can diffuse itself through a quantity of matter equal to what it did before death, and thus reconstitute the same individual. This prefigures Leibniz's later doctrine of *transformationism*, according to which death is merely a transformation of the organism in such a way that the domain of influence of its dominant monad shrinks to a physical point.[42] Mercer is surely right to see the origins of this biological doctrine in these speculations of 1671.

But although Mercer has identified several important continuities in Leibniz's thought, in accentuating them she has perhaps glossed over some real discontinuities. Chief among these is the difficulty that the atoms Leibniz entertains in 1676 are explicitly described as 'indissectible' (*insecabilis*), as 'simplest bodies' which lack variety in all respects but size, and which (unlike his *bullae*) 'did not originate through motion' (A VI.iii 524; *Labyrinth*, 61). They are 'perfect solids', moving in a perfect fluid constituted by infinitely small points lacking any original cohesion. That is, like classical atoms, they are maximally hard. And although a mind is indissolubly planted in the matter of each, 'this matter is of a definite

---

[41] 'Yet if there were no true substantial unities there would be nothing substantial or real in such a collection. It was this that forced M. Cordemoy to abandon Descartes and adopt Democritus' doctrine of atoms' (*New System of the Nature of Substances* (1695); quoted from the translation of R. S. Woolhouse and Richard Francks, *Philosophical Texts* [*Texts*] (Oxford: Oxford University Press, 1998), 148–9. See also his letter to Arnauld (8 Dec. 1686), *Texts*, 119.

[42] A representative statement of this is given in Leibniz's *Specimen Inventorum* of *c.* 1686: 'Indeed, just as some people have proposed that every generation of an animal is a mere transformation of the same animal now living, and a kind of accretion that renders it sensible, so by parity of reason it seems defensible to hold that every death is a transformation of the living animal into another smaller animal, and is a kind of diminution by which it is rendered insensible' (A VI.iv 1623–4; *Labyrinth*, 317). Cf. Leibniz's letter to Arnauld of 9, Oct. 1687, where he cites both Leeuwenhoek and Swammerdam in support of his belief in transformation.

magnitude (*esse certae magnitudinis*)' (A vi.iii 477; *Labyrinth*, 51), unlike that of his earlier corporeal substances, or indeed his later ones, of which he writes in 1683: 'A corporeal substance has no definite extension (*nullam habet extensionem definitam*)' (A.vi.iv 1466; *Labyrinth*, 265). Granted, the atoms of 1676 differ from classical atoms in that each contains a mind which organizes matter as a kind of accretion that may vary over time. But this matter is described as organized not around the mind, but around the atomic body itself: 'Body is as incorruptible as mind, but the various organs around it are changed in various ways' (A.vi.iii 510; *Labyrinth*, 119). This suggests that the atoms of 1676 are not to be directly identified with corporeal substances, but are instead their indestructible cores or centers.[43]

This in turn invites a similar re-reading of the theory Leibniz proposed to Duke Johann Friedrich in his letter and accompanying essay on the immortality of the soul in May 1671. Here, too, mind is encased in an indestructible center, analogous to the *Luz* of the Rabbis, organizing matter around this central core. Only at this juncture Leibniz considered the central core or kernel to be a 'physical point', containing the soul at a mathematical point inside it: 'this kernel of substance, consisting in a physical point (the proximate instrument and as it were vehicle of the soul constituted in a mathematical point) remains always' (A ii.i 109); 'Mind endures forever, safe and sound in its point' (A ii.i 113). Thus the *corporeal substance* would be the whole complex of mind together with an organized portion of matter of varying magnitude, as Mercer has observed; but this would not be the *atom*, which would instead be the indestructible core. Leibniz says as much in his *De resurrectione corporum*, which he appended to the essay that he sent to Duke Johann Friedrich. For in his discussion of cannibalism there he equates the physical point that contains the soul or mind with an atom: 'even if not even an atom (other than that point in which the mind is implanted) is now left of me' (A ii.i 115).[44]

---

[43] The mind-containing atoms are also the centers of the associated vortices, as Catherine Wilson has observed (in her unpublished paper 'VORTEX: The significance of inertial circular motions in Leibniz's Paris notes, with reference to Aristotle, Hobbes, and Descartes'). She suggests that Leibniz's strong association of mind with vortical motion in this period is connected with his identification of the latter with the eternal circular motion of Aristotle's fifth element. Mind occupies a singularity, as it were, at the center of the vortex, encased in an indivisible material kernel. Wilson suggests that this way of conceiving mind comes to an end with Leibniz's 'Thought is Not Motion' at the end of the Paris period (A vi.iii 586–7).

[44] As noted above, this seems to accord with Robinet's interpretation of points as atoms. But Leibniz distinguishes the (concrete) physical point from an (abstract) mathematical point, or

Second, although there is a clear continuity in Leibniz's belief that an incorporeal principle of activity is necessary to explain the perdurance of a corporeal substance and its means of individuation, the precise way in which mind is supposed to organize matter seems to have been an open problem for Leibniz in this period, and one on which he changed his views more than once. Indeed his thinking throughout the whole ten years from 1668 onwards is characterized by constantly changing views on how mind is relevant to the cohesion of matter. We have already noted how the young Leibniz was elated to be able to explain what the atomists could not, the cohesion of their primary particles, in terms of his endeavour theory of original cohesion. Cohesion around the equator and latitudinal lines of his *bullae* is explained by the spin of the particle, forming a closed chain of overlapping points. To be sure there is a continuity between the atoms of 1676 and the *bullae* or *terrellae* that preceded them, for in each case the particle is immersed in a fluid at the center of a vortex, and each such particle-vortex is associated with a mind. But whereas in 1671 the *bulla* is actually created by the action of light on the aether causing a vortex, and its cohesion is explained in terms of this spinning about its own axis, in 1676 the atom is a perfectly solid body whose solidity is perhaps explained by mind and whose firmness is the cause of the associated vortex: 'It is necessary that as many vortices are stirred up as there are firm bodies in nature, solely by the motion of the firm bodies. And there are in the world as many minds, ôr little worlds, as there are vortices'.[45] So we see that, on the one hand, Leibniz does not in 1676 separate the problems of metaphysical unity of a body from its physical cohesion, as he later would, after he has finally rejected atomism; and on the other, the idea that mind or soul accounts for body's cohesion and unity is more a statement of an ongoing research program than a solution to a problem that remains constant.

---

indivisible, in much the same way as he does much later in the *New System*: 'when a corporeal substance is contracted, all its organs together make what to us is only a *physical point . . . mathematical points* are their *points of view* for expressing the universe' (GP iv 483; Woolhouse and Francks, *Texts*, 149).

[45] A vi.iii 393; *Labyrinth*, 59. Cf. also 'There are as many vortices . . . as there are indissectible bodies' (A vi.iii 525; *Labyrinth*, 63), 'there are as many minds as vortices, and as many vortices as solid bodies' (A vi.iii 509; *Labyrinth*, 117).

3. LEIBNIZ AND CHEMICAL ATOMISM

At this point it may seem that all we have done is to muddy the waters. For apart from still having to explain how Leibniz could uphold infinite division and atoms simultaneously, we are now also faced with elements seemingly extraneous to atomism as normally understood: the individuation of substances, the indestructibility of minds or souls, and the biological theory of transformation. In addition we have the problem of why in 1676 Leibniz should have reverted to atoms lacking all variety except size, and subsequently replaced them with his theory of corporeal substance.

In what follows I shall argue that not only the original enigma, but also the seemingly extraneous elements of Leibniz's atomism, are all resolvable once the traditions of atomism on which Leibniz is drawing are properly identified. For the resistance on the part of Beeley and Mercer to ascribing atoms to Leibniz is due at least in part to their conceiving atoms as *absolutely indivisible, purely passive chunks of extension, devoid of any qualities, forces or internal complexity*, in evident opposition to the hard core of Leibniz's metaphysics. This is indeed one notion of atom that became prevalent after what we may term the 'Cartesian Revolution'. But it is not the conception of atom that was most prevalent in the first half of the seventeenth century, when many authors proposed atoms that were regarded not only as divisible, but also as possessing a variety of qualities, powers, and inner complexity.[46] This is worth elaborating on in some detail.

Classically, atoms were posited as homogeneous lumps of 'being' moving around in the 'non-being' or void. In contrast, the Stoics posited a plenum of matter which was indefinitely divisible. Accordingly we are wont to assume that there could hardly be a more clear-cut alternative than that open to a mid-seventeenth-century matter theorist: either, on the one hand, infinitely hard atoms and the void, as advocated by Epicurus and revived by Gassendi, or, on the other, the infinitely divisible corpuscles moving in a plenum advocated by Descartes in his Stoic-inspired cosmology. But the starkness of this opposition does not seem to have been evident to many of the players themselves. Robert

---

[46] Ironically, the existence of this tradition is recognized by Beeley, who acknowledges that Leibniz advocated 'chemical atoms' that were internally divided.

Boyle's refusal to commit himself one way or the other is well documented, although this is usually attributed to a distrust of meta-physical reasoning. Yet the lack of acknowledgement of any such polar opposition between atomism and plenism seems to have been almost universal. Hobbes, for instance, was unequivocally opposed to the vacuum even in the face of Boyle's experiments. Nevertheless, despite opting for a plenist metaphysics and the actually infinite divisibility of body,[47] he was quite happy to talk of *atoms* in his physics:

> Since we already supposed earlier that innumerable atoms, some harder than others and having several simple motions of their own, are intermingled with the aethereal substance; from this it necessarily follows that . . . some of these atoms on colliding with others, and to the extent that their motions and mutu-al contact demand, will attach to one another and cohere together; and that, seeing as there is no vacuum, it will not be possible for them to be pulled apart, except by as much force as is necessary to overcome their hardness.[48]

Nor is this mix of atoms and the plenum some Hobbesian oddity; rather, it is a feature of much seventeenth-century thought. Hobbes had been preceded in this by his compatriot Sir Kenelm Digby, who had also asserted divisible atoms and denied the void. And before them the French atomist Sébastien Basson, whilst urging the merits of classical atomism, had rejected the interstitial vacuum, appealing instead to the Stoics' all-pervading aether, 'an extremely tenuous corporeal substance, which in the rarefaction of air, for example, insinuates itself among the particles of air', and which produces all material changes, including the arrangement of the atoms.[49] Likewise the early seventeenth-century

---

[47] '*There is no minimum divisible thing*: whatever is divided, is divided into parts that are further divisible; ôr, there is no minimum divisible thing; ôr, as most geometers express it, for any given quantity, a smaller one can be assumed' (*De Corpore*, II, ch. 7, §13; *LW* i 386). 'Therefore there is no tininess of a body that is impossible . . . For we know there to be certain animalcules so tiny that their whole bodies can scarcely be discerned; yet these too have their embryos, their little veins and other vessels, and their eyes perceptible by no microscope' (*De Corpore*, IV, ch. 27, §1; *LW* i 363).

[48] *De Corpore*, IV, ch. 28, §8: *LW* i 386. Cf. also: 'In the first place, therefore, I suppose that the immense space we call the world is an aggregate of bodies: both of those that are consistent and visible, [*viz.*] the earth and the stars; and of those that are invisible, [*viz.*] the minutest atoms which are scattered in the gaps between the earth and the stars; and finally, of a very fluid aether, occupying every remaining place, wherever it is in the universe, in such a way that no place is left empty' (*De Corpore*, IV, ch. 26, §5; *LW* i 347–8).

[49] Sebastiano Basso, *Philosophiae naturalis adversus Aristotelem Libri xii In quibus abstrusa Veterum physiologia restauratur, & Aristotelis errores solidis rationibus refelluntur* (Geneva: Pierre de

German chemical atomist Daniel Sennert had made no appeal to the void as a principle in his influential work; and in England, Sir Francis Bacon had advocated atoms or *semina rerum* (seeds of things) whose *virtutes* enabled them to assume any shape by folding and unfolding so as to fill any space. This made the vacuum redundant, and Bacon denied that there was one in nature, whether aggregated or interstitial.[50] Even later atomists such as Huygens and Newton speculated freely about subtle fluids penetrating all apparent vacua. In this vein Leibniz himself introduces his *New Physical Hypothesis* with the disclaimer that 'It is all the same whether you affirm or deny the *vacuum*, since I freely acknowledge that whatever is exhausted of air is filled up with aether; in short, whether little empty spaces are left is irrelevant to the gist of our hypothesis' (*TMC*; A.VI.ii 246).

Now accompanying this non-classical mixing of atoms and plenum were distinctly non-classical conceptions of the atoms themselves, with few scholars upholding the traditional conception of atoms as passive, rigid, and strictly indivisible units of matter. Sennert, for instance, inferred his atoms from phenomena such as sublimation, solution of metals in acids, and putrefaction, and equated them with the Aristotelian *minima naturalia* promoted by Julius Caesar Scaliger, that is, with the smallest but qualitatively different indivisible particles of which each of the four elements is composed, rather than with the homogeneous and infinitely hard atoms of the philosophical tradition.[51] In this he was followed by Kenelm Digby, who asserted that

it is evident that the Elements must remaine pure in every compounded body in such extreme small parts as we use to call atomes: for if they did not, the variety of bodies would be nothing else, but . . . so many pure homogeneall

la Rouiere, 1621), 335. See also J. R. Partington, *A History of Chemistry* [*History*] (London: Macmillan 1970), 388.

[50] For an excellent study of the atomisms of this period, see Antonio Clericuzio, *Elements, Principles and Corpuscles: A Study of Atomism and Chemistry in the Seventeenth Century* [*Elements*] (Dordrecht and Boston: Kluwer, 2000), 82. I am indebted to Dan Garber for bringing this valuable resource to my attention; it confirms (and goes well beyond) many of the conclusions I had reached previously in my own research in primary sources.

[51] Daniel Sennert, *De Chymicorum Cum Aristotelicis et Galenicis Consensu ac Dissensu, Liber I* [*De Chymicorum*] (i.e. 'On the Agreement and Disagreement of the Chemists with Aristotelians and Galenists, Book I'), (Wittenberg 1619), 356. Sennert's most elaborate presentation of atomism is in his *Hypomnemata Physica* (Frankfurt, 1636). See also Partington, *History*, 273.

Elements, and not bodies composed of heterogeneall parts: . . . nor could produce the complicated effects which proceed from them.[52]

And while Digby denied that there were any strictly indivisible particles of matter at all, Sennert characterized his atoms as merely physically but not mathematically indivisible, 'not further divisible through natural processes', and 'so small as to escape detection by the senses'.[53] As Robert Boyle wrote in an early manuscript summarizing this tradition, the assertors of atoms do not understand them to be

indivisible or Mathematicall points which are so void of quantity that the subtle rasor of Imagination it selfe cannot dissect them, but *minima Naturalia* or the smallest particles of bodyes, which they call Atomes not because they cannot be suppos'd to be divided into yet smaller parts . . . but because tho they may be further subdivided by the Imagination, yet they cannot by Nature, which not being able in her resolutions of Naturall bodyes to proceed *ad infinitum* must necessarily stop somewhere.[54]

These atomist conceptions of Bacon, Sennert, Digby, Hobbes, and Boyle should be compared to Descartes's comment in his *Principles*: 'No one ever rejected Democritus' atomic theory because it admitted particles that are so small that they elude the senses, . . . but [*inter alia*] because it supposed the atoms to be indivisible' (*Principles of Philosophy* IV. 202; AT viii 1. 325). It is interesting to note that shortly after Descartes wrote this, his compatriot Magnen (teaching in Pavia, Italy) had advocated 'simple atoms' which, though physically indivisible and insensible, were not only infinitely divisible in the mathematical sense but able to undergo radical changes of shape, just like Descartes's particles of the third element. No wonder, then, that Descartes's

---

[52] Kenelm Digby, *Two Treatises: A Treatise of Bodies* [*Two Treatises*], (Paris: Blaizot, 1644), 143; (London: J. Williams, 1645), 178; cf. Clericuzio, *Elements*, 82.

[53] Andrew van Melsen quotes Sennert as saying: '[atoms or minima of nature] owe their names to the fact that they cannot be further divided through natural processes, and, reversely, form the building blocks of all natural bodies. They are, however, so small that they escape detection by the senses' (*Opera* i, 151; in van Melsen, *From Atomos to Atom: The History of the Concept of Atom* (New York: Harper, 1960), 85). I was unable to find this edition of Sennert's works.

[54] Robert Boyle, 'Of the Atomicall Philosophy', Royal Society Boyle Papers, xxvi, fos. 162–75 (dated as 1651–3); 227–35 in *The Works of Robert Boyle*, ed. Michael Hunter and Edward B. Davis (London: Pickering & Chatto, 2000), vol. 13; also quoted in Clericuzio, *Elements*, 117. Cf. Digby: 'By which word *Atome*, no body will imagine we intend to expresse a perfect indivisible, but onely, the least sort of natural bodies' (*Two Treatises*, 1644 edn., 38; 1645, 48).

corpuscles were often assimilated by his contemporaries to atoms,[55] since seventeenth-century atoms were regarded not as absolutely indivisible—they were not beyond God's power of dividing them, but beyond ours.[56] Leibniz himself drew attention to this point in his reading notes on Descartes's *Principles of Philosophy* in 1675. To the latter's claim that 'There cannot be atoms, since they could at least be divided by God', he adds laconically: 'this Gassendi would not have denied' (A.VI.iii 215; *Labyrinth*, 25).

It should not be thought, however, that the divisible atoms of Sennert, Hobbes, and others were indistinguishable from Cartesian corpuscles. The latter, whose parts cohere only by virtue of their being mutually at rest, would eventually be divided and dissolved by the jostling of other particles in the plenum. An atom, on the other hand, is naturally indissoluble, indivisible by natural means, so that atoms of various kinds form the building blocks of all matter (Sennert), even if they do not maintain the same shape or size (Bacon, Hobbes, Magnen). Their different properties are posited above all to explain the different natures of chemical elements or principles. But a second major reason for positing them, as I shall discuss below, is that atoms—or rather certain molecules formed from them—are able to serve as units for the propagation of natural kinds, with their indivisibility ensuring the assumed incorruptibility of forms; they were also generally assumed to have the power to fashion other particles. Clearly there is nothing analogous to these properties in a purely mechanical natural philosophy like that of Descartes.

In sum: in order to understand Leibniz's atomism it is vital to recognize that there was a flourishing tradition of atomism in the seventeenth century deriving from chemical, biological, and medical sources, rather than from the classical metaphysical tradition. Thus the term 'atom' did not necessarily, or even usually, carry the connotation of a corpuscle that is absolutely indivisible, remaining rigid, perfectly hard, and possessing the same shape and size for all eternity (Democritus, Epicurus, Lucretius),

---

[55] Famously, Gerauld de Cordemoy will substitute atoms for divisible Cartesian corporeal substances. Henri LeRoy (Regius), in his *Philosophia naturalis* of 1661, and Adriaan Heereboord were other prominent Cartesians to advocate atomism (see Clericuzio, *Elements*, 185–6).

[56] Cf. Descartes to More, 5 Feb. 1649: 'It implies a contradiction for there to be atoms, . . . since although God could have made things so that they are not divided by any created being, we certainly cannot understand him as having been able to deprive himself of the faculty of dividing them' (AT v. 273).

or at least for the duration of the created universe (Gassendi); these we may agree to call *classical atoms*. In the chemical tradition represented by Sennert, the basic meaning of 'atom' is a particle that is not further divisible by any physical or chemical process, with no particular connotation of sameness of shape or rigidity.[57] Thus an atom is rather a corpuscle of matter of a particular element (air, fire, water, etc.) that is the irreducible building block of that element, and which remains intact through all chemical reactions. These are generally called *chemical atoms*. Now because chemical reactions can be quite violent, many writers in this tradition endowed their atoms with powers—energy, sympathy, etc.—properties that were incompatible with a purely mechanical interpretation of classical atoms as purely passive chunks of extension devoid of qualities.

Here I must immediately add that the latter conception of classical atoms is not necessarily to be thought of as historically more accurate. The interpretation of atoms as biological seeds can be found in Lucretius, Epicurus' atoms were endowed with an innate tendency to action or *energeia*, and there was a strong tradition of regarding Plato's atoms not simply as geometrical shapes, but as being attracted to atoms of the same kind by a force of sympathy. Thus the division between classical and chemical atoms is by no means a strict dichotomy. It was certainly possible, for example, to maintain that atoms are absolutely indivisible and perfectly hard, yet still possess active powers of various kinds. Indeed, Gassendi himself not only strove to correct the interpretation of classical atoms as purely passive, but was no stranger to the chemical tradition, as recent scholarship has established.[58] He did not, as a matter of record, subscribe to the narrow mechanist program of reducing the whole of nature to the motions of a purely passive matter, but allowed activity,

---

[57] It can, of course, be seen as a beautiful irony that the early seventeenth-century conception of atoms is far closer to the modern one than the classical conception that was later re-established by Dalton and nineteenth-century chemistry.

[58] As Olivier Bloch notes in his *La philosophie de Gassendi* [*Gassendi*] (The Hague, 1971), Gassendi had explicitly responded to Campanella's imputation of an inert matter to Epicurus, objecting that 'Epicurus dreams of nothing less than passive matter, unmitigatedly assigning a restless motion to his atoms, from which he also deduces the actions of all concrete things' (B. N. Nouv. acq. lat. 2643, fos. 49^v–50^r, Bloch, *Gassendi*, 212, n. 39). See also Gassendi's comment in (Tours 709 fo. 185^r): 'Epicurus believes all atoms to be endowed with a certain internal energy, ôr inborn vigor, by which they set themselves in motion' (Bloch, *Gassendi*, 215, n. 55). Bloch gives a good account of Gassendi's views in relation to the chemical tradition. On this, see also Clericuzio, *Elements*, 63–74.

forces, and even formative powers in his atoms and molecules.[59] For although he agreed that all phenomena or effects should be explained in terms of matter in motion, this did not for him entail that all *causes* were so reducible. And contrariwise, just as Gassendi was influenced by the chemical tradition, so authors in that tradition were not shy of claiming Democritus, Epicurus, and Plato as precedents for their views.

In any case, taking into account this well-established alternative tradition which justified atoms through chemical and medical arguments enables us to remove the apparent inconsistency in most of Leibniz's statements about atoms in the early 1670s. We may grant that, having opted for the moderns, Leibniz would not have accepted, say, atoms that were qualitatively different for each specific element, nor 'sympathies' and 'attractions' as original properties of atoms.[60] Nevertheless, the properties Leibniz singles out in his rejections of atoms—their absolute indivisibility, their passivity, and their rigidity—are all properties of classical atoms interpreted according to a strict mechanical philosophy. The atoms he rejects are 'bodies whose parts never separate' (A.VI.ii 280; *Labyrinth*, 344), 'perfect solids' or 'bodies so firm that they do not suffer any subdivision or bending' (A.VI.iii 561; *Labyrinth*, 199), or bodies containing nothing but extension (A.VI.iv 1799; *Labyrinth*, 279). On the other hand, the 'atoms' he upholds are very small, very hard corpuscles which are 'naturally indissoluble', yet still divisible, and which have an internal complexity—all of which are properties of chemical atoms, and for which there were also precedents in Gassendi, Hill, Bacon, Hobbes, Digby, Bérigard, van Goorle, and others not usually thought of as chemical atomists. Certainly, Leibniz's own primary corpuscles in the *HPN*, the *bullae*, are of this kind: although not perfectly hard, they will endure for the duration of the present world. Thus we may say of Leibniz's atomism in the early 1670s: he rejects classical atoms (which indeed he

---

[59] Cf. Clericuzio: 'Gassendi's theory of *semina* and spirits . . . are to be understood as part of a theory of matter which does not dispense with forces, activities, and powers' (*Elements*, 63).

[60] More accurately, Leibniz accepted the idea of bodies sympathizing with one another, but tried to give it a reductive interpretation, first in terms of motion in common (see A VI.iii 80, 104; *Labyrinth*, 4–5) and later in terms of his doctrine of expression (A VI.iv 1618; *Labyrinth*, 309). He takes this kind of rational reduction a step farther with his later rehabilitation of the atomists' *appetitus* in the guise of an instantaneous tendency to change state. Given the other correspondences (though not necessarily influences) of Basson's views and Leibniz's in the *HPN*, particularly the predominant role of aether, the relationship between these thinkers is probably deserving of further study.

may never have espoused, except perhaps in his adolescence), but, like many of his contemporaries, advocates flexible and divisible atoms that are indissoluble by natural processes, but which possess considerable (indeed, for Leibniz, infinite) internal complexity. His atoms, like theirs, are indivisible in the sense that they remain intact, but divisible in the sense of possessing internal parts.

There is in fact more than circumstantial evidence for Leibniz's indebtedness to the chemical atomist tradition. As Beeley has observed, his *HPN* is replete with references to the chemical literature, and his theory of *bullae* may be seen as a reinterpretation of chemical atoms (or, better, molecules) along acceptable mechanical lines.[61] Indeed, as I have suggested elsewhere,[62] the theory of cohesion of his *bullae* offered by Leibniz bears a close affinity to the theory of chemical composition or mixtion (*mistio*) of Julius Caesar Scaliger, which was widely accepted in the seventeenth century, and with which Leibniz would probably have been familiar both in the original and through the work of Sennert, who had adopted it. Instead of regarding mixtion simply as 'the union of the miscibles', as had Aristotle, Scaliger defined it as 'the motion of minimum bodies towards mutual contact so that a union is made' (a definition that Sennert explicitly endorsed).[63] In the same Exercise Scaliger comments: 'For it is not just that they touch one another, like Epicurean atoms; so do our corpuscles, but in such a way that a continuous body and unity is made. For it becomes one by a making continuous of the boundaries, which is common to all that has entered into the mixtion.'[64] This theory was adopted not only by Daniel Sennert but also by Robert Boyle, according to whom the concretions of particles that form the basis of chemical processes (what Gassendi had termed 'molecules' and

---

[61] See Beeley, *Kontinuität* ch. 7. See also his 'Response', in which he writes 'Leibniz also provides an ingenuous model of the chemical atom, composed of cortex and nucleus, which he is without difficulty able to adapt to his theory of the infinite dividedness of matter, while at the same time serving to explain the chemical processes of decomposition and synthesis' (75).

[62] See references cited in n.26.

[63] *Julii Caesaris Scaligeri Exotericarum Exercitationum Libri XV de subtilitate ad Hieronymum Cardanum* [*Exotericarum*] (i.e. 'Fifteen Books of Exoteric Exercises on Subtlety, for Hieronymus Cardan,' by Julius Caesar Scaliger), (Paris 1557), Ex. 101, 143: *mistio est motus corporum minimorum ad mutuum contactum, ut fiat unio*. This was endorsed by Sennert in ch. xii of his *De Chymicorum*, 356: 'I confess I am now won over by the opinion of Scaliger, who defines mixtion to be the motion of minimum bodies towards mutual contact so that a union is made.' See also Clericuzio's discussion of Scaliger's *minima naturalia* on 9–15 of his *Elements*.

[64] Scaliger, *Exotericarum*, 143.

Boyle calls 'corpuscles of the second order') are formed by a close union of *minima naturalia*.[65] Although in his early work Boyle had interpreted these *minima* as Sennertian atoms, in his published works he reinterprets them as simple corpuscles possessing only mechanical properties.[66] It does not seem too fanciful to regard Leibniz as extending this kind of rationalization of Sennert's theory begun by Boyle. The difference in Leibniz's case is that, unlike Boyle, Scaliger, and Sennert, he did not have to presuppose primary particles whose original cohesion is unexplained: cohering bodies are formed from an actual infinity of overlapping points, as exist in the circles of latitude around the axes of the spinning *bullae*.

There is, however, a second difference in Leibniz's understanding of the internal composition of atomic particles that is crucial to the resolution of our enigma. We have seen that his *bullae* are held together by the cohering bands of overlapping points in their surfaces, and that, like the naturally indivisible molecules of his contemporaries, they contain within themselves smaller particles possessing their own individual motions. But for Leibniz the differing internal motions of the parts of a body are precisely what constitute these parts as individually different, *and therefore divide the body within*. As he wrote in an unpublished tract of 1672,

It is manifest that a body is constituted as definite, one, particular, distinct from others, by a certain motion or particular endeavour of its own, and if it is lacking this it will not be a separate body . . . And this is what I have said elsewhere, that cohesion comes from endeavour or motion, that those things which move with one motion should be understood to cohere with one another.[67]

Thus the cohesion of the *bullae* is explained by the motion in common of the points in each concentric band of its surface (the cohesion of the bands being further explained by means of a principle of minimization of disturbance of motion). The *bullae* themselves, however, are composite, divided within by the differing motions of their component parts. And it

---

[65] See Clericuzio, *Elements*, 122–3.

[66] On Sennert as the source of Boyle's early atomism, see W. R. Newman, 'The Alchemical Sources of Robert Boyle's Corpuscular Philosophy', *Annals of Science* 53 (1996), 567–85. See also A. Clericuzio, 'A Redefinition of Boyle's Chemistry and Corpuscular Philosophy', ['Redefinition'], *Annals of Science* 47 (1990), 561–89, and Clericuzio, *Elements,* 103–48, esp. 117, 123.

[67] Proposition 14, *Propositiones Quaedam Philosophicae* (A VI.iii 28). Leibniz wrote this tract, probably intended for publication, in early to mid-1672.

is the individual motions or endeavours of these parts that individuate them as actually differing parts, dividing them off from one another.[68]

This conception of parts being individuated by their differing motions is in fact Cartesian in origin, and forms the basis for Leibniz's argument for the actually infinite division of matter.[69] It derives from the argument Descartes gave in his *Principles* for the 'division of certain particles of matter to infinity' (*Principles of Philosophy* II. 34; *Labyrinth*, 358). Although Descartes had further qualified this to mean an *indefinite* division in certain spaces, Leibniz habitually took it to demonstrate the actually infinite division of matter everywhere. Descartes's argument was that in order for motion to occur through unequal spaces in a plenum, 'all the imaginable particles of [a certain] part of matter . . . must be to some degree displaced from one another; and such a displacement, however slight, is a genuine division'. There is therefore 'a division of matter into actually indefinite particles, although these are incomprehensible to us' (ibid.). In a typical comment on this passage in 1675 Leibniz writes: 'In Part II, §3[4] [of Descartes's *Principles*] matter is admitted to be really divided into parts that are smaller than any assignable, and therefore actually infinite' (A.VI.iii 214; *Labyrinth*, 25). He had made implicit reference to this argument in support of his claim for the actually infinite division of the continuum in the *TMA*, but he spells it out explicitly in many other places. Thus in 'Created Things Are Actually Infinite' he writes: 'Any body whatever is actually divided into several parts, since any body whatever is acted upon by other bodies' (A.VI.iv 1393; *Labyrinth*, 235).[70] But the internal division of bodies does not detract from the spinning motion that gives them coherence. This privileged nature of circular motion for individuating bodies is a recurring theme in 1671. Thus in 'On Primary Matter', Leibniz attributes the origins of bodies to 'particular circulations' of matter, arguing that bodies have infinite parts and that 'there are infinitely many

---

[68] Indeed, without motion to give these parts their individuality, Leibniz argues on several occasions, matter, being undifferentiated, is nothing at all. See e.g. 'On Primary Matter' (A VI.ii 280; *Labyrinth*, 344).

[69] See the analysis given in Richard T. W. Arthur, 'Russell's Conundrum: On the Relation of Leibniz's Monads to the Continuum', in J. R. Brown and J. Mittelstrass (eds.), *An Intimate Relation* (Dordrecht: Kluwer, 1989), 171–201, esp. 182–9.

[70] See also: A VI.iii 474, 281, 553–4; *Labyrinth*, 47, 113, 183, A VI.iv 1399, 1623, 1799; *Labyrinth*, 245, 317, 279.

creatures in any body whatever' (A.VI.ii 280; *Labyrinth*, 344). In the *Hypothesis de systemate mundi*, as we saw above, he describes space as 'filled with globes' spinning on their axes, these being 'the only integral bodies', the 'naturally indissoluble' atoms. But he also says that 'it suffices for a body to be integral only at its surface', and to be 'again composed of infinite globes inside' (A.VI.ii 294; *Labyrinth*, 344–5).

So there are two senses of division here: a body is actually divided *within* by the differing motions of its internal parts despite the fact that, if it is atomic (i.e. 'integral' or 'indissoluble'), it will not be dividable by any natural process from *without*. That is, an atom for Leibniz can quite literally be a *terrella* or little world, if it has an impenetrable crust. Beneath that crust, as if beneath the Empyrean, is a world of inner motion and activity that is perhaps in principle explicable in the same terms as our world but on a vastly smaller scale. Hence Leibniz's sustained commitment to the thesis of 'worlds within worlds to infinity', often in the very same tracts in which he defends atoms.

With respect to the latter thesis, however, it must be observed that Leibniz's conception of actually infinite division is highly unorthodox. For he appears to hold that the thesis of the division of matter into worlds within worlds without end *entails* its division into 'points'. Thus as late as spring 1676 he writes: 'if it is true that any part of matter, however small, contains an infinity of creatures, i.e. is a world, it follows also that matter is actually divided into an infinity of points' (A.VI.iii 474; *Labyrinth*, 49). In one sense this seems to be a rewriting of Descartes's argument, with the latter's 'indefinite particles' reinterpreted as actual Galilean points. But this runs counter to the Anaxagorean conception of 'worlds within worlds to infinity', which would normally be interpreted as precluding such least elements or minima. Leibniz seems to have believed that he could finesse this difficulty and assimilate the two conceptions by rejecting the existence of minima and redefining points as 'parts smaller than any assignable'. It is almost as if 'part smaller than any assignable' is a 'syncategorematic' formula, as Beeley suggests (*Kontinuität*, 59–60, 244), not denoting points as independently existing entities but standing for the idea of an unlimited containment of spheres within spheres. But this leaves it hard to understand how matter could be regarded as composed of such points. I will return to this issue in the next section. For now let it suffice to note that well into 1676 Leibniz seems to have regarded the worlds within worlds thesis as entailing the composition of matter from infinitesimal points.

To summarize: the solution I am offering to the enigma posed in the first section is this. I had said that *if* we take Leibniz's atoms in the orthodox sense of finite parts of matter that are not further divided, then his thesis that matter is actually infinitely divided would indeed preclude them. But the point is that the atoms he upholds are not such orthodox atoms; rather they *are* further divided within. Like the chemical atoms of Sennert and the young Boyle, Leibniz's atoms are complex corpuscles that are naturally indivisible (physically unbreakable), even though they possess internal parts. But the very fact that they have internal parts with different motions entails that they are actually divided within; and the fact that there is an infinity of different motions means that the division is an actual division to infinity.

4. THE ROAD TO CORPOREAL SUBSTANCES

So far I have argued that our original enigma is resolved by a comparison of Leibniz's atoms with the naturally indestructible yet composite corpuscles of many of his contemporaries. For by the Cartesian criterion of actual division subscribed to by Leibniz, every such corpuscle containing internal parts in differing motions is actually divided, and if every part of matter is individuated by its motion, then each of its parts is further divided. This would explain how Leibniz could advocate atoms and the infinite division of matter at the same time, and also why he advocated actually infinite division. But it does so at the expense of raising other perplexities. For it does not explain what motivated him to be attracted to atomism in the first place, nor why he came to abandon it. Nor does it explain why, if Leibniz did not originally conceive atomism to be incompatible with infinite division, he eventually came to think it so. It is to these issues that I want to turn in this section of the essay.

With regard to Leibniz's motivations for atomism, again the connection I have sketched between his atoms and those of the chemical atomist tradition is illuminating. Indeed, a reconsideration of Leibniz's views in relation to those of Sennert and Gassendi will also throw some light on the seemingly extraneous elements of his thought on atoms mentioned above: the individuation of substances, the indestructibility of minds or souls, and the biological theory of preformation.

As we have seen, Leibniz was from the beginning concerned to argue the inadequacy of a purely mechanical account of body. His argument, already articulated in the *Catholic Demonstrations* of 1668, was that Cartesian *res extensa* does not contain the basis for motion or the activity of a body, that a purely passive substance would be unable to act, and therefore could not qualify as a substance in the proper sense.[71] This may seem incompatible with any meaningful commitment by Leibniz to the 'material atomism' of Gassendi.[72] But it appears in a different light when it is compared to the actual views of Gassendi, for whom matter is intrinsically and incessantly active. In this respect Leibniz was largely echoing the criticisms of Descartes which Gassendi had published in his *Disquisitio metaphysica*:

Concerning body, I note only this, that if its whole nature consists in the fact that it is *res extensa*, then every action and the faculty of every acting thing is out-side corporeal nature, since extension is purely passive, and whoever says a thing is only extension says, among other things, that it is not active. Therefore there will be no action, and no faculty of acting, in bodies.[73]

---

[71] 'It must be demonstrated against Descartes that space and extension are really different from body because otherwise motion would not be a real thing in body' (A VI.i 510); 'Substance is a being which subsists in itself . . . A being which subsists in itself has a principle of action within it . . . If that which has a principle of action within itself is a body, it has a principle of motion within itself . . . No body has a principle of motion in itself apart from a concurrent mind' (A VI.i 508–12).

[72] Christia Mercer, for example, in rejecting any important role for Gassendi on the forma-tion of Leibniz's thought, seems to understand him as having advocated material atoms that are purely passive. This may be why she persists in ascribing to me the view that 'Leibniz flirted with material atomism in the 1660s and 1670s' (*Leibniz's Metaphysics*, 295) on the basis of my taking seriously Leibniz's admission of having subscribed to Gassendi's atomism. On the contrary, I agree with her about Leibniz's eclecticism, and his attempts after 1668 to found mechanism in a metaphysics that is basically Aristotelian and Neoplatonic (for which I refer readers to her excellent book). But I do not see this as incompatible with his interpreting Gassendi's active atoms as containing an immaterial principle of action.

[73] Pierre Gassendi, *Disquisitio Metaphysica*, III 305b in *Opera Omnia [Opera]*, (Lyons: Anisson, 1658); quoted by Bloch, *Gassendi*, 207. Leibniz acknowledges his debt to Gassendi on this point even while rejecting Gassendi's atomism. In December 1676, in the context of an indignant response to Honoré Fabry's accusation that he favoured Democritus and Gassendi over Aristotle, he asserts 'Truly, I hold for certain that there are incorporeal substances, that motion does not come from body but from outside; . . . Nonetheless I agree with Gassendi rather than Descartes that the essence of body does not consist in extension' (A II.i 289).

Gassendi, in fact, was not the only proponent of the New Philosophy to ascribe an innate activity to matter: Beeckman, Hill, Hooke, Charleton, and others all subscribed to the same thesis.[74] However, he was the most explicit in assigning it a cause that was not in keeping with the mechanical philosophy narrowly conceived. Atoms, he claimed, following Epicurus, possess an *impetus* or *energeia* by which they spontaneously resume their motions after collisions.[75] Although in his posthumous *Syntagma philosophicum* (1658) Gassendi repudiated his ascription of innateness to the atoms' impetus, he continued to uphold the idea of an active matter resulting from the incessant activity of atoms, and in an essay on this subject in 1669 Boyle took the same position.[76] Moreover, Gassendi was explicit that such activity in bodies required a principle of action, just as the young Leibniz would insist. Indeed, when he talks about agents and principles of action in matter, as he does in the following passages from the *Syntagma*, Gassendi sounds a lot like Leibniz:

> But certainly in natural things there is an Agent operating inside them, and it is indeed distinguished from matter in part, but not from matter as a whole . . . since in everything there is a principle of action and of motion, . . . and as it were the flower of the whole of the matter, which is also the very thing that is usually called Form.[77]

[74] John Henry, in his 'Occult Properties and the Experimental Philosophy: Active Principles in Pre-Newtonian Matter Theory' (*History of Science* 24 (1986), 335–81), argues that many English philosophers regarded matter as endowed with activity, among them Petty, Glisson, and even Boyle. Clericuzio disagrees ('Redefinition', 572), quoting passages showing Boyle's trenchant opposition to ascribing self-motion to matter. Nevertheless, Boyle certainly upheld the incessant motion of matter, and in his *New Essays* Leibniz mentions only Boyle in this connection, citing 'Mr. Boyle's book attacking absolute rest' in support of his view that 'there is never a body without movement', which 'is one of my proofs that there are no atoms' (i.e. classical atoms): G. W. Leibniz, *New Essays on Human Understanding*, ed. and trans. Peter Remnant and Jonathan Bennett (Cambridge: Cambridge University Press, 1981), 53.

[75] 'Whence also the motive force which is in each concrete thing owes its origin to atoms; nor is it in fact distinct from their weight (*pondus*) or impetus' (Gassendi, *Animadversiones*, 309). 'Supposing (as Democritus did not deny) that motion is ascribable to atoms, he judged it absurd not to attribute to them a special force by which such motion is initiated: of this kind is gravity or weight, or impulsion, and also the impetus by which whatever moves is made to act' (*Syntagma Philosophicum* [*Syntagma*], *Opera*, i 280; cf. Clericuzio, *Elements*, 64).

[76] In the *Syntagma* Gassendi wrote that the thesis 'that atoms have in themselves a motive force or impetus must be disapproved' (*Opera*, i 280); see Clericuzio, *Elements*, 64–5. Boyle also considered and rejected this Epicurean thesis in *An Essay of the Intestine Motions of the Particles of Quiescent Solids; where the Absolute Rest of Bodies is called in Question* (*The Works of Robert Boyle*, ed. Hunter and Davis, vi. 189–211). This is the book by Boyle referred to by Leibniz (see n. 74).

[77] Gassendi, *Syntagma*, *Opera*, I 336a, 337a; cf. Bloch, *Gassendi*, 216.

In these same passages, however, Gassendi attempts to account for this principle of action as 'that most mobile and active part' of the matter, a materialist construal that Leibniz evidently did not find convincing. Nevertheless, it is difficult to resist seeing something of Gassendi's *flos materiæ* ('flower of matter') in Leibniz's talk of a *flos substantiæ* ('flower of substance') in his letter to Duke Johann Friedrich in May 1671 and subsequent writings. Indeed, it seems to me that once it is realized that Gassendi advocated a principle of action in every body, and indeed 'forms' in matter whose effects would always be motions of parts of matter, one can begin to appreciate that Leibniz's later remarks about his early debt to Gassendi may not have been framed simply for their rhetorical effect.

Particularly important for assessing Gassendi's possible influence on Leibniz is his interpretation of *semina rerum* ('the seeds of things') as clusters of atoms of a certain type. Having already followed Sennert in distinguishing certain concretions of atoms (his *molecules*) as the principles of most chemical reactions, Gassendi also followed him in identifying certain of these compound corpuscles as *semina*, created by God at the beginning of things, containing all the 'genetic information', as it were, needed for the generation and development of minerals, stones, gems, and biological organisms.[78] Although there was a longstanding interpretation of seeds as active principles originating with the Stoics' *logoi spermatikoi*, to which Plotinus and Augustine gave an immaterialist interpretation that was later adopted by van Helmont, the identification of these seeds (*semina*) with certain atoms or compound corpuscles also had the warrant of the whole tradition of atomism from Epicurus and Lucretius to Bacon and Boyle. Here I do not think it necessary to say that Leibniz was influenced by atomism *as opposed to* Neoplatonism.[79] But I would urge that the dual roots of the idea of seminal principles (and the resulting ambiguity of the term) were particularly useful for his

[78] For a good recent account of Gassendi's views, see Clericuzio, *Elements*, 63–74. Leibniz could also have been influenced by Gassendi through his reading of Boyle, who followed Gassendi's identification of primary concretions of particles with seminal principles. See Clericuzio, 'Redefinition', 583.

[79] As Mercer has explained in her recent book, Leibniz inherits the doctrine of *rationes seminales* of Plotinus and Ficino through his teacher Thomasius, and is seriously committed to it (*Leibniz's Metaphysics*, 200 ff., 223 ff.); see also Catherine Wilson, 'Atoms, Minds, and Vortices', in S. Brown (ed.), *The Young Leibniz and his Philosophy (1646–1676)* (Dordrecht: Kluwer, 1999), 223–43, at 226.

conciliatory purposes: every atom or *bulla* is a seed precisely because it contains a seminal reason or mind.

At any rate, to return to Gassendi, the importance of his interpretation of *semina rerum* as indivisible compound particles is that it constitutes the theoretical basis for his advocacy of *preformationism*, which explained the growth of complex organisms from a pre-existing invisible seed. In this it was opposed to the rival hypothesis of *epigenesis*, which explained growth and development in terms of the action of a vital spirit acting on a purely passive matter.[80] Gassendi (again following Sennert) interpreted the pre-existing seed as an invisibly small and indivisible body which is itself active, containing an active principle or form responsible for taking it through the organic changes and accretions it would undergo. The indivisibility of the molecules by natural processes thus accounts for the persistence of natural kinds from the beginning of time, even if the individual organisms developing from these seeds do not so persist.

This feature of preformation, finally, is of great importance for Gassendi, because of its connection with the doctrine of the propagation of souls that he favored: *traducianism*. This doctrine, upheld by most Lutherans, had been promoted by Sennert before him, and Leibniz too was committed to it from an early age.[81] It maintained that souls are propagated *per traducem*, i.e. through the parents' seeds, as opposed to being introduced at conception from the outside. Gassendi's preformationism thus puts this theological doctrine on a firm natural philosophical footing by identifying the seeds as indestructible corpuscles containing forms or souls (immortal souls in the case of humans), passed on in biological generation.

Leibniz's transformationism can therefore be seen as a modification or variant of Gassendi's preformationism.[82] What Gassendi holds to be

---

[80] For a succinct account of the opposition between epigenesis and preformationism, see Richard S. Westfall, *The Construction of Modern Science* (Cambridge: Cambridge University Press, 1977), 99 ff.

[81] On Sennert's traducianism, see E. Michael, 'Daniel Sennert on Matter and Form: At the Juncture of Old and New', *Early Science and Medicine* 2/3 (1997), 272–99. For an interpretation of Leibniz as piously committed to Lutheranism, see Ursula Goldenbaum, 'Leibniz as a Lutheran', in A. P. Coudert, R. H. Popkin, and G. M. Weiner (eds.), *Leibniz, Mysticism, and Religion* (Dordrecht: Kluwer, 1998), 169–92.

[82] As noted in n. 42, Leibniz saw the microscopists Leeuwenhoek and Swammerdam as agreeing with his transformationism; they are usually regarded as among the most prominent seventeenth-century preformationists.

true of the natural kinds generated by the seeds, is for Leibniz true of the individual substances. In each case the forms were created at the beginning of the world by God, and will last for all creation. And for the young Leibniz, as for Gassendi, their indestructibility is explained in terms of indestructible material casings, with the growth and development of the organism explained in terms of an accretion of matter around this indivisible core, organized by the active principle within. But what Gassendi holds to be the case for human souls is generalized by Leibniz into a general solution for 'the vexatious problem of the origin of forms': for him all forms, not just human souls, are principles of individuation, and all forms are immortal. This immortality, in turn, follows from their immateriality. Thus Leibniz's main divergence from Gassendi lies in his rejection of materialism, and his persistent attempts to explain by means of rationalistic principles how mind organizes matter around the nucleus. Not to be forgotten too, of course, is the Anaxagorean strain in Leibniz's thought: since the physical continuum is not merely finitely divided into atoms, but infinitely divided, each atom is as it were a miniature world.

To summarize: even if we do not take Leibniz at his word for his claimed debt to Gassendi's atomism, a comparison of their views does much to explain the motivations for his own atomism. The hypothesis of active atoms containing an organizing principle or form explains the origin and persistence of natural kinds, as well as the indestructibility of souls, and the generation of biological organisms and minerals from seeds. It also grounds the theological doctrine of traducianism, which is strongly linked to the biological doctrine of preformation. Two marked differences of Leibniz from Gassendi, though, are his hypothesis of the infinite dividedness of matter, and his insistence on the immateriality of souls, from which he wanted to derive their immortality.

But if Leibniz's thought is distinguished from Gassendi's in his insisting on the immateriality of forms, this does not distinguish him from Daniel Sennert, who was perfectly explicit that forms, in keeping with religious orthodoxy, must be immaterial. In his *De chymicorum*, Sennert wrote

Forms are the divine and immutable principle that determines all actions and passions of a natural thing; and they are, as it were, the instrument and hand of the most wise Creator and Workman God, who in creation freely bestowed this force and efficacy onto these his instruments, than which nothing more marvellous can be thought. This is what J. [C.] Scaliger has rightly also taught . . . For there is in every natural thing, and in the parts of body, besides the matter that the elements supply, a certain divine principle and fifth nature, by which they are that which they are, and are reduced to a certain family of a natural kind. For the elements are material, and so are not capable of giving rise to action.   (353, 358)

Thus Leibniz's investing of his atoms with an immaterial form is in keeping with the views of one of the chief proponents of seventeenth-century atomism. For both him and Sennert it is the immaterial form or soul that makes matter organic and able to sense, and is the source of its actions and passions. In fact, this contextualizing of Leibniz's thought within the atomist tradition sets his 'rehabilitation' of substantial forms in quite a different light. For Sennert had effectively already proposed such a rehabilitation when, in his *Hypomnemata physica* of 1636, he opposed the rejection of substantial forms by the atomist Basson. Now, I am not claiming here that Leibniz was directly influenced by Sennert, or by any particular texts, only that certain key features of his position were implicit in the atomist tradition with which he was certainly familiar. There is also the very great difference that Leibniz was concerned to give a rehabilitation that was consistent with mechanical principles. In the important manuscript 'Metaphysical Definitions and Reflections' (summer 1678–winter 1680/1), for instance, Leibniz argues that 'Even though all things are animate, nonetheless they all act according to the laws of mechanics, for sensation and appetite are determined by organs (i.e. parts of a body) and objects (i.e. by surrounding bodies)' (A VI.iv 1400; *Labyrinth*, 247).

The discussion so far has given us some insight into Leibniz's continued motivation for upholding a kind of atomism, namely one in which each atom constitutes the indivisible kernel of a corporeal substance, and contains a form or mind which individuates the substance and constitutes its active principle. But it leaves some features of the enigma of Leibniz's atomism outstanding: it still does not explain why he returned to perfectly solid atoms in 1676, nor why he eventually abandoned them altogether.

A full answer to these questions would take us too far afield, and must await another occasion. But let me sketch what I take to be the key to understanding these developments. In a nutshell, the answer I propose is that the changes in Leibniz's position on atoms are precipitated in large measure by changes in his understanding of the physical continuum, and the implications of this for his theories of cohesion and division. In particular, these changes make it impossible for him to sustain the endeavour theory of original cohesion that was foundational to his theory of *bullae*. As we have seen, this depended on the idea that a body impelling another has already begun to enter its place at the moment of impact by a part smaller than any given part, i.e. by an actually infinitely small part of space. But when Leibniz begins to doubt that the continuum can be regarded as composed from actual infinitesimal parts, the idea that a body's cohesion can be explained through the spatial continuity of such overlapping physical points becomes untenable. Once that theory is abandoned, however, Leibniz has no explanation of original cohesion, or of how it is that a body does not dissolve into its constituent points. It is at this juncture that he reconsiders the possibility of atoms in the strict sense: bodies that are indissectible, perfect solids, which are discrete aggregates of minima or physical points held together by minds. For if a body is actually infinitely divided into 'all the parts into which it can be divided', these must be, he supposes in February 1676, otherwise unconnected physical points. In order to compose an atom, some principle seems required other than what can be derived from matter and motion alone. Leibniz therefore proposes that this is 'mind': once 'thought has entered into a portion of matter' this portion becomes indissectible, or a 'perfect solid'. Mind, as we saw above, is no longer contained in a mathematical indivisible, but organizes matter around an atomic nucleus which is its indestructible kernel.

During this same period, however, Leibniz develops a new understanding of the infinite that militates against this conception of a body's being divided into an infinity of distinct points. We saw earlier that he seemed in his early work to understand infinitesimals as somehow standing for an unending containment of spheres within spheres. But this is at variance with his formula for an infinitesimal: a part smaller than any assignable. The latter is naturally paired with the *categorematic* infinite, to use the medieval term, that is, a number greater than any assignable. But in 1676 Leibniz comes to reject infinite number in this categorematic sense in favor of a properly *syncategorematic* understanding: to say that there are infinitely many things in this sense is to say that there are so many things that, no matter how large a (finite) number one assigns to them, there are more. This leads Leibniz to abandon the idea that an infinitely divided body does issue in 'all the parts into which it can be divided', as if it is the mere collection of these parts. 'If we suppose any body we please is actually resolved into still smaller bodies,' he writes in late April 1676, 'i.e. if some worlds are always supposed within others, would it thereby be divided into minimum parts? Thus being divided without end is different from being divided into minima, in that there will be no last part, just as in an unbounded line there is no last point' (A VI.iii 510; *Labyrinth.* 119). To say that the body is actually infinitely divided is to say rather that, no matter how many parts are assigned, there are more, but not that there is an infinite number of them. This syncategorematic understanding parallels Leibniz's interpretation of infinite series, which he reached in the same period: to say that an infinite series has a sum is not to say that one collects together and adds an infinite number of terms; rather it is to say that there is a number such that, for any specifiable error, some finite series with the same rule and first term will sum to that number within the specified error.[83]

This position reaches fruition in November 1676 in the dialogue *Pacidius Philalethi*, mentioned at the beginning of this essay. For there Leibniz explicitly rejects the 'perfect solids' and 'perfect liquids' he had entertained in the spring, replacing this conception of matter with one more reminiscent of Bacon's, where *plicae materiae* fill all of space through their folding and unfolding, with no need for a void or perfect fluid composed of points:

If a perfectly fluid body is assumed, a finest division, i.e. a division into minima, cannot be denied; yet a body that is everywhere flexible, though not without a certain and everywhere unequal resistance, still has cohering parts, although these are opened up and folded together in various ways. Accordingly the division of the continuum must not be considered to be like the division of sand into grains, but like that of a sheet of paper or tunic into folds. And so although there occur some folds smaller than others infinite in number, a body is never thereby dissolved into points or minima.—(A VI.iii 555; *Labyrinth*, 185)

This explains why Leibniz denies the existence of atoms in the *Pacidius*: all that exist are portions of matter that are themselves further subdivided. In accordance with his denial of the categorematic infinite, Leibniz

---

[83] Cf. Leibniz's '[to say] that a certain infinite series of numbers has a sum . . . [is to say] that any finite series with the same rule has a sum, and that the error always diminishes as the series increases, so that it becomes as small as we would like' (A VI.iii 503; *Labyrinth*, 99). See my defence of this interpretation of Leibniz on the infinite in my exchange with Gregory Brown in the *Leibniz Review*, culminating in 'Leibniz on Infinite Number, Infinite Wholes and the Whole World: A Reply to Gregory Brown', *Leibniz Review* 11 (2001), 103–16.

conceives worlds to be contained within worlds to infinity without this infinite division ever issuing in minima:

Accordingly I am of the following opinion: there is no portion of matter that is not actually divided into further parts, so that there is no body so small that there is not a world of infinitary creatures in it . . . This does not mean, however, either that a body or space is divided into points, or time into moments, because indivisibles are not parts, but the extrema of parts. And this is why, even though all things are subdivided, they are still not resolved all the way down into minima. (A VI.iii 565–6; *Labyrinth*, 209–11)

Thus there are no actual infinitesimals, or parts of a continuum smaller than any assignable part. Nonetheless, one can still treat infinitesimals as fictional parts, on the understanding that they are (finite) parts small enough that no error will arise.[84] In parallel with this, there are no atoms, in the categorematic sense of bodies so small that they cannot be further divided. Nevertheless, it is permissible to hypothesize them for the sake of physics or chemistry: an atom on this syncategorematic understanding would be a part assumed small enough that no error will arise, although in reality no part is so small that it is not further subdivided. An atom in this sense is what Leibniz also calls a 'physical point'.[85] All this is in keeping with Leibniz's interpretation of the infinite as exceeding every finite number that can be assigned, but not as a number greater than all finite numbers. It is to this syncategorematic conception, I submit, that Leibniz is referring in the passage in the *Phoranomus* I quoted at the beginning of this essay, when he writes that he was not able to abandon atoms and the void until he finally 'grasp[ed] that in reality there were parts in things exceeding every number, as a consequence of motion in a plenum'.

Still unexplained by this new position on division, however, is the problem of substance. We have seen that Leibniz is deeply committed to minds in matter, acting as principles of individuation, bearers of genetic

---

[84] For a lucid explanation of Leibniz's syncategorematic interpretation of infinitesimals in his mature work, see Hidé Ishiguro, *Leibniz's Philosophy of Logic and Language*, 2nd edn. (Cambridge: Cambridge University Press), ch. v, 79–100. In a paper in preparation, I trace the development of Leibniz's thought on infinitesimals in his early work, and how this evolves into a syncategorematic interpretation in 1676.

[85] Thus in a chemical manuscript dating from 1678–81, Leibniz writes: '*Physical minima* are those parts into which every single one of the components of a mixture is divided, but here they are taken as points. This portion may also be called an atom' (A VI.iv 2024 ff., N367₄). For the distinction between physical, mathematical, and metaphysical points, see n. 44 above.

information, organizing principles for chemical reactions and biological and mineral growth, and the font of a substance's actions and passions. But until he can explain how it is that mind enables a given substance to be the same over time, Leibniz cannot claim to have solved the metaphysical problem of substance. For if there are no atoms, and matter is a mere aggregate of parts, how is it that a form or mind is attached to this aggregate of parts at one time, and to that at another? What Leibniz appears to be actively seeking in the late 1670s is some principle which would explain the self-identity of a corporeal substance through time: if it is not conservation of a certain mass, then it appears likely that mind is connected with the conservation of motion.[86] 'Anyone seeking the primary sources of things,' he writes in his 'Metaphysical Definitions and Reflections' (summer 1678–winter 1680), 'must investigate how matter is divided into parts, and which of them is moving' (A VI.iv 1401; *Labyrinth*, 251).

But by 1678 Leibniz has finally found a solution to this problem, with his recognition that 'matter is divided not even into parts of equal bulk (*moles*) as some have supposed, nor into parts of equal speed, but into parts of equal power, but with bulk and speed unequal in such a way that the speeds are in inverse ratios to the magnitudes' (A VI.iv 1401–2; *Labyrinth*, 251). Something is the same corporeal substance, as I interpret this, not when it retains the same or equal matter, nor simply when it conserves the same quantity of motion through collisions, but when its parts before and after a collision have equal power (mv^2). (Here it must be remembered that Leibniz held that no force is transferred in collisions, 'but each body moves by an innate force, which is determined on the occasion of, i.e. with respect to another' (A VI.iv 1620; *Labyrinth*, 333).[87] Any apparent loss of force in an inelastic collision is carried away by invisible parts.) This discovery of conservation of mv^2 in early 1678 then clears the way for Leibniz's new reinterpretation of substantial forms as forces. This change is evident in the 'Conspectus for a Little Book on Physics' composed later that year, where, after rejecting atoms, Leibniz argues that the laws of motion follow from the equality of cause

---

[86] In 'On Motion and Matter' (early April 1676) Leibniz favours the idea that it is the universal mind that effects the conservation of motion, not the individual minds in each body: 'For when two bodies collide, it is clear that it is not the mind of each one that makes it follow the law of compensation, but rather the universal mind assisting both' (A VI.iii, 493; *Labyrinth*, 77).

[87] Cf. also: 'Rigorously speaking, no force is transferred from one body to another, but every body is moved by an innate force (*insita vi*)' (A VI.iv 1630; *Labyrinth*, 333).

and effect, from which the conservation of power is derived.[88] But from this there follows the necessity of souls or forms:

> It must also be demonstrated that every body is actually divided into smaller parts, i.e. that there are no such things as atoms, and that no continuum can be accurately assigned in body . . .

> Following this, the subject of incorporeals: There turn out to be certain things in body which cannot be explained by the necessity of matter alone. Such are the laws of motion, which depend on the metaphysical principle of the equality of cause and effect. Here therefore the soul must be treated, and it must be shown that all things are animated. Unless there were a soul, i.e. a kind of form, a body would not be an entity, since no part of it can be assigned which would not again consist of further parts, and so nothing could be assigned in body which could be called *this something*, or *some one thing*. That it is the nature of a soul or form to have some perception and appetite, which are passions and actions of the soul . . .   (A VI.iv 1988; *Labyrinth*, 233)

Thus I interpret the final configuration of Leibniz's thought on atoms as follows: there are no atoms, in the sense of parts of matter that are not actually divided. Nevertheless, one can proceed in natural philosophy on the assumption that there are atoms, provided these are understood to be parts assumed to be small enough that no error will arise on their being supposed undivided. On the other hand, metaphysically there must be atoms in the sense of substances having a real unity. These are the sources of actions and passions, and their conservation is necessary in order to explain a thing's self-identity, and its development according to its own nature. The essence of these metaphysical atoms is force, and they are manifested in physics in the form of a substance's conserving its own force, rather than a constant quantity of matter or of motion.

5. CONCLUSION

As was perhaps only to be expected, the enigma of Leibniz's atomism has required a rather complex resolution. I have argued here that his

---

[88] 'Force or power . . . must be estimated from the quantity of the effect. But the power of the effect and of the cause are equal to each other, for if that of the effect were greater we would have mechanical perpetual motion, if less, we would not have physical perpetual motion. Here it is worth showing that the same quantity of motion cannot be conserved, but that on the other hand the same quantity of power is conserved' (A VI.iv 1989; *Labyrinth*, 235).

long attachment to atoms is only explicable once it is seen in the context of the rich variety of atomisms current in the early seventeenth century. For Leibniz never (except perhaps in his teens) subscribed to atoms in the sense of purely material chunks of extension devoid of any internal complexity. Like Gassendi, whom he claimed to have followed, and also like Sennert, he appealed to atoms (or concretions of them) as the physically indivisible seed-cases within which the soul or organizing principle of organic bodies was contained. This allowed him to give a similar solution to Gassendi's of the problem of the origin of forms—namely a version of preformation—and by this means to uphold traducianism, the Lutheran doctrine of the transmission of souls through the parents' seed. On this interpretation of atoms, derived from those of Sennert, Sperling, Gassendi, Hobbes, Digby, and Jungius, they are physically indivisible in the sense of not being further divisible by natural processes, especially chemical ones, and thus as lasting for the duration of this world; but they are further divided within by intestine motions, and so are not indivisible in this sense.

This latter property of inner complexity and heterogeneity is one Leibniz's atoms shared with those proposed by a great variety of early modern thinkers. What distinguished Leibniz's various attempts in atomist physics from those of his predecessors, however, is his commitment to a 'modern' conception of qualities and forces. Where Magnen appealed to sympathy as an original quality of atoms of the same element, Leibniz construed it in terms of motion in common; where Gilbert and Kepler appealed to magnetism as an attractive force, Leibniz attempted to explain it in terms of a minimization of disturbance of motion. But, most importantly, where other atomists had supposed the cohesiveness of the atoms themselves as an original quality, Leibniz sought to give an explanation in terms of matter in motion.

But where Leibniz differed most decisively from Gassendi and other atomists was in his conception of matter as not merely mathematically divisible, but actually infinitely divided by the differing motions within it. This, of course, accentuated the difficulty of accounting for cohesion. In 1670, however, Leibniz thought he had found a way of reconciling infinite division with 'atoms' of a certain kind, these being the *terrellae* or *bullae* of his *HPN*. On this theory, matter is infinitely divided into points or indivisibles, which differ in size in proportion to their corresponding indivisible motions, or endeavours; the overlapping of such points then explains the cohesion around meridian lines of the surface of each *bulla*. Thus in this period we find Leibniz rejecting classical atoms, but nevertheless making positive references to atoms in the sense of chemical units or biological seeds, containing a soul or mind which individuates them.

Two further threads lead Leibniz to a final resolution of these issues. One is his reinterpretation in 1676 of actually infinite division as not issuing in a least part or minimum. An atom then becomes a hypothetical minimum part of matter, a part assumed small enough that no error will arise, although in reality no part is so small that it is not further subdivided. The second thread concerns the principle of activity and individuation that must be supposed in any body, no matter how small, if it is not to be a mere phenomenon. When in 1678 Leibniz locates this in his new conception of force, he is finally free to abandon the idea of a physically indestructible atomic core to corporeal substance. The sameness of a substance, formerly explicated by means of its possession of a mind, is now construed in terms of the conservation of living force. Not only is the self-identity of a certain quantity of matter organized by the soul now no longer required, the atomic core itself becomes redundant. Thus it is that after 1678 atoms are firmly rejected by Leibniz, their only role being as hypothetical minimal parts of elements enabling certain explanations in natural philosophy.

The enigma I set out to resolve in this essay was how in his youth Leibniz could have advocated atoms for so many years after he had reached the conclusion that matter is actually infinitely divided. For if atoms are taken in the sense of finite bodies that are not further divided, then this conclusion directly precludes them, as Leibniz himself urged in his mature writings. I have argued that the enigma is resolved once it is realized that Leibniz never did subscribe to atoms of this sort. His atoms, far from being devoid of internal complexity, were further divided within by the intestine motions of their parts, and contained within them a mind or soul that is the principle of their activity, and is responsible for their individuation and the accretion and organization of surrounding matter into an organic body. In all these respects Leibniz's atomism, for all its modernism regarding forces and qualities, is best regarded as continuing the lively seventeenth-century tradition of atomism articulated by Sennert and Gassendi.

McMaster University

9

Answering Bayle's Question: Religious Belief in the Moral Philosophy of the Scottish Enlightenment

JAMES A. HARRIS

1. 'Bayle states the question,' wrote Lord Kames in his *Sketches of the History of Man*, 'Whether a people may not be happy in society and be qualified for good government, upon principles of morality singly, without any sense of religion'. 'The question is ingenious,' he continues, 'and may give opportunity for subtle reasoning'.[1] In this essay I examine some answers given to Bayle's question in the moral philosophy of the Scottish Enlightenment. Calvin had claimed that 'natural' man is so depraved 'that he can be moved or impelled only to evil';[2] and the Westminster Confession too affirms that, because of the sin of Adam and Eve, all human beings are 'made opposite to all good and wholly inclined to all evil' (VI. iv). Hutcheson, Kames, Smith, and Reid all reject this kind of pessimism. Breaking with the view that the human will is only steered away from evil by the gift of grace from God, they revive a Greek and Roman confidence in the potential of ordinary human nature. As their opponents were quick to point out, it seems to be a consequence of this faith in human nature that a man does not need to be a Christian in order to be virtuous. But this is not to say that they are prepared to countenance Bayle's idea of a prosperous community of virtuous atheists. Religious belief, albeit of a minimal, 'natural' kind, remains integral to virtue as they understand it. To doubt that there is a providential order to the universe and that there is a life after death, is to endanger one's natural preference for virtue over vice, for it renders one vulnerable to being embittered by the difficulties and disappointments

---

[1] Henry Home, Lord Kames, *Sketches of the History of Man* [*Sketches*], 2nd edn. 4 vols. (Edinburgh, 1778), iv. 344.

[2] John Calvin, *Institutes of the Christian Religion* [*Institutes*], ed. John T. McNeill, trans. Ford Lewis Battles (Philadelphia: The Westminster Press, 1961), 296 (II. iii. 5).

of everyday life. Natural religion, so Hutcheson and his successors hold, provides a framework of belief in which innate benevolence grows and flourishes into a secure and reflective commitment to the life of virtue.

The only moral philosopher of the Scottish Enlightenment to take seriously Bayle's hypothesis of the possibility of virtue without religion is Hume. In the final section of this essay I shall make some tentative suggestions as to what distinguishes Humean moral psychology from that developed by his most significant Scottish contemporaries. To leave Hume until last is, of course, to risk neglecting his role in the development of moral philosophy in eighteenth-century Scotland; and it would be absurd to suggest that Hume had no positive influence upon the theorizing of Kames, Smith, and Reid. My justification for turning to Hume only at the end of the essay is, however, that I am concerned here principally with what is *unique* in his work on the principals of morals. There has been a tendency in modern scholarship to emphasize Hume's debt to Hutcheson, and Smith's debt to Hume.[3] I shall focus on the similarities between Hutcheson, Kames, Smith, and Reid, and on the differences between them taken as a group and Hume. With respect to the relation between Hutcheson and Hume, I follow the lead especially of James Moore and M. A. Stewart, who have done much to bring to light the continuity between Hume's sceptical account of the understanding and his sceptical moral philosophy.[4] The relation between Smith and Hume has not received the same kind of revisionist attention, and what I say about it below must remain rather speculative until further work has been done. For the moment, my claim is simply that to recognize the role played by belief in providence in the moral theories of such as Hutcheson, Kames, Smith, and Reid is to be forced to recognize also

---

[3] Hume's debt to Hutcheson is stressed in, e.g. Norman Kemp Smith, *The Philosophy of David Hume: A Critical Study of its Origins and Central Doctrines* (London and New York: Macmillan, 1941) and in David Fate Norton, *David Hume: Common-Sense Moralist, Sceptical Metaphysician* [*David Hume*] (Princeton: Princeton University Press, 1982). Adam Smith's debt to Hume is a central feature of Knud Haakonssen's work on Smith: see, e.g. *The Science of a Legislator: The Natural Jurisprudence of David Hume and Adam Smith* [*Science of a Legislator*] (Cambridge: Cambridge University Press, 1981), ch. 3.

[4] See, e.g. James Moore, 'Hume and Hutcheson', in M. A. Stewart and J. P. Wright (eds.), *Hume and Hume's Connexions* (Edinburgh: Edinburgh University Press, 1994), 23–57, and M. A. Stewart, 'Two Species of Philosophy: The Historical Significance of the First *Enquiry*', in Peter Millican (ed.), *Reading Hume on Human Understanding* (Oxford: Clarendon Press, 2002), 67–96. The distinctiveness of Hume's contribution to eighteenth-century moral philosophy is well characterized in Isabel Rivers, *Reason, Grace and Sentiment, ii: Shaftesbury to Hume* (Cambridge: Cambridge University Press, 2000), ch. 4.

one respect in which Hume is at odds with the moral philosophy prevalent in the Scotland of his day.

2. Bayle's case for the possibility—indeed, actual existence—of virtuous atheists is made in the *Pensées diverses sur la comète* of 1683, which was translated into English in 1708.[5] The paradox took on a life of its own when, extracted from the layers of irony of the *Penseés diverses*, it became the principal theme of Book I of Shaftesbury's *Inquiry concerning Virtue, or Merit*. Shaftesbury takes as his theme 'What honesty or virtue is, considered by itself; and in what manner it is influenced by religion: how far religion necessarily implies virtue; and whether it is a true saying that "it is impossible for an atheist to be virtuous, or share any real degree of honesty or merit".[6] Before he addresses this question, Shaftesbury proposes some definitions which will be useful for my purposes in this essay. To be a 'perfect theist', he says, is '[t]o believe . . . that everything is governed, ordered or regulated for the best by a designing principle or mind, necessarily good and permanent', while to be a 'perfect atheist' is '[t]o believe nothing of a designing principle or mind nor any cause, measure or rule of things but chance, so that in nature neither the interest of the whole nor of any particulars can be said to be in the least designed, pursued or aimed at'.[7] There were, of course, many in the eighteenth century who found Shaftesbury's definition of theism, with its omission of the necessity of belief in the Trinity or the Resurrection, unacceptable; but I shall assume that the definition captures the essence of the creed espoused by Hutcheson, Kames, Smith, and Reid. For these men, as for Shaftesbury,

---

[5] See Pierre Bayle, *Pensées diverses sur la comète* [*Pensées diverses*], ed. A. Prat, 2nd edn. rev. P. Rétat, 2 vols. (Paris: Société des Textes Français Modernes, 1994), especially the long series of proofs 'Que l'Atheïsme n'est pas un plus grand mal que l'Idolatrie'. See also Elisabeth Labrousse, *Bayle*, trans. Dennis Potts (Oxford: Oxford University Press, 1983), 52–4. As Labrousse notes, in addition to arguing for the existence of virtuous atheists, Bayle also proposes that a society of perfect Christians would soon be ruined by its own virtuousness. This was a paradox developed aggressively by Mandeville in his argument that 'private vices' are necessary to the economic health of a state. Dugald Stewart wrote in 1820, in his 'Dissertation' for the *Encyclopædia Britannica*, that 'The influence . . . of [Bayle's] writings on the taste and views of speculative men of all persuasions, has been so great, as to mark him out as one of the most conspicuous characters of his age' (*The Works of Dugald Stewart*, ed. Sir William Hamilton, 11 vols. (Edinburgh, 1854–60), i. 315). For a brief account of the context and argument of the *Pensées diverses*, see Walter Rex, *Essays on Pierre Bayle and Religious Controversy* (The Hague: Martinus Nijhoff, 1965), ch. 2.

[6] Anthony Ashley Cooper, Third Earl of Shaftesbury, *Characteristics of Men, Manners, Opinions, Times* [*Characteristics*], ed. Lawrence E. Klein (Cambridge: Cambridge University Press), 163–4 (*Inquiry*, I. i. 1).   [7] Ibid. 165 (*Inquiry*, I. i. 2).

belief in God is first and foremost belief in Providence, and to deny the existence of God is to affirm what was often termed 'Epicureanism'. The question, then, was whether virtue was possible for one who believed that death is the end, and that there is no supernatural force ensuring that apparent evils have a place in the larger scheme of things.

Having defined virtue as 'a certain just disposition or proportionable affection of a rational creature towards the moral objects of right and wrong', Shaftesbury goes on to consider what in a rational creature can 'exclude a principle of virtue or render it ineffectual'.[8] He concludes, first, that no purely speculative opinion can damage the natural sense of right and wrong; secondly, that atheism cannot be responsible for setting up false ideas of right and wrong; and thirdly, that 'without an absolute assent to any hypothesis of theism, the advantages of virtue may be seen and owned and a high opinion of it established in the mind'.[9] The Baylean notion of a non-Christian life of virtue entered Scottish currents of thought via Hutcheson's explanation and defence of Shaftesburian principles; and nowhere is the voice of Shaftesbury more plainly heard in Hutcheson's work than in the final section of the *Illustrations on the Moral Sense*, entitled 'How far a Regard to the Deity is necessary to make an Action virtuous'. Here Hutcheson addresses the opinion that, in view of God's infinite goodness, 'to act from Love to [God's creatures] without *Intention* to please God, must be infinitely evil'.[10] To act from a natural love of others, without thought of God, so some believe, is to ignore the fact that all that is good in men comes from God. All gratitude and benevolence should be directed towards God alone, and not towards the mere vessels of his grace. The atheist, no matter how naturally virtuous, will fail to fulfil his higher obligations; and, so argues the opponent Hutcheson sets up for himself, because he is not good, he must be evil. '[A]nything in profane men that appears praiseworthy must be considered worthless', Calvin wrote; 'where there is no zeal to glorify God, the chief part of uprightness is absent'.[11] As already noted, in the Calvinist tradition the will of the 'natural man' is in the aftermath of the Fall permanently bent towards sin: in the words of

---

[8] Anthony Ashley Cooper, Third Earl of Shaftesbury, *Characteristics of Men, Manners, Opinions, Times* [*Characteristics*], ed. Lawrence E. Klein (Cambridge: Cambridge University Press), 177 (*Inquiry*, I. iii. 1).　　　　　　　　　　　[9] Ibid. 189 (*Inquiry*, II. iii. 3).

[10] Francis Hutcheson, *An Essay on the Nature of the Conduct of the Passions and Affections, with Illustrations on the Moral Sense* [*Essay*] (London, 1728), 302 (*Illustrations*, VI. i).

[11] Calvin, *Institutes*, 294 (II. iii. 4).

Thomas Boston's extremely popular *Human Nature in its Fourfold State*, the will is 'now turned traitor, and rules with and for the devil'.[12]

Hutcheson accepts that 'the most virtuous Temper is that in which the *Love* equals its *Causes*':[13] love of someone should be, at the least, proportionate to the benefits one has received from him. To love someone is to seek to increase his happiness. And so long as we assume that God's happiness is increased by the happiness of his creatures, love of God will, as Hutcheson puts it, 'directly excite us to all manner of *beneficent Actions*'.[14] There need, then, be no tension between love of God and love of his creatures, so long as it is accepted that it is appropriate to have stronger affections of love and gratitude for God than for anyone else. But suppose you love God's creatures without any idea at all that there is a God? Is this evidence of an evil disposition? Hutcheson's answer is that 'No Object which is entirely *unknown*, or of which we have no *Idea*, can raise *Affection* in the best Temper'; 'consequently *want of Affection* to an unknown Object evidences no evil'.[15] Hutcheson knows that this is likely to be countered by the objection that, in matters divine as in matters legal, ignorance is no excuse. Men have always been under an obligation to recognize the truth of theism, it is said by some. Hutcheson replies that, while it is true that reflection quickly discovers the existence of God and of (moral) laws of nature, men have to know that they must reflect before the process of discovery can begin; and 'if the *Idea of a Deity* be neither imprinted [as an innate idea], nor offer itself even previously to any *Reflection*, nor be universally excited by *Tradition*, the bare *Want* of it, where there has been no *Tradition* or *Reflection*, cannot be called criminal upon any Scheme'.[16]

The atheist is one who has reflected upon the evidence that there is a God and who refuses to be persuaded by it. Hutcheson's principal point in this section of the *Illustrations* is that such a person is not necessarily less virtuous than one who devotes his love to the divinity. There are degrees of 'goodness of temper', according to Hutcheson, and, so he says,

'tis plain, that in *equal Moments* of good produced by two agents, the *Goodness of the Temper* is inversly as the several *additional Helps*, or *Motives* to it. So that *more*

---

[12] *The Whole Works of the Late Reverend Thomas Boston of Ettrick*, ed. Samuel McMillan, 12 vols. (Aberdeen, 1850), viii. 56. *Human Nature in its Fourfold State* was first published in 1710, and was in its 20th edn. by 1771.   [13] Hutcheson, *Essay*, 305 (*Illustrations*, VI. ii).
[14] Ibid. 307 (*Illustrations*, VI. iii).   [15] Ibid. 317 (*Illustrations*, VI. v).
[16] Ibid. (*Illustrations*, VI. v).

Virtue is evidenced by any given *Moment* of Beneficence from good Affections only toward our *Fellows*, or particular Persons, than by the *same Moment* produced from the joint Considerations of the Deity, or of a general *System* or Species.[17]

Hutcheson is not easy to follow here, but the point seems to be that where the amount, or 'moment', of good is produced by two actions, one of which is performed only with a view to the benefit of one of our fellow men, and the other of which is performed with the same view *but also with a view to expression of gratitude to God*, then there is in fact *more* virtue in the former action than in the latter. The reason for this is that the goodness of an action is equal to the love it expresses divided by the causes of that love.[18] Because the action done to please God has a greater cause of love than one done merely to benefit a fellow human being, its goodness turns out to be less. It is hard to know how seriously to take this example of Hutcheson's fondness for moral algebra, but the larger message is clear: 'that Temper must really be very *deficient* in Goodness, which needs to excite it to any good Office, to recal the Thoughts of a Deity, or a *Community*, or a *System*'.[19] Hutcheson, indeed, is much more explicit than Shaftesbury about the damage that false ideas of what God demands of us can do to both the workings of the moral sense and the motivating power of our natural benevolence. He complains that Christianity has too frequently neglected the attribute of benevolence in its characterization of the divinity; and says that to imagine God to be 'cruel, wrathful, or capricious' is 'apt to raise a *Resemblance* of Temper in the Worshipper, with its attendant *Misery*'.[20]

3. The idea that virtue is to any extent independent of Christian belief was a permanent bugbear of the 'Orthodox' or 'Popular' opponents of the 'Moderate' wing of the Church of Scotland.[21] The philosophers under discussion here were not part of the 'Moderate' faction, but their

---

[17] Hutcheson, *Essay*, 323 (*Illustrations*, VI. vii).   [18] See Ibid. 304–5 (*Illustrations*, VI. ii).

[19] Ibid. 328 (*Illustrations*, VI. viii). Hutcheson is quick to modify this sentiment with admission that thoughts of God and of the good of humankind considered as a whole *strengthen* all good affections.

[20] See, e.g. § 9 of 'Reflections on the Common Systems of Morality', in Francis Hutcheson, *On Human Nature*, ed. Thomas Mautner (Cambridge: Cambridge University Press, 1993); and Hutcheson, *Essay*, 176–7 (VI. iii).

[21] For an account of the controversy between Moderates and Orthodox, see Ian D. L. Clark, 'From Protest to Reaction: The Moderate Regime in the Church of Scotland, 1752–1805', in N.T. Phillipson and Rosalind Mitchison (eds.), *Scotland in the Age of Improvement* (Edinburgh: Edinburgh University Press, 1970), 200–24.

work was taken by the Orthodox to provide the theoretical foundation for the all-too-worldly sermons of such as Hugh Blair, John Home, and William Robertson.[22] Naturally enough, the Orthodox exaggerated the independence of morality and religion in their polemics. In *Ecclesiastical Characteristics*, his satire on 'Moderation', John Witherspoon advises that the would-be Moderate man should in his preaching confine himself to the inculcation of social duties, and that these duties should be recommended only from rational considerations, '*viz.* the beauty and comely proportions of *virtue*, and its advantages to the present life, without any regard to a future state of more extended self-interest'.[23] The truly Moderate man draws his authorities 'from Heathen writers, none, or as few as possible, from scripture', and he avoids the word 'grace' as much as he can. Witherspoon mocks the Hutchesonian claim 'That virtue is founded upon instinct and affection'.[24] Virtue, he says, 'was once stiff and rigid, like ice or cold iron; now she is yielding as water, and like iron hot from the furnace, can easily be beaten into what shape you please'.[25] This last point is returned to by George Anderson, the man largely responsible for the abortive attempt of 1754–5 to prosecute Lord Kames and Hume for atheism.[26] Writing on 'the profit and loss of religion', Anderson declares abhorrence for what he calls the 'sensitive philosophy' on the grounds that it 'takes morality off the old and solid foundation, to place it upon an internal sensation, to be understood according to everyone's fancy'.[27] To rely on a moral *sense* to

---

[22] For the Edinburgh 'moderate literati', see Richard Sher, *Church and University in the Scottish Enlightenment: The Moderate Literati of Edinburgh* (Edinburgh: Edinburgh University Press, 1985). Sher calls the religion of the Moderates 'Christian Stoicism'. The central tenet of this religion, he writes, 'is that to attain true happiness people should concentrate on being benevolent in thought and deed, leaving results, outcomes, and consequences in the capable hands of the deity' (179). The contrast between Christian Stoicism and Epicureanism is, according to Sher, particularly clear in Adam Ferguson's work on the history of the Roman Republic, where Epicureanism is taken to represent 'maximization of personal pleasure, the denial of Providence, the reduction of all ethical issues to pleasure and pain, and the insistence that all goodness is restricted to private affairs' (200).

[23] John Witherspoon, *Ecclesiastical Characteristics: or, the Arcana of Church Policy* [*Ecclesiastical Characteristics*], 5th edn. (Edinburgh, 1763), 26.   [24] Ibid. 65.

[25] Ibid. 51.

[26] For an account of the controversy, see Ian Simpson Ross, *Lord Kames and the Scotland of his Day* (Oxford: Clarendon Press, 1972), ch. 5.

[27] George Anderson, *An Estimate of the Profit and Loss of Religion, personally and publicly stated* [*Estimate*] (Edinburgh, 1753), 10. Anderson devotes an entire section of his book to Bayle's claim that virtuousness does not depend upon belief in, in Anderson's words, 'a providence which distributes rewards and punishments, according to the merit, or demerit, of rational

inform us of the distinction between right and wrong is to give up on the possibility of our grasping what is *obligatory* about virtue and what is *forbidden* about vice. '[H]uman nature, and human reason,' Anderson argues, 'abstracting from divine authority, doth not furnish us with a law to regulate our conduct.'[28] No matter how 'exquisite' one's feelings may be, it is a 'beastly morality' which has no place for law and its unconditional obligation.[29]

What Witherspoon and Anderson are claiming is that there is an important difference between doing the right thing because one's character and sentiments prompt one to, and doing the right thing because one *recognizes* that it is the right thing to do. Acting out of respect for law is, they believe, the essence of virtue. Full-blown moral worth requires there to be a sense of obligation, and a sense of obligation requires belief in a supremely powerful being able to endow moral laws with absolute authority. According to Witherspoon and Anderson, then, the non-Christian is unable to merit genuinely moral approbation. Like William Warburton in *The Divine Legation of Moses*, they reply to the claim that an atheist may have a 'natural' idea of the difference between good and evil with arguments to the effect that one without belief in God, in Warburton's words, 'can never come to knowledge of the *Morality* of actions properly so called', since, as Warburton continues, the morality of an action lies in its obligatoriness, and the obligatoriness of an action 'necessarily implies an Obliger'.[30] This was not a line of thought that the second generation of Scottish Enlightenment moral philosophers was inclined simply to dismiss. Kames, Smith, and Reid recognized that Hutcheson's lack of interest in the notion of duty left his moral philosophy seriously incomplete.[31] But they were not prepared to follow the Orthodox in looking to the will of God for the source of the concept of

creatures' (66–7). The essence of atheism, according to Anderson, is not so much the denial of theological doctrines as the undermining of the direct influence that belief in God should have on human conduct. He sees the watered-down natural religion of the moderates as indistinguishable from deism in its obfuscation of the connection between faith and practice.

[28] Ibid. 85.   [29] Ibid. 95–7.

[30] William Warburton, *The Divine Legation of Moses* [*Legation*], 4th edn. (London, 1765), 92, 95.

[31] See, in addition to the texts discussed below, Hugh Blair's review of Hutcheson's *System of Moral Philosophy* in the *Edinburgh Review*, i (1755), 9–23. In a generally sympathetic review, Blair writes that 'Mr. Hutcheson's scheme would have been much more compleat, if he had distinguished, in a more explicit manner, betwixt a sense of duty, and a simple approbation of moral sense' (18). He concludes the long paragraph devoted to this subject: 'In general, we may

moral obligation. A source of normativity, therefore, had to be found within the self.[32]

One of the first to seek to supplement Hutchesonian moral theory with a central role for the concept of duty had in fact been Kames, the principal target of Anderson's *Estimate of the Profit and Loss of Religion*. Though the terms 'duty' and 'obligation' 'are of the utmost importance in morals', Kames says in his essay 'Of the Foundation and Principles of the Law of Nature', 'I know not that any author has attempted to explain them, by pointing out those principles or feelings which they express'.[33] Shaftesbury shows only that virtue is in our interest; Hutcheson 'founds the morality of acts, on a certain quality of actions, which procures approbation and love to the agent'.[34] Both fail to account for the distinction between our approval of benevolent and generous actions, on the one hand, and the feeling of the authority of considerations of 'justice, faith, and truth' on the other:

> Benevolence and generosity are more beautiful, and more attractive of love and esteem, than justice. Yet, not being so necessary to the support of society, they are left upon the general footing of approbatory pleasure; while justice, faith, truth, without which society could not at all subsist, are the objects of the above peculiar feeling, to take away all shadow of liberty, and to put us under a necessity of performance.[35]

The 'peculiar feeling' is the work of conscience, which Kames describes as 'the voice of God within us which commands our strictest obedience, just as much as when his will is declared by open revelation'.[36] Kames

---

observe, concerning the strain of this part of our author's philosophy, that it represents virtue rather in the light of a beautiful and noble object, recommended by the inward approbation of our minds, than as a law dictated by conscience; and may be calculated rather for making virtuous men better, than for teaching the bulk of mankind the first principles of duty' (19–20).

[32] Warburton claims that 'The Obliger must be different from, and not one and the same with the obliged' (*Legation*, 95): it is, of course, not only in Scotland that a good deal of eighteenth-century energy is expended in showing this claim to be wrong.

[33] Henry Home, later Lord Kames, *Essays on the Principles of Morality and Natural Religion* [*Essays*] (Edinburgh, 1751), 54. [34] Ibid. 55.

[35] Ibid. 61.

[36] Ibid. 63–4. Kames acknowledges the importance of Butler's examination of the foundations of moral duty in the preface to the *Sermons*, but argues that Butler 'has not said enough to afford that light the subject is capable of': there is more to conscience than mere disapprobation; conscience 'is none of our principles of action, but their guide and director'; and 'the authority of conscience' does not consist merely in an act of reflection, but 'arises from a direct feeling' (*Essays*, 61–3).

does not, however, suggest that we need to *know* that conscience is the voice of God in order to bind ourselves to its dictates. The moral sense has a natural authority over the principles of action. When it disapproves of something we have done, it produces 'the sense of merited punishment, and dread of its being inflicted upon us', a feeling which, Kames says, can rise to 'a degree of anguish and despair'.[37] Human nature itself is the source of the dictates of conscience: we do not need to wait for religion, or positive law, to tell us that some actions are obligatory and others forbidden.

In *The Theory of Moral Sentiments* Smith develops more fully this notion of a natural sense of duty.[38] He describes a process of self-examination in which, as he puts it, a man is divided into two persons, making him at the same time agent and spectator of his actions. The spectator Smith calls 'the man within the breast',[39] and it is he who overcomes and corrects the biases inherent in feelings which are too weak to prompt us to genuinely impartial acts of generosity and justice. We find it hard to make an objective assessment of our own particular passions and affections, Smith observes; and '[t]his self-deceit, this fatal weakness of mankind, is the source of half the disorders of human life'.[40] Yet '[o]ur continual observations upon the conduct of others, insensibly leads us to form to ourselves certain general rules concerning what is fit and proper either to be done or to be avoided'; and a regard to general rules is what 'institutes the most essential difference between a man of principle and honour, and a worthless fellow'.[41] The importance we attach to these rules is enhanced by the opinion—'first impressed by nature, and afterwards confirmed by reasoning and philosophy'—that they are the commandments and laws of God.[42] But neither insight into the content of the rules, nor acceptance of their binding force, derives in the first instance from belief in their divine origin. The sense of duty is

---

[37] Kames, *Essays*, 64.

[38] In his discussion of justice, Smith expresses a debt to 'that remarkable distinction between justice and all the other social virtues, which has of late been insisted upon by an author of very great and original genius'—that is, by Kames: see Adam Smith, *The Theory of Moral Sentiments* [*Theory*], ed. D. D. Raphael and A. L. Macfie (Indianapolis: Liberty Fund, 1984), 81 (II. ii. i). See also the anonymous *Some Late Opinions concerning the Foundation of Morality* (Edinburgh, 1753), which also commends Kames for 'stating so clearly the sentiment of duty or moral obligation, and distinguishing it from the sentiment of simple moral approbation' (8).

[39] Smith, *Theory*, 130 (III. ii).   [40] Ibid. 158 (III. iv).

[41] Ibid. 159, 163 (III. iv, v).   [42] Ibid. 163 (III. v).

'natural', and religion serves only to give it reinforcement.[43] Like Shaftesbury, Smith believes that one's natural sense of right and wrong provides a way of distinguishing between false and true religions. The true religion reveals itself as such, not through Scripture or miracles, but rather through its consonance with and reaffirmation of what we already know to be admirable moral principles.

Smith is sceptical of the idea that *all* our actions ought only to arise from a sense of duty. 'As a person may act wrong by following a wrong sense of duty,' he says, 'so nature may sometimes prevail, and lead him to act right in opposition to it.'[44] Reid moves further away from Hutcheson than does Smith. He holds that 'those actions *only* can truly be called virtuous, or deserving of moral approbation, which the agent believed to be right, and to which he was influenced, more or less, by that belief'.[45] But he too rejects the idea that a regard for the will of God must be where the agent gets his notion of right from. Reid looks to *reason* for the source of the idea of duty, and to the *moral sense* or *conscience* for the means whereby to translate the deliverances of reason into principles of action. 'The subject of law must have the conception of a general rule of conduct, which, without some degree of reason, he cannot have. He must likewise have a sufficient inducement to obey the law, even when his strongest animal desires draw him the contrary way.'[46] The notion of duty, Reid says, is 'too simple to admit of a logical definition'.[47] It certainly cannot be resolved into considerations of interest or happiness; and nor, one infers, can it be resolved into considerations of what God demands of us. As is the case in Smith's moral theory, acting in accordance with duty is best seen as a man's obedience to his better self. Reid, it is true, holds that '[t]hat conscience which is in every man's breast, is the law of God written in his own heart'; and also says that '[r]ight sentiments of the Deity and his works . . . add the authority of a Divine law to every rule of right conduct'.[48] Nevertheless, when we disobey the dictates of conscience, we stand 'self-condemned': the rules

---

[43] Ibid. 170 (III. v).   [44] Ibid. 177 (III. vi).

[45] *The Works of Thomas Reid, D. D.* [*Works*], ed. Sir William Hamilton, 6th edn. (Edinburgh, 1863), 647 (*Essays on the Active Powers*, V. iv); emphasis added.

[46] Ibid. 586 (*Essays on the Active Powers*, III. iii. v).

[47] Ibid. 587 (*Essays on the Active Powers*, III. iii. v).

[48] Ibid. 638, 639 (*Essays on the Active Powers*, V. i).

of right conduct have their own authority, independent of their being recognized as the law of God.

In opposition to the Calvinist tradition as represented by Witherspoon and Anderson, the moral philosophers that followed Hutcheson portray virtue as a natural expression of principles intrinsic to the human constitution. When we respond to our sense of right and wrong, we are beholden, not to a softening of the heart caused by God's unmerited grace, but rather to motivational principles rooted in what Kames calls 'the very frame of our nature'.[49] There is more to virtue than simple Hutchesonian benevolence: there are times when benevolence has to be stiffened or even corrected by the concept of duty. But even then, we are, to use the Pauline idiom later taken up by Kant, giving the law to ourselves, in the sense that we do not need to be aware of the divine provenance of the moral law in order to recognize its bindingness. However, this naturalism about virtue is of a distinctive kind. It will be helpful for the purpose of the comparison with Hume that will be the concern of Section 5 of this essay to note the fact that there is a very strong sense among the moral philosophers discussed thus far that the frame of our nature is the work of God. Their naturalism is what has been called 'providential naturalism'.[50] Providentialism is obvious in the writings of philosophers of the 'common sense' tradition such as Kames and Reid.[51] It is perhaps less obvious in Smith. Most recent work on Smith has wanted to downplay its importance in *The Theory of Moral Sentiments*, as if there is a risk that to take seriously Smith's frequent invocations of the work of an intelligent and benevolent designer is to jeopardize his achievement as a scientist of the mind.[52] I believe that there is no such risk, and that careful attention needs to be paid to Smith's talk of evidence of providence in the human constitution if his moral

[49] See Kames, *Essays*, 94: 'abstracting altogether from [God's] will, there is an obligation to virtue founded in the very frame of our nature'.

[50] This phrase was coined by David Fate Norton, and is given a comprehensive definition in Norton, *David Hume*, esp. pp. 170–3, 202–5.

[51] See, e.g. the peroration to Kames's *Essays on the Principles of Morality and Natural Religion*, sometimes taken to have been written by Hugh Blair ('[D]o not all these wonders, O *Eternal Mind*! Sovereign Architect of all! form a hymn to thy praise?' (*Essays*, 389); and so on); and Reid's Preface to the *Essays on the Intellectual Powers*, where he quotes Burke's declaration that 'The more accurately we search into the human mind, the stronger traces we every where find of his wisdom who made it' (Thomas Reid, *Essays on the Intellectual Powers of Man*, ed. Derek R. Brookes (University Parle, PA: Pennsylvania State University Press, 2002), 15; Reid, *Works*, 218).   [52] See, e.g. Haakonssen, *Science of a Legislator*, 77–9.

science is properly to be understood.[53] To take a particularly relevant example, Smith sees it as contingent that awareness of a spectator's sympathetic identification with an agent's sentiments generally prompts actions that have beneficial social consequences. We could have been created in such a way that the mechanism of sympathy engaged with other principles of human nature so as to generate actions with very different consequences. Smith devotes much of the *Theory* to illuminating a variety of similarly fortuitous ways in which the principles of human nature are such as to maximize human happiness. Like the common-sense philosophers, he frequently intimates that there is much in our nature that should cause us to be grateful to our maker.[54] Smith's account of the origins of the notion of justice is much more complicated than that of Kames or Reid, but the hold that justice has upon the human will is secured for all three philosophers by providential design, rather than being, as it is for Hume, the result of the calculated acceptance of a convention.

4. I have suggested that it is a characteristic feature of the moral philosophy of the Scottish Enlightenment that firmness of Christian belief is not, contrary to the position of Calvinist Orthodoxy, essential to the worth of a man's character and actions. Hutcheson, Kames, Smith, and Reid all refuse to accept that virtue is incomplete where there is no self-conscious orientation of action towards conformity with the will of the Christian God. Our sentiments are naturally orientated towards virtue, they believe; and natural benevolence is turned into full-blown virtue by principles of self-criticism also derived from the constitution of the mind. But there is, nevertheless, a limit to the trust that these philosophers are willing to place in the natural virtuousness with which all human beings are born. They all see innate goodness as likely to be corrupted by adherence to an Epicurean cosmology which denies the reality of providential design, and which asserts that the death of the body marks the end of personal existence. The virtuous person may not need to be a believer in the value of the Atonement; but he does have to believe in the principles of natural religion, in divine providence, and in a life after death. Thus the moral philosophers of the Scottish

---

[53] Here I follow Richard A. Kleer, 'Final Causes in Adam Smith's *Theory of Moral Sentiments*', *Journal of the History of Philosophy* 33 (1995), 275–300.

[54] See, e.g, the footnote at Smith, *Theory*, 76–8 (II. i. v).

Enlightenment are (for the most part) unable to go as far as Bayle himself did when he argued 'Que l'exemple de Lucrèce et ses semblables prouve manifestement, que la Religion n'estoit pas la cause des idées d'honnêteté qui étoient parmi les Payens', and when he extolled the virtues of the notorious atheist Lucilio Vanini.[55]

Shaftesbury holds that it is *possible* for virtue to be sustained without any religious beliefs at all. But he speaks with the Scottish philosophers when he argues that 'the natural tendency of atheism' is to corrupt the belief men have in the advantages of virtue:

Nothing indeed can be more melancholy than the thought of living in a distracted universe, from whence many ills may be suspected and where there is nothing good or lovely which presents itself, nothing which can satisfy in contemplation or raise any passion besides that of contempt, hatred, or dislike. Such an opinion as this may by degrees embitter the temper and not only make the love of virtue to be less felt but help to impair and ruin the very principle of virtue, namely, natural and kind affection.[56]

Different philosophers have different understandings of what, exactly, it might be to live without belief in a providential order. For Shaftesbury, it seems, it would be to be unable to believe that there is anything at all 'good or lovely' in the universe. No matter how ordered and comfortable things might appear, if they are not the result of intelligent design, they can excite only 'contempt, hatred, or dislike'; and the virtuous inclinations with which we are born would quickly turn into bitterness at having been placed in such a world. Hutcheson, by contrast, worries about the effect of loss of belief in providence in a world in which experience of the undeniably good is intermingled with experience of the apparently bad. Hutcheson dwells in the *Essay on the Nature and Conduct of the Passions* on the aptitude that men have 'to let their Imaginations run out upon all the *Robberies, Piracies, Murders, Perjuries, Frauds, Massacres, Assassinations*, they have ever heard of, or read in History'.[57] We all too easily exaggerate the amount of evil that there is in the world; and even

---

[55] Bayle, *Pensées*, ii. 111, 135–8 (§§ 174, 182). For an account of Vanini's life and works, see J. S. Spink, *French Free-Thought from Gassendi to Voltaire* (London: Athlone Press, 1960), 27–42. Voltaire claims that Bayle was wrong, first to describe Vanini as an atheist, and secondly to say that he was particularly virtuous: see the article 'Athéisme' in the *Dictionnaire philosophique: Œuvres complètes de Voltaire*, 52 vols. (Paris, 1879), xvii. 472.

[56] Shaftesbury, *Characteristics*, 189 (*Inquiry*, I. iii. 3).

[57] Hutcheson, *Essay*, 184 (VI. iv).

if we recognize that, in fact, the amount of good is much larger, we may still find it hard to understand why there is any evil at all. The solution is to see that there may be 'some unseen Necessity for the greatest Good, that there should be an *Order of Beings* no more perfect than we are, subject to Error and wrong Affections sometimes'.[58] 'This Belief of a Deity', Hutcheson continues, 'a Providence, and a *future State*, are the only sure Supports to a good Mind'.[59] In the posthumous *System of Moral Philosophy*, Hutcheson writes that 'Tis a needless inquiry whether a society of *Atheists* could subsist? or whether their state would be better or worse than that of men possessed with some wicked superstition?'[60] 'The best state of religion is incomparably happier than any condition of *Atheism*', he continues, even while it may be admitted that 'the corruptions of the best things may be the most pernicious'.[61]

The incompatibility of an Epicurean denial of providence and a future state with a firm commitment to virtue is asserted also by Kames, who writes in his essay 'Of our Knowledge of the Deity' that 'There certainly cannot be a more discouraging thought to man, than that the world was formed by a fortuitous concourse of atoms, and that all things are carried by a blind impulse':[62]

We can have no solid comfort in virtue, when it is a work of mere chance; nor can we justify our reliance upon the faith of others, when the nature of man rests upon so precarious a foundation. Every thing must appear gloomy, dismal and disjointed, without a Deity to unite this world of beings into one beautiful and harmonious system.[63]

Kames here introduces a still different worry about the consequences of Epicureanism. Virtuousness that is the result of accident rather than design is not something that can be its own reward in demanding situations; and if human nature is not the result of providential design, why should we trust other people not to take advantage of us whenever they can? If human nature is the product of chance, then there is no reason to expect that motives for the pursuit of virtue are universally distributed. James Balfour of Pilrig develops a similar line of thought when he argues that atheism undermines the 'painful' feeling of conscience that goes with knowledge of having done wrong. Without belief in a divine

---

[58] Ibid. 187 (VI. iv).   [59] Ibid. (VI. iv).

[60] Francis Hutcheson, *A System of Moral Philosophy* [*System*], 2 vols. (London, 1755), i, 219.

[61] Ibid. 220.   [62] Kames, *Essays*, 320.   [63] Ibid. 321.

framer of our constitution, 'We must discover the apprehension of merited punishment to be chimerical, and the sense of wrong to be the mere off-spring of our minds.'[64] Balfour, like the other philosophers discussed here, believes that our natural disposition is to pursue virtue and avoid vice; and like Reid, he believes that reason is all that is needed to turn Hutchesonian benevolence into what he calls 'dispassion'; but, he argues, to come to believe that this is all the result of a fortuitous concourse of atoms would be to lose one's confidence in the rightful authority of moral sentiments over base ones.

It might seem perverse to try to find a place for Smith among these proponents of conventional piety. After all, Smith is a philosopher particularly sensitive to the harm that religion can do to the sense of duty. He claims, in fact, that '[f]alse notions of religion are almost the only causes which can occasion any very general perversion of our natural sentiments'.[65] As we have seen, he sees men as able to regulate their actions with rules derived from nothing more transcendent than the internalization of the perspective of the impartial spectator on human affairs. But Smith is not so unrealistic as to expect that everyone listens to what 'the man within' says. He sees clearly that it is often that 'violence and artifice prevail over sincerity and justice'.[66] And when we see this happen, Smith writes, 'we naturally appeal to heaven, and hope, that the great Author of our nature will himself execute hereafter, what all the principles which he has given us for the direction of our conduct, prompt us to attempt even here'.[67] In virtue of the fact that our sentiments are as they are, God has taught us to check injustice wherever we find it: we believe that it is in the nature of things that virtue should flourish, and vice be stamped out. When we find ourselves unequal to this task, we must hope that God 'will complete the plan which he himself has taught us to begin; and will, in a life to come, render to every one according to the works which he has performed in this world'.[68] Smith does not rest belief in a future state on selfish desires of reward for duteous and faithful behaviour; yet life after death *is* essential to the completion of a moral scheme only imperfectly realized in this life. Moreover, the idea of a future state provides a motive to virtuous action for those presented with opportunities for the secret or impunible

[64] James Balfour, *A Delineation of the Nature and Obligation of Morality* [*Delineation*] (Edinburgh, 1753), 37.   [65] Smith, *Theory*, 176 (III. vi).

[66] Ibid. 169 (III. v).   [67] Ibid.   [68] Ibid.

satisfaction of immoral desires. Smith writes that 'The idea that . . . we are always acting under the eye, and exposed to the punishment of God, the great avenger of injustice, is a motive capable of restraining the most headstrong passions, with those at least who, by constant reflection, have rendered it familiar to them'.[69] It is for this reason, he says, 'that mankind are generally disposed to place great confidence in the probity of those who seem greatly impressed with religious sentiments'.[70]

From the sixth edition of the *Theory of Moral Sentiments*, published in 1790 just before his death, Smith excises a passage on the value of the Atonement.[71] But in the same edition he *adds* new paragraphs which reiterate the ideas just summarized. He dwells in particular on the need for belief in life after death on the part of those who find themselves blamed for what they did not do, and concludes that

> Our happiness in this life is . . . , upon many occasions, dependent upon the humble hope and expectation of a life to come: a hope and expectation deeply rooted in human nature; which can alone support its lofty ideas of its own dignity; can alone illumine the dreary prospect of its continually approaching mortality, and maintain its cheerfulness under all the heaviest calamities to which, from the disorders of life, it may sometimes be exposed.[72]

Without this 'humble hope and expectation', one infers, life would be insupportable. Even the virtuous man would be reduced to despair at the disorder and injustice obvious in all times and in all places. The fact that Smith adds this kind of passage to *The Theory of Moral Sentiments* long after the end of his professorial career is surely sufficient to allay suspicion that references to the doctrines of natural religion in the book are merely a matter of deference to what was expected from a university teacher in eighteenth-century Scotland.

Smith is followed by Reid in his insistence on the need for belief in a future state. Atheism, Reid says in his *Lectures on Natural Theology*, would

---

[69] Ibid. 170 (III. v).

[70] Ibid. Haakonssen suggests that there is a sceptical aspect to Smith's presentation of religious belief as a natural phenomenon: see *Science of a Legislator*, 74–7. He is right to say that Smith's own religious convictions are very far from obvious, in the *Theory* or anywhere else; and that Smith does not claim legitimacy for the inference to a providential order. All that I need for my argument, however, is the fact that Smith finds a role for religious belief in his conception of virtue, while Hume does not.

[71] See Smith, *Theory*, 91–2n. (II. ii. 3).   [72] Ibid. 132 (III. ii).

plunge what he calls 'the thinking part of mankind' into 'distress, anxiety and despair':[73]

I do not deny that when in high spirits and hurried away by the pleasing gales of prosperity, [the atheist] may banish remorse and all forbodings of futurity, but yet in his more serious moments when brought down by calamities to which all are liable, and especially when he has a near prospect of his dissolution, then all these thoughts let loose upon him and he is plunged into despair.[74]

These sentiments are similar to those found in the passages of Beattie's *Essay on Truth* where Beattie is most savage in his condemnation of the effects of Hume's scepticism. Beattie goes so far as to call those who would rid men of religious belief 'traitors to human kind' and 'murderers of the human soul':[75]

Caressed by those who call themselves the great, ingrossed by the formalities of life, intoxicated with vanity, pampered with adulation, dissipated in the tumult of business, or amidst the vicissitudes of folly, [our modern sceptics] perhaps have little need or little relish for the consolations of religion. But let them know, that in the solitary scenes of life, there is many an honest and tender heart pining with incurable anguish, pierced with the sharpest sting of disappointment, bereft of friends, chilled with poverty, racked with disease, scourged by the oppressor; whom nothing but trust in Providence, and the hope of a future retribution, could preserve from the agonies of despair. And do they, with sacrilegious hands, attempt to violate this last refuge of the miserable, and to rob them of the only comfort that had survived the ravages of misfortune, malice, and tyranny![76]

It seems to have been a matter of consensus in the Scotland of the eighteenth century that a minimal 'natural' form of religion, affirming providence and a future state, is essential to ensuring that a natural orientation towards virtue does not decay into despair. There may be various understandings of the damage that Epicurean belief might do, but we can say that, in general, the moral philosophers of the Scottish Enlightenment hold that the virtuous agent needs to be able to find a place for himself within a larger providential scheme if he is not to be driven to despair by, in Reid's words, 'the calamities to which all are

---

[73] Thomas Reid, *Lectures on Natural Theology* [*Lectures*], transcribed from student notes and ed. Elmer H. Duncan (Washington, DC: University Press of America, 1981), 8.

[74] Ibid. 9.

[75] James Beattie, *An Essay on the Nature and Immutability of Truth* [*Essay*], 2nd edn. (Edinburgh, 1771), 528.   [76] Ibid. 527–8.

liable'. The Scottish philosophy of the eighteenth century is thus very far from being secular in spirit. It is likely that neither Hutcheson, Kames, Smith, nor Reid would have been acknowledged a Christian by John Knox and Andrew Melville; but, still, religious beliefs are central to their conception of the moral life. On this matter there was only one dissenting voice, and it is to the more resolute Bayleanism of David Hume that I now turn.

5. Where Hume writes about the influence of religious belief upon moral practice, his concern is often with the harm that religion can do.[77] In the *Natural History of Religion*, he argues that monotheism has an inevitable tendency towards intolerance, in so far as its 'unity of object seems naturally to require the unity of faith and ceremonies, and furnishes designing men with a pretence for representing their adversaries as profane, and objects of divine as well as human vengeance'.[78] Furthermore,

Where the deity is represented as infinitely superior to mankind, this belief, though altogether just, is apt, when joined with superstitious terrors, to sink the human mind into the lowest submission and abasement, and to represent the monkish virtues of mortification, penance, humility, and passive suffering, as the only qualities which are acceptable to him.[79]

And a devotion to the monkish virtues, Hume points out in the second *Enquiry*, tends to 'cross all . . . desirable ends, stupify the understanding and harden the heart, obscure the fancy and sour the temper'.[80] There is, however, nothing unique in such opinions. The moral philosophers discussed thus far are also keenly sensitive to the damage that can be done by false religion to the moral sentiments. The views of Hutcheson and Smith on this matter have been alluded to above; and in the *Sketches on the History of Man*, Kames echoes Hume's criticism of devotion to the monkish virtues,[81] while letters written by Reid soon after his arrival in

---

[77] Balfour remarks that Hume appears to think of religion 'as opposite to the natural principles of morality, and tending to prevent the exertion, and display of our virtuous inclinations' (*Delineation*, 138).

[78] David Hume, *Dialogues concerning Natural Religion and Natural History of Religion* [*Dialogues and Natural History*], ed. J. C. A. Gaskin (Oxford: Oxford University Press, 1993), 161.

[79] Ibid. 163.

[80] David Hume, *Enquiry concerning the Principles of Morals*, ed. Tom L. Beauchamp (Oxford: Oxford University Press, 1998), 146. One might also cite, of course, Philo's animadversions on superstition in Section XII of the *Dialogues concerning Natural Religion*.

[81] See Kames, *Sketches*, iv. 392–9.

Glasgow indicate his distaste for the severities of 'Popular' Calvinism.[82]
Where Hume differs decisively from his contemporaries in his estimate
of the ability of belief in providence to provide reassurance to the belea-
guered man of virtue. Hume does not claim that all religious belief is
harmful to the economy of the moral sentiments. His position is better
characterized as the view that, once religion has been stripped down to
its rational or 'natural' core, it becomes simply irrelevant to moral practice. When they do not produce fanaticism or intolerance, speculative
beliefs are impotent, because they do not engage with the mechanisms
responsible for the everyday life of the mind.[83]

This is a position distinct from Hume's scepticism about the rationality of belief in the tenets of natural religion. The question here is not
whether natural religion has philosophical credibility, but whether the
doctrines of natural religion are able to counteract feelings of resent-
ment and despair as Hutcheson, Kames, Smith, and Reid believe they
can and do. In Part XII of the *Dialogues*, Philo says that '[i]t is certain,
from experience, that the smallest grain of natural honesty and benevolence has more effect on men's conduct, than the most pompous views
suggested by theological theories and systems';[84] but Hume's doubts on
this score come into focus most clearly at the end of the essay 'Of Liberty
and Necessity', where he considers the problem of evil, and the solution
to the problem that postulates a larger providential scheme in which
everything is in fact for the best. Hume writes that while the view that
every event is, despite appearances, 'an object of joy and exultation' may
be 'specious and sublime', it is, alas, also 'weak and ineffectual':

You would surely more irritate than appease a man lying under the racking pains
of gout by preaching up to him the rectitude of those general laws, which produced the malignant humours in his body, and led them through the proper

---

[82] Reid writes to David Skene in 1765 that the common people of Glasgow are 'fanatical in
their religion', and then says that '[t]he clergy encourage this fanaticism too much, and find in
it the only way to popularity. I often hear a gospel here which you know nothing about, for
you neither hear it from the pulpit, nor will you find it in the bible' (*Works*, 41b). It should be
added, however, that in an earlier letter to Skene's father, Reid admits that this 'gloomy, enthu-
siastical' religion makes the people 'tame and sober' (ibid. 40b).

[83] I take it that this is why Philo feels able to endorse 'the philosophical and rational kind'
of religion at the end of the *Dialogues*. One of the conditions that he imposes on acceptance of
the proposition 'that the cause or causes of order in the universe probably bear some remote
analogy to human intelligence' is that it be understood to 'afford no inference that affects
human life' (*Dialogues and Natural History*, 129).   [84] Ibid. 123.

canals, to the sinews and nerves, where they now create such acute torments. These enlarged views may, for a moment, please the imagination of the speculative man, who is placed in ease and security; but neither can they dwell with constancy on his mind, even though undisturbed by the emotions of pain and passion; much less can they maintain their ground when attacked by such powerful antagonists.[85]

Moral evils are equally unlikely to be overcome by 'philosophical meditations' which establish that 'everything is right with regard to the whole, and that the qualities, which disturb society, are, in the main, as beneficial . . . as those which more directly promote its happiness and welfare'.[86] The natural sentiments of the mind, Hume concludes, 'are not to be controuled by any philosophical theory or speculation whatsoever'.[87] This is, of course, a fundamental principle of the Humean psychology. We are permanently disabled from bringing our natural beliefs into line with the productions of pure reason: as Hume says at the end of Book I of the *Treatise*, 'very refin'd reflections have little or no influence upon us'.[88]

Bayle argues forcefully in the *Pensées diverses* 'que l'homme n'agit pas selon ses principes'.[89] It is this fact, according to Bayle, that proves that an atheist is as able to live a virtuous life as a Christian; and nowhere, I believe, is Bayle's influence on Hume clearer than in Hume's separation of the realm of theory from the realm of practice. Having dismissed the practical efficacy of 'enlarg'd views' with respect to physical ills, Hume turns to the moral sphere, and writes that

The mind of man is so formed by nature that, upon the appearance of certain characters, dispositions, and actions, it immediately feels the sentiment of approbation or blame; nor are there any emotions more essential to its frame and constitution. The characters which engage our approbation are chiefly such as contribute to the peace and security of human society; as the characters which excite blame are chiefly such as tend to public detriment and disturbance: Whence it may

---

[85] David Hume, *Enquiry concerning Human Understanding*, ed. Tom L. Beauchamp (Oxford: Oxford University Press, 1999), 163. [86] Ibid. 164.

[87] Ibid.

[88] David Hume, *A Treatise of Human Nature*, ed. David Fate Norton and Mary Norton (Oxford: Oxford University Press, 2000), 174 (I. iv. vii). Of course, Hume immediately questions this principle, in light of how '[t]he *intense* view of these manifold contradictions and imperfections in human reason has so wrought upon me, and heated my brain'; but it is 'nature herself', rather than further reasoning, that provides the cure.

[89] See Bayle, *Pensées diverses*, ii. 11–13 (§ 136).

reasonably be presumed, that the moral sentiments arise, either mediately or immediately, from a reflection of these opposite interests.[90]

Speculative beliefs are irrelevant to an account of moral character because our sentimental reactions easily overpower them. No matter how sincere one's attachment might be to the doctrines of natural religion, those doctrines are unable to alter the course of the natural reactive mechanism. If virtue survives disappointment and frustration, therefore, the explanation must lie not where Hume's contemporaries think it does, in belief in providence, but rather in the strength of the hold upon us of concern for 'the peace and security of human society'. Hume's moral philosophy fleshes out such an explanation, and grounds respect for justice in utilitarian considerations, that are in turn grounded in sympathy: in what in the second *Enquiry* he terms 'a warm concern for the interests of our species'.[91] And when the principles of justice are taken to be human artefacts, inventions suited to our purposes, rather than elements of a divinely crafted human frame that are only contingently related to the maximization of human welfare, then there is a straightforward and this-worldly answer to the question 'Why should I act justly?' Whether or not there is a providential intelligence responsible for the order of things might well seem irrelevant when the rationale for and origin of justice is taken to be, simply, '[t]hat there be a separation or distinction of possessions, and that this separation be steady and constant'.[92]

Hume's aetiology of respect for the demands of justice was taken by his contemporaries, whether 'Orthodox' or not, to have the Hobbesian implication that the only motive for conformity to law is fear of the magistrate. The *Letter from a Gentleman to his Friend in Edinburgh* reports that the Moderate William Wishart and his cronies had charged Hume 'with sapping the Foundations of Morality, by denying the natural and essential Difference between Right and Wrong, Good and Evil, Justice and Injustice; making the Difference only artificial, and to arise from human Conventions and Compacts'.[93] But a respect for justice has its roots in human nature, on Hume's view as on the view of the other

---

[90] Hume, *Enquiry concerning Human Understanding*, 163–4.

[91] Hume, *Enquiry concerning the Principles of Morals*, 113 (V. ii).

[92] Ibid. 174 (Appendix III).

[93] [David Hume], *A Letter from a Gentleman to his Friend in Edinburgh* (Edinburgh, 1745), 18. For other versions of the same charge, see, e.g. Kames, *Essays*, 103–19; Reid, *Works*, 651–63 (*Essays on the Active Powers*, V. v).

philosophers we have discussed here: the difference lies in the character of the roots. Where his contemporaries look to a distinct and irreducible faculty of conscience, given us by our Maker, and productive of generally beneficial consequences by virtue of our Maker's benevolence, Hume anchors our concern with justice in what he terms 'the present necessitous condition of mankind'.[94] Justice *is* natural, in the sense that it is something one will expect to be a feature of every human society. 'If self-love, if benevolence be natural to man', Hume says in Appendix III of the second *Enquiry*, 'if reason and forethought be also natural; then may the same epithet be applied to justice, order, fidelity, property, society':'In so sagacious an animal, what necessarily arises from the exertion of his intellectual faculties may justly be esteemed natural.'[95] The debate between Hume and his opponents over the source of the notion of duty turns out in the end to be a debate about the work done by reason in moral life; and it is interesting to note that it is Hume, the sometime proponent of the view that reason is the slave of the passions, who gives reason a central role in the construction of rules of justice.[96] Can the rules governing the acquisition of property, he asks, can principles of inheritance and contract, really be rooted in original instincts? 'Does nature, whose instincts in men are all simple, embrace such complicated and artificial objects, and create a rational creature, without trusting anything to the operation of its reason?'[97]

6. It would not do to underestimate the significance of Hutcheson's break with the Calvinist tradition. His revival of Greek and Roman conceptions of the life of virtue was a revolutionary move. It is hardly surprising that his appointment to the moral philosophy chair at Glasgow was strenuously contested by those persuaded of the truth of

---

[94] Hume, *Enquiry concerning the Principles of Morals*, 83 (III. i).   [95] Ibid. 173.

[96] The Hume of the *Treatise* has a penchant for dramatic phrase-making that, it seems to me, all too often obscures the real character of his thought.

[97] Hume, *Enquiry concerning the Principles of Morals*, 96 (III. ii). As already noted, Reid insists on the rational nature of moral demands; but the first principles of morals, on his account, are first principles of common sense. On Reid's view, reason is the faculty by which we *discover* the principles of morality; on Hume's view, reason's role is in the *construction* of those principles. (I do not mean, however, to depict Hume as a 'rationalist' in his moral philosophy: Humean virtue is always ultimately grounded in sentiment and sympathy. What differentiates Hume from his contemporaries, I am suggesting, is his sense of the limited scope of the sentiments and faculties we are born with, and of the consequent need for sentiment and sympathy to be refined and developed by reasoning. I am grateful to an anonymous referee for forcing me to be clearer about this.)

the Calvinist assessment of human nature.[98] Hutcheson's religion looked like no religion at all to his opponents, and opposition to such 'moderating' ideas persisted throughout the eighteenth century, to be rewarded by the great renewal of evangelical Calvinism that took place in the early decades of the nineteenth. But we should not be misled by Orthodox rhetoric into believing that Enlightenment Scotland saw a great burst of secularization. Religious belief, as I have sought to show here, remains at the heart of the conception of virtuous agent found in the philosophies of Hutcheson, Kames, Smith, and Reid. From the point of view of the Orthodox, the beliefs in question are so minimal as not to be recognizably Christian; yet it remains the case that an insistence on a role for belief in a providential order and in a life after death serves sharply to distinguish mainstream Scottish from Humean moral theory.

Hume's relation with Baylean scepticism is a complex matter, but it appears fair to say that he endorses wholeheartedly Bayle's claim that there is simply no connection between speculative principles of any sort, whether conventional or subversive, and motives to action.[99] Hume, however, unlike Bayle, is interested in construction as well as destruction, and his great innovation lies in a detailed elaboration of a theory of virtue that makes it irrelevant whether or not there is, in Shaftesbury's words, 'nothing of a designing principle or mind nor any

[98] See William Robert Scott, *Francis Hutcheson: His Life, Teaching and Position in the History of Philosophy* (Cambridge: Cambridge University Press, 1900), 54–5. I am told by M. A. Stewart, however, that there is no evidence for the frequently repeated claim that Hutcheson was prosecuted for atheism by the Glasgow Presbytery for 'teaching to his students in contravention of the Westminster Confession the following two false and dangerous doctrines, first that the standard of moral goodness was the promotion of the happiness of others; and second that we could have a knowledge of good and evil, without, and prior to a knowledge of God' (cf. ibid. 83–4).

[99] Hume's early memoranda provide a fascinating record of his youthful encounter with Baylean scepticism: see Norman Kemp Smith, 'Hume's Early Memoranda, 1729–40: The Complete Text', *Journal of the History of Ideas* 9 (1948), 492–512, and esp. 500–3. (Particularly suggestive with respect to the topic of this essay is the tenth memorandum of Section II: 'Atheists plainly make a Distinction betwixt good Reasoning and bad. Why not betwixt Vice and Virtue? Baile.') For specfic suggestions as to the Baylean texts read by Hume, see J. P. Pittion,'Hume's Reading of Bayle: An Inquiry into the Source and Role of the Memoranda', *Journal of the History of Philosophy* 15 (1977), 373–86. For accounts of the nature of Bayle's influence on Hume's thought, see, e.g. Richard Popkin, 'Bayle and Hume', in *The High Road to Pyrrhonism* (San Diego: Austin Hill Press, 1980); and James Moore, 'Natural Law and the Pyrrhonian Controversy', in Peter Jones (ed.), *Philosophy and Science in the Scottish Enlightenment* (Edinburgh: John Donald, 1988).

cause, measure or rule of things but chance, so that in nature neither the interest of the whole nor of any particulars can be said in the least designed, pursued or aimed at'.[100] I have not, however, done any more in this essay than gesture towards an interpretation of Hume's moral psychology that would make clear what it is about Humean virtue that enables it to do without support from religious belief.[101]

St Catherine's College, Oxford

[100] Shaftesbury, *Characteristics*, 165 (*Inquiry* I. i. 2).

[101] An ancestor of this essay was presented at a conference on the Scottish Enlightenment in its European context held at the University of Glasgow in March 2001, and I benefited greatly from the subsequent discussion. I am grateful for comments on more recent drafts to Knud Haakonssen, James Moore, Isabel Rivers, and John Robertson, as well as to an anonymous referee.

Index of Names